DATE DUE

DE 16 98			

DEMCO 38-296

Embracing
Victory

———

Also by Mariah Burton Nelson

The Stronger Women Get, the More Men Love Football:
Sexism and the American Culture of Sports

Are We Winning Yet?
How Women Are Changing Sports
and Sports Are Changing Women

Embracing Victory

Life Lessons
in Competition and Compassion

Mariah Burton Nelson

William Morrow and Company, Inc.

New York

Library of Congress Cataloging-in-Publication Data

Nelson, Mariah Burton.
    Embracing victory: life lessons in competition and compassion / Mariah
Burton Nelson.
        p. cm.
    Includes bibliographical references.
    ISBN 0-688-14649-X
    1. Women—United States—Psychology. 2. Competition (Psychology)—
United States. 3. Women athletes—United States—Psychology.
4. Women in business—United States—Psychology. I. Title.
HQ1206.N385 1998
158.1'082—dc21   97-30454
                                                                               CIP

To my mother,

Sarah Burton Nelson

Preface

This has been a difficult book to write because I desperately wanted it to be really good. Here's why: I'm competitive. I always want to win. As a writer I want my books to win praise, win awards, win readers over to my way of seeing things. That's scary to admit. You might think I'm *too* competitive.

At one point I gave up. The first two versions of the proposal had been rejected. I said to my agent, Felicia Eth, "I don't want to write this book anymore."

"Why not?" she asked, baffled. "It's a great idea! The proposal just needs more work! Why would you abandon the project?"

"I'm tired," I said, "and discouraged, and—"

"Afraid of losing?" she asked gently.

"That's not it," I insisted.

She pressed: "I was wondering if you're reluctant to face another rejection."

Moi? The competitor? The lifelong athlete? Afraid to lose?

Well, maybe. I finally admitted to myself (though never to Felicia) that maybe I *had* been tempted to drop out of the race altogether rather than risk another defeat.

It's a tricky thing, competition: complex and challenging.

This book may not win awards. It may not win good reviews, it may not win my parents' approval, and it may not win you over to my way of understanding competition. But despite periodic setbacks, I still attempted to win. In this attempt the book grew stronger, tighter, livelier, funnier, more interesting. In this attempt I suffered but also enjoyed myself, because after all, as a writer, I like to write. As an athlete I like to work hard, even though that includes blisters and sore muscles. Regardless of the final score (reviews, sales figures, fan letters), I now feel successful, satisfied, and even victorious.

That's what this book is about: not winning necessarily, but trying to win. Believing that it is possible, noticing that it's entertaining (some of the time), and trusting that it's worth the effort. Not giving up, or not for long. Trusting that in the process of trying to win, good things happen.

—MARIAH BURTON NELSON

Contents

COMPETITION

I like to swim naked
I like to swim fast
swimming next to you I swim faster
shed more layers of flesh
learn your rhythms as well as my own
Each time I breathe I see you
breathe
stroke
breathe
stroke
and see you again
You can tell by my stroke that I need you
You can tell by my stroke
by the way that I breathe
that I need your stroke, your breath
that to be my best I need you
swimming beside me

—M.B.N.

Part One

Beyond Conquering and Cheerleading

Chapter 1

Seeking Excellence Together:
An Introduction

As a college basketball player I used to claim that I wasn't competitive. In my mind, being athletic was okay but being competitive was not. I told myself I just "happened" to be the star of the Stanford University team, the leading scorer and rebounder. I wouldn't admit that I competed with my teammates to maintain that position.

Don't many of us delude ourselves this way, striving for success while pretending not to compete?

I met my match when I turned pro and played for a year in France with an American teammate, Heidi Wayment. Suddenly I was no longer the star. Heidi was. One night after a game I demanded, "How am I supposed to score more than nineteen points if you won't pass me the ball? Why are you so competitive with me?"

"Look who's being competitive!" she countered. "Since when is nineteen points something to be ashamed of? Only when compared to my twenty-nine, right?"

Later I told a good friend, "I've realized that I am in fact very competitive."

"No," she said sarcastically. "You?"

Despite our great strides in sports, business, and politics, some women still avoid competition, and many women feel ambivalent about it. We want to win but think it's somehow wrong to admit that. We're tired of competing with other women over who looks better in a bathing suit. We're wary of the barbaric tactics some men use in unacknowledged competitions with their wives and girlfriends. We've been wounded by contests at work in which we didn't understand the rules of the old-boy game. Raised to be concerned about the feelings of others, we don't want anyone else to lose.

So we pretend not to compete. Or we try not to compete. But just because competition can be difficult and confusing and painful doesn't mean we should retreat into a world in which no one's allowed to keep score. She who never plays the game never wins. We need to compete. But competition does not have to be cruel or destructive or hateful. Games don't have to be battles. Opponents need not exhibit "killer instinct." Winning doesn't have to be the only thing.

We need to figure out *how* to compete without losing our dignity and integrity and sense of humor. Then we need to practice competing, so we get better at it. Then we need to pass these lessons along to other women, to children, and, if they're interested, to men.

In this book I encourage women to compete openly and honorably. I present original ways of thinking about competition and offer guidelines for competing compassionately, ethically, and effectively in all areas of life. I insist that we must embrace victory—and defeat—on our own terms.

A few years ago the editors of *Women's Sports + Fitness* magazine asked me to write an essay on the benefits of competition. They asked Alfie Kohn, author of *No Contest: The Case Against Competition*, to write an opposing essay on the hazards of competition. I'd read his book, so I knew pretty much what he'd say: Competition can make people feel like losers and turn friends into enemies. Cooperation, by contrast, fosters a sense of inclusion and mutual respect.

I agree with him. Competition can devastate self-esteem and destroy relationships.

But I also disagree with him. Competition can enhance confidence and intimacy. Competition and cooperation are not opposites. I see competition as (ideally) a *form* of cooperation, a framework for doing one's best in concert with other people who are simultaneously doing their best, thus inspiring you to do even better.

I'll write the best essay I can, I thought. *I hope it's better than his.*

Apparently Alfie Kohn didn't think like that, not if he's a purist: no contests, ever. His essay ("No-Win Situations") was good, however, as was mine ("Who Wins? Who Cares?"). Both have been reprinted more than a dozen times.

After a while Alfie called me. We had never spoken before. "How much do you think we should be charging these publications for reprint rights?" he asked.

"I've been asking for two hundred dollars," I told him.

He said, "I've been asking for two-fifty."

I found this amusing. "Alfie!" I said. "I guess you're winning!"

He chuckled but countered, "No one has to win. Or lose. I had no idea what you were charging, so I called to make sure there was no disparity. We shouldn't see ourselves as rivals at all."

He was right, at least in terms of our little price-fixing scheme, and I appreciated his call.

For me, competition is like that: One minute I'm competing; the next minute I'm not. To compete all the time would be foolish, exhausting, and counterproductive. But nowadays, many years after my epiphany with Heidi on the basketball court, I admit it: I love to compete. I like to laugh, at myself or the situation, because I find competition humorous. Often it's more fun than frustrating, more amusing than immobilizing. And often there's room for everyone to succeed.

I like to win—if the contest has been fair and close and fun or if the rewards are meaningful. I believe in winning. In particular I want women to win—not in some battle of the sexes (why, when women compete with men, does it always become a battle of the sexes?) but in the human effort to excel. I believe in excellence.

I enjoy the process of competing: effort, intensity, risk, challenge, rewards. I see competition as a compass that can point one toward one's own goals and also toward intimacy with one's rivals.

I enjoy the intimacy, the *connection* that competition brings. If I'm swimming alone, my mind can wander. Challenge me to race you, and suddenly all distractions are gone. I'll focus on swimming fast, faster than you. After the race I'll thank you, not because I won or lost but because you offered me a gift: the opportunity to relish the improvisational dance called competition.

Women who enjoy competition are fortunate because all of us need to compete at least sometimes, in some situations, in order to survive and thrive, given the competitive structure of our society. Competition constitutes an integral part of families (siblings compete for parental affection and resources), capitalism (companies compete for market share), education (students compete for grades), and democracy (leaders compete for votes). Those who fail to enter competitive arenas invariably fail to win.

But I've met few women who enjoy competition without any shame or fear or confusion. I get confused too. It wasn't until writing this book that I realized I sometimes compete too much, or not enough, or with the wrong attitude. When I feel unsuccessful or inferior as a writer, it's often because I'm competing with the wrong people or at the wrong time. As an athlete I've been too competitive, injuring my body en route to victory.

Other women suffer from other competitive conundrums: reluctance to defeat anyone else, fear of retribution from losers, self-doubts about their potentials for success, and confusion about feminism, which has shunned competition as male while at the same time using the competitive democratic process to advance toward equal rights. Family background; cultural, racial, ethnic, and religious heritage; and sport or lack of sport experience all affect how women compete, or don't compete, and how we feel about competition.

This book is for women because we have this in common: Society was not designed to accommodate or reward female winners. We all wade in competitive waters that were designed for men, with men's interests and capabilities in mind. We all face sexist stereotypes. Influential physician Benjamin M. Spock writes in *Decent and Indecent*, "I think that when women are encouraged to be competitive too many of them become disagreeable."[1] Dr. Spock was a gentleman; nowadays competitive women get called bitches or ball breakers or worse. The sentiment is the same: Women should not compete and especially should not defeat men.

Women also struggle with competition because men have defined it. When men talk about competing, they rarely use the words I used: "humor" and "inspiration" and "intimacy" and "connection" and "excellence." They tend to talk about domination over enemies, whether those enemies are individuals or companies or armies or countries. This is what I call the Conqueror's way of competing, the winning-is-the-only-thing mentality during which, in the single-minded quest for victory, pleasure and process seemingly become irrelevant.

Women are ambivalent about competition because we know what it's like to be conquered, or can imagine it. As a group we have been losers in the game of sexism, whereby men try to win by proving their masculinity through the subjugation of women and weaker men. We know how painful it can be to lose. So most of us don't like the Conqueror's way.

Plus, most of us were never taught to how win—or only how to win a man. We were excluded from competitive sports and businesses and negotiations and hence haven't gotten comfortable with the language, custom, nuance of competition; we haven't come to see it as fun, challenging, and exciting. We never learned the rules. We didn't get the experience. So we tend to shun competition as too male: too heartless and exclusive, too cutthroat and cruel. We don't want to play that game.

Nor are most women willing to resign themselves to the traditional feminine form of competition, what I call the Cheerleader's way. Cheerleaders compete only on the sidelines, and only with other girls, and only over beauty and boyfriends and popularity. They're allowed on the main floor but only for a few moments at a time, when the boys are busy in the locker room. They celebrate other people's victories, not their own.

Because of our history of exclusion and limitation, many women have become wary of competition itself, uncomfortable in the Conqueror or Cheerleader role, unwilling to risk alienating men, and reluctant to confirm our suspicions that we are failures, second rate, second best. So we disavow our own competitive strivings, avoid competitive situations, or temper our efforts with smiles and denials.

Fortunately there's an alternative. Competition doesn't have to mean domination, and it doesn't have to involve kicking up your heels to show off your underwear.

I call it the Champion's way. The Champion competes openly, aggressively, joyously, with respect for her opponents, and without apology for her own desire for excellence. She competes honestly and ethically. She refuses to conquer anyone, but she also refuses to accept the second-class status of Cheerleader. Hers is a competitive philosophy exemplified by the wisest, most gracious athletes, many of whom are women.

The Champion's way requires a healthy self-esteem, a recognition of one's own competence, and a generosity of spirit. Because a Champion has experienced victory, she feels adequate, capable, up to the task. Because she has experienced defeat, she knows that it's not fatal, and she is neither paralyzed by the likelihood that she will lose again nor hesitant to inflict defeat on her rivals. She believes in herself enough to risk competing. She supports her peers without perceiving their gains to be her loss.

Champions define for themselves what counts as victory, what constitutes defeat, what it means to compete. I don't think we need one consensual female definition of competition, but I do think it's crucial that we define it for ourselves, rather than accept the definitions handed to us by sports editors, political editors, even dictionaries. The late poet Audre Lorde warns in *Sister Outsider,* "If we do not define ourselves for ourselves, we will be defined by others—for their use and to our detriment."[2] Susan Faludi writes in *Backlash* that women must "be free to define themselves—instead of having their identity defined for them, time and again, by their culture and their men."[3]

In this book I define "competition" this way: seeking excellence together. I offer this five-part framework for understanding competition: It's a relationship, it's a process, it's an opportunity, it's a risk, and it's a feminist issue.

The most important point is the first: Competition is a relationship. Competitors are always in relation to their rivals. The word "compete" comes from the Latin *competere,* meaning "to seek together." (*Com* means "to come together, agree, be suitable." *Petere* means "to seek.") So competing has its roots here, in relationship: in seeking together.

To seek: To search, to pursue, to try to discover or acquire, to make an inquiry.

Together: As a group, in relationship, in agreement or harmony, with each other.

To seek together: To search for excellence as a group. To pursue greatness in relationship with others. To try to discover or acquire anything worthwhile in agreement or harmony with sister seekers or brother seekers. To make an inquiry with each other.

Competition is also a process. It takes time. Winning and losing are part of the process, and they matter, but how we compete matters the most. It matters because it affects other people, and it matters because it affects how we feel about ourselves: our self-esteem, our integrity, our dignity.

Competition is an opportunity. It's a chance to get to know yourself and other people. It's a chance to push yourself beyond what you thought was possible. Opponents can be annoying. They can feel like obstacles or obstructions. Or they can be welcomed as opportunities.

Competition is a risk. Sooner or later you will fail, be disappointed, disappoint others. You will learn what you can't do as well as what you can. Others will notice your failings as well as your victories, and they'll respond. To compete, you must acknowledge your desires, declare your intentions, and trust that you can handle the outcome, as well as the process, with some degree of grace. It's scary. It takes courage.

And competition is a feminist issue. Because of sexism, women know what it's like to be subordinate, to be defeated, to be losers. We have been denied opportunities to compete with men on an equal basis. We've seen men react to female victory as if it signified male defeat. All this cultural conditioning affects how we compete, and with whom. But everything changes as we begin to define competition for ourselves.

B oys learn to compete through sports. Now girls too are learning through sports what it takes to succeed: practice, teamwork, consistency, flexibility, stamina, and hard work. We're learning how it feels to be victorious, to be the best, to be subordinate to no one. We're noticing that winning is fun but that losing is no disgrace. We're developing respect, even gratitude for our rivals. We're learning that the harder we push our teammates, the stronger the team becomes. We're learning to compete successfully against men—regardless of male approval or disapproval.

We're defining what it means to be Champions. Female athletes often compete in ways that leave no one feeling vanquished. Women team up even in situations where individual competition is expected. We say things like "There's more than one way to win." We understand that winning and losing are not the black-and-white dichotomy they seem to be.

This book is for women who cherish opportunities to compete, who live to compete, who never feel more alive and sensuous and happy than when they're skiing fast down a mountain, working hard to meet a deadline, or campaigning for a cause they believe in.

But this book is also for the "I hate competition" crowd. Despite the recent influx of girls into sports, most American women over about age thirty-five were not encouraged to compete, neither in sports nor in the rest of life. No one cheered for them when they were young and impressionable. They lined up to play but watched helplessly as team captains chose everyone else first. They felt humiliated by rope-climbing tests, push-ups, and sprints for which they weren't trained. They felt fat or awkward or weak or embarrassingly *female*, adolescent breasts bouncing conspicuously under ill-fitting gym suits. Jog bras had not been invented. There were no commercials featuring attractive, perspiring women. Given a chance to run, these women ran as far from sports as they could. Competition itself—with its inherent prospect of more defeat, more loss of self-esteem—often became scary or loathsome.

Curious about the relationship between sports and competition, in 1996 I designed a sixty-question anonymous survey.[4] With the help of 42 teachers, coaches, and administrators, I distributed 2,150 surveys to middle school, high school, and college students (aged eleven to forty-nine) in nineteen states plus the District of Columbia and two Canadian provinces. I distributed the survey only to female students. I didn't want to use men as the standard, measuring women against them, then concluding that women are more or less competitive than men are. I didn't want to discover or emphasize gender differences. I just wanted to ask women and girls some questions about competition. Some surveys were distributed to athletic teams, and others to required classes. Almost half the questionnaires (1,030) were completed and usable.

I'll discuss the results throughout the book. First, here's the big picture: Athletes were much more likely than nonathletes to think of themselves as competitive, to describe themselves as bold, to enjoy competing with friends or lovers, to feel positive when comparing their achievements with those of others, and to expect to win in new situations.

Nonathletes were more likely to be uncomfortable with competition, to avoid competitive situations, and to believe friends shouldn't compete. Yet nonathletes were just as likely as athletes to believe that "learning to win and lose are essential skills in today's society." They were equally likely to agree that "competitive women tend to be successful." More than half of both groups agreed that "Often, women can compete without being cutthroat about it."

Few of the women talked about competition "with friends, family, or co-workers." That's what I'm here for: to talk about it. To name problems, propose solutions, and encourage you to think about your own competitive attitudes, behaviors, and goals.

In this book I ask the question, Why are we still acting like Cheerleaders? Why is popularity such a driving force in our lives? What would happen if we allowed ourselves to compete with men? Not like men, but with men?

What does it mean to be a Champion? How does a Champion act? How can we compete with integrity and compassion? Is there a way to care about others *and* care about ourselves while striving for victory?

The lessons in this book can be applied to rivalries at work, in the gym, on Wall Street, on Capitol Hill. But unlike other books about women and competition, this book is not designed to teach women how to play by men's rules. I don't sing along with Rex Harrison: "Why can't a woman be more like a man?" I've never wanted to be a Conqueror, and haven't met too many women who do. This book does not assume female deficiency. It will not use football analogies. Men are not, in my opinion, better competitors than women are; in fact, my second book (*The Stronger Women Get, the More Men Love Football*) criticizes the masculine-dominance-at-all-costs paradigm.

This book is for women who are willing to make up their own rules. It's for women who love to win and women who are afraid to win and women who hate the word "winning." It's not only about winning. It's about how women can compete without losing our spouses and friends and codes of ethics. It's about how women can see the world if we let competition be fun. If we let it be a game.

In Part One I elaborate on my model of Conquerors, Cheerleaders, and Champions. In Part Two I describe my five-part framework for conceptualizing competition. In Part Three I discuss how the sporting experience is changing women's approach to competition and why even athletes struggle. In Part Four I examine how sexist influences and our diverse backgrounds make competition complicated. And in Part Five I offer such advice as: Give yourself permission to compete. Be willing to lose. Decide when to compete and when not to. See men as your peers. And think of yourself as a Champion.

The book is a love story, really. It's about how to compete with your heart open. It's about the joy and pain and humor of competition. I encourage you to love yourself enough to compete for what you want. To let go of the feminine conditioning that women shouldn't win or shouldn't defeat men. To demand victory—for yourself and for your "team," whether your teammates are poker players or IBM executives. To cheer for your teammates, but not instead of pursuing your own goals. And to stop competing over popularity and prettiness and thin thighs.

While researching this book, I interviewed some women who have been wounded by competition and are wary of it and are intimately acquainted with the ways it can hurt. I interviewed experts, female and male. But I searched for ordinary successful women who compete well. Who love to compete. Who know how to integrate their respect for their opponents with their own desire to succeed. Who pay attention to the process—competing respectfully—and the result: who wins. These women demonstrate what most of my survey respondents believe: that competition doesn't have to be cutthroat. That Champions can compete both triumphantly and tenderly.

I interviewed about two hundred women and girls and surveyed more than a thousand of them and read everything I could find on the subject, but this is also a personal book, based on the wisdom I've gained from a lifetime of competing in sports, at work, and in my family. Competition is a process of aspiring to be greater than you are. It's a process of seeking excellence with others. It's a process I've been studying all my life.

Maybe your perspective is different. Maybe you (or Alfie Kohn) could write a better book. Go ahead. I'll read it, learn something, and thank you for the inspiration—and the opportunity to compete. Meanwhile here's everything I know.

Chapter 2

What Men Are Doing in This Book

While investigating how women compete and what keeps us from competing, I noticed that it's impossible (for me) to write a book about women without also writing about men, because male styles of competition, male beliefs about who should compete with whom, and male-erected barriers to female success affect how women compete.

Men often control what women do. Even when men aren't in control and aren't necessarily trying to be in control, women often wonder what men might do if they were in control, if men felt threatened. Many women care what men think, and these women make decisions about their own competitive behavior on the basis of what they presume men think. Decisions about whom to compete with, and when and how, are filtered through women's awareness of male power, male egos, and male reluctance to lose to women.

Two stories—one about a butler, the other about mice—illustrate these points.

I heard the butler story from a playwright, Carolyn Gage, who writes about strong women like Joan of Arc and Louisa May Alcott. She has noticed a disturbing trend: Whenever there's a male character in one of her plays, audiences assume he's the main character. "For instance, say there's a butler, and he brings in the tea," she explains. "It's an insignificant role. Yet he will draw an inordinate amount of focus from the audience." From postperformance discussion sessions with audience members, Gage has learned that "they will see the butler as central. Crazy though it seems, the women are perceived in terms of what they mean to the butler. It becomes a play about the butler."

I notice the same dynamic when I tour the country, talking to college and professional audiences about women's empowerment through sports. Women are the subject of my talks. I mention male coaches or fathers or husbands, but they are not usually my intended focus. Yet often, especially in mixed-gender audiences, people's questions and comments pertain to men. Men assert that female athletes are inferior to male athletes. Women ask questions about how to be athletic or competitive yet still be pleasing to men.

So it was when I interviewed women for this book. Many of them spoke hesitantly and self-consciously, as if they were wondering, *Are there any butlers in the room? Is there anyone around who might think me immodest, who might think me unfeminine, who might feel intimidated by my success?*

Gage notes that this dynamic occurs "in any situation in which people have dominant and subordinate status. The members of the subordinate group will alter their behaviors in response to the members of the dominant group."

One way women alter their behavior is by avoiding competitions with men. A little story about mice helps explain this.

First, this background: Male mice tend to fight. Female mice don't. Place two male mice in a cage together and often they battle until one rolls onto his back and exposes his throat, indicating submissiveness. It's mouse language for "Uncle!" or "I give in" or "If you wanted to, you could kill me, so go ahead and feel superior, and let's get on with living in peace."[1]

By mistake, scientists at Johns Hopkins University recently discovered that when male mice are genetically altered so they lack nitric oxide, they become so aggressive that two males placed in the same cage will battle to the death. When the submissive mouse rolls onto his back and exposes his throat, the dominant mouse rips it apart.

Nitric oxide is a gaseous molecule that allows nerve cells to communicate with each other. In addition to this effect on male mouse aggression, it has an effect on male mouse sexuality. Usually, when a male mouse is placed in a cage with a female who is not in estrus, the male will try to mount her once or twice but then give up. Genetically altered mice "keep trying to mount the female, no matter how much she screams."

The authors of a paper on this subject are not as cautious as scientists usually are about extrapolating to humans. They say that nitric oxide "may be a major mediator of sexual and aggressive behavior . . . in humans as well as mice." Presumably they mean in human men, since female mice lacking nitric oxide do not become aggressive and since sexual assailants and murderers are rarely women.

My intention here is not to curtail men's sexually aggressive or murderous behavior through molecular manipulations (though I'd be all for it). Nor am I attempting to attribute human rape or murder to biochemistry. Surely there are other reasons besides an imbalance of nitric oxide that account for men's violence toward other men and women (and mice, but that's another story). But I think this little mouse tale can go a long way toward explaining why women avoid competing with men.

Note the correlation between mouse murder and mouse rape. Note that when dominance displays are carried to an extreme, they include not only deadly assaults on males but also sexual assaults on females. Note that when male mice become aggressive in the presence of female mice, that aggression takes a sexual form. Note that between male and female mice, sex becomes a form of dominance.

Sound familiar?

Even if it has no relevance to humans at all, I think the mouse story validates a feeling that many women have: that some men—perhaps men who lack some molecule in the brain, perhaps men who lack common courtesy—take winning to extremes. That they go for the jugular. That they try to win, to dominate, even when having sex. That all they want to do is dominate. That domination is their *modus operandi*, the name of their game.

The mouse story validates women's discomfort with competition as men have defined it. It reminds me of this human story: Most women desire neither to be dominated nor to dominate. They know all about having to roll over and say, "I submit," so someone will stop picking on them. They have read about other women who got their throats slashed open. They know about rape, attempted rape, date rape, and the myriad other ways men try to be "on top." Women know, of course, that not all men equate competition with domination, and that, of course, not all men assault women. Nevertheless, it's not always easy to distinguish men who see women as peers from men who might suddenly use force or other nasty tactics to assert their supposed supremacy over women. As a result, women tend to be wary about competing with men. Sometimes they're wary of competition itself.

So they say, "Let's not compete. Let's construct a system in which no one is dominant over anyone else, and no one gets hurt."

I say, "Let's think about competition some other way. Let's separate domination from competition, power-over from power-to. Let's think about whether displays of dominance ever belong in the bedroom. Let's devise ways to compete in which no one gets his or her neck ripped open and no one gets conquered."

There was a time when women learned about competition and victory and teamwork without men. In locker rooms, in women's gyms, and in the privacy of all-female physical education classes and sports teams, girls and women in the first part of this century were to some degree free from male influence, free from concerns about how female competition and victory would affect male ego, pride, and desire to control.

This was not an accident. Female physical educators deliberately created all-female spaces in which women could sweat and strive, and win or lose, in privacy, without male cheers or jeers. Responding to the violence, scandal, and commercialization that already plagued men's sports (as well as to men's limitations on women's access to sports), these coaches taught sportswomanship as well as sports skills, emphasizing the values they thought important: health, cooperation, participation, respect, friendship, and high moral conduct. Games took place in the refuge of the "girls' gym," where the referees and coaches were women. Sometimes they forbade men to watch.

We don't have those spaces anymore. We don't have women's gyms anymore because women of my generation rightfully demanded access to the larger "men's" gyms. We don't play in private anymore because spectators, male and female, come to watch. Nowadays, most coaches in women's sports are men. Most administrators are men. Many recreational sports, from youth soccer to corporate softball, are co-ed.

There aren't too many all-female environments left outside the sporting world either. There aren't many women's colleges anymore. There aren't women's occupations anymore. Men have proved themselves capable of serving food on airlines, changing hospital linens, answering telephones, and typing. Women simultaneously have become investment bankers, firefighters, airline pilots, and heavy-equipment operators.

So we no longer live in separate spheres. Instead women compete with men every day: in sports, in relationships, at work, for political office, and often for political rights. As demonstrated by the gender gap (the difference between how women vote and how men vote), women tend to compete with men to determine who our leaders will be and what our laws will be. We also compete with male assailants, individually and collectively resisting various forms of sexual harassment, exploitation, and assault.

Some men compete compassionately and wisely: like Champions. Some of them are quoted in this book because I appreciate their expertise and I hope female readers can learn from them. (I also hope male readers can learn from this book.) But men appear in this book mostly because they have defined competition in ways that confuse and hurt women, because men compete with women in ways women need to understand, and because women worry, often with good reason, about male reactions to female success. If women are going to learn to compete effectively, we'll have to do so in the presence of men.

Chapter 3

Conquerors

Ross Perot, writing in his autobiography about his competition for a computer service contract, says, "I am going to kill those guys, then I'm going to bury them, and then I am going to dance on their graves until the stench gets so bad I can't stand it."[1]

How many women can embrace a competitive style like *that*? Yet this is how men often talk about competition.

I think of this as the Conqueror's way.[2] To a Conqueror, competition is about defeating, vanquishing, subduing, subjugating, displaying dominance. It's about killing and slaughtering and humiliating enemies, then dancing gleefully on their graves. Boston psychotherapist Tracy Wallach says, "Competition becomes and feels destructive when . . . the person must win at all costs and cannot tolerate others winning also."[3] The Conqueror's way is about winning *at the expense* of others, who must lose. Let's hope Gore Vidal was joking when he said, "It is not enough to succeed. All others must fail."[4] Yet this is the Conqueror's way: All others must fail.

The Conqueror's way is also about manliness. It's not an exclusively male perspective, and many men do not see themselves as Conquerors, but men have developed it, embellished it, and associated it with masculinity itself. To be masculine is to be forceful, aggressive, and dominant, over women and over other men. To be masculine is to win. Losing is emasculating.

The Conqueror's way is most obvious in the manly sports arenas (football, baseball, boxing, hockey, and basketball), where games can become bloody battles. But like polluted air, the Conqueror's approach seeps out beyond sports: to the military, which is gaining more of a reputation for assaulting women than for national defense, and also to the business world, where competition is increasingly described in terms of winning—the bottom line, the final analysis. The Conqueror's way implies scarcity: resources in short supply, limited rewards based on performance. One person wins the job, the lover, the gold medal. One company wins the highest percentage of the market share. One person or team or company becomes the Conqueror, the hero who intentionally vanquishes "the enemy." And someone else—or everyone else—must lose.

Because the Conqueror mentality pervades the way we think and talk about competing, competitiveness has become synonymous with hostility, argumentativeness, belligerence, and militancy. To many women, competitiveness has become synonymous with the least appealing aspects of masculinity.

The gender hierarchy itself—in which women are told they're either inferior or superior but are rarely treated as teammates or colleagues or equal partners—has also given competition a bad name. Having been on the conquered end of the Conqueror's quest, most women don't aspire to be Conquerors themselves. Having watched male leaders "spar" over everything from federal budgets to foreign policies, many women have grown weary of a world view in which compromise is a sign of weakness. Having watched men brutalize one another ("knock 'em dead") and their own bodies ("no pain, no gain") in the name of athletic conquest ("in your face") and the spirit of war ("killer instinct"), some women have come to abhor competition of all kinds. Having watched men's disagreements over sneakers and jackets end in murder, women feel wary of rivalries. They condemn macho maneuverings that mask feelings of impotence, anxiety, or

loneliness. They're turned off by abuses that seem endemic to competition: insider trading, harassment of "subordinates," and a philosophy that "cheating isn't cheating if the refs don't see."

"Competition is male," women say. Or, "That's a competitive,
male way of doing things."

So while men congratulate each other on their competitive businesses and competitive colleges and competitive armies, women complain, "Oh, I'd never work with her. She's too competitive."

While fathers scream at their children from the sidelines of the
soccer fields, mothers comfort their crying kids and look at each other
quizzically. "Isn't this league too competitive for five-year-olds?"

Mona Harrington has researched female attorneys' responses to
the Conqueror model in the legal system. Though some women thrive
on this form of competition, most abhor it, says Harrington, author
of *Women Lawyers: Rewriting the Rules*.[5] They denounce the hierarchy among colleagues and the combative method of settling disputes. They complain that men intimidate, brag about their victories,
and engage in "silly war games." They contend that the adversarial
method is an inefficient way to solve problems and that it "too often
fosters game-playing as opposed to problem-solving or truth-finding
or justice-dealing.

"Drawn to the law by its promise of fairness," many women "shun
chronic engagement in battle," Harrington says. These women prefer
being open with people, looking for shades of gray, finding common
ground. "Women like to roundtable it and come out with everybody
feeling a little bit the winner and a little bit the loser." They find the
legal profession's male culture alienating, too competitive, and not
compatible with being a caring human being.

As women enter the paid work force in greater numbers, will they
get accustomed to the Conqueror's way and adopt it as their own? In
a 1994 book called *Hardball for Women: Winning at the Game of
Business,* Pat Heim advises, "If you're vying with your coworker Bob
for the opportunity to head the plum project and you're competitive,
you may do anything within your ethical boundaries to ensure that

you achieve your goal: Drop comments about his incompetence, point out his past cost overruns to your superiors, or even conveniently 'lose' his files and sabotage his progress—in short, pull out all the stops to undermine his winning the project." Just doing a good job yourself, Heim warns, is not enough.[6]

The women I've talked with tend to resist such advice. They seek ways to compete that preclude sabotaging others in order to advance themselves. Maybe I'm not looking in the right places, but I don't see too many female Conquerors. I've met women who enjoy domination and intimidation, but not many.

Sure, one time a crazed Texas mother arranged for the murder of her daughter's friend's mother, hoping that the young rival would be too distracted to make the cheerleading squad. But that's hardly an everyday occurrence. Sure, Tonya Harding's henchman hit her rival on the kneecap, but this hardly signifies an upward trend in female violence. More women are imprisoned now than ever before, but their crimes remain primarily prostitution and drug use. Some female bosses are bossy, and some female lawyers and surgeons and stockbrokers are more greedy than graceful. But don't we notice them and comment on them because they stand out? I once read about an Olympic swimmer who refused to shake hands with her rival, saying, "I hope she drowns," but I've never heard that since. I don't see women being ejected from athletic events for fighting, for spitting on referees, for unsportsmanlike conduct. I don't see female members of Congress being censured by the Senate or House of Representatives for ethical violations or sexual harassment. Few women lie in bed at night dreaming of becoming conquering heroes. It's not our myth, our quest. So I'm not terribly concerned that women will follow in men's footsteps. I'm more concerned that boys will follow in men's footsteps, but that's beyond the scope of this book. Carolyn G. Heilbrun writes in *Reinventing Womanhood:* "If women adopt the male models of achievement, must they take on its meaner aspects as well? I would answer that the meaner aspects of competitive male behavior are despicable in men and would be equally so in women. But to insist that women shun competitive behavior solely for that reason is to condemn women to continued failure, while doing nothing to redeem the sins of the male."[7]

The Conqueror's way affects how all of us think about competition. Conquering is what we're objecting to when we say we hate competition. Conquering is what we're not doing when we say we're not competing. Conquering is what we're up against when men compete with us.

So we can't talk about competition without talking about domination and power and manliness. Even if that's not how we compete, and not how we'd like to compete, and not how we're raising our sons or daughters to compete, the Conqueror's way demands our attention, complicating and influencing any female or feminist form of competition that we might imagine.

Chapter 4

Cheerleaders

A few years ago two teenage girls approached me with a dilemma. They wanted to try out for the high school basketball team I was coaching, but they also wanted to cheer for the boys' team. They couldn't do both.

I was mystified. How could anyone choose cheerleading over basketball?

"Play basketball," I implored them. "We have more fun."

I figured that was part of my job, recruiting girls for my team. I was open about my bias. Cheerleading relegates girls to a support role. Cheerleaders get to feel like winners only if the athletes—usually male— win. Girls need to learn about winning (and losing) on their own.

I wasn't persuasive, apparently, because both girls chose cheerleading. An administrator later reprimanded me for telling girls that basketball is better than cheerleading.

Basketball *is* better than cheerleading. Cheerleading is a relic of the past and should be abolished.

But the incident got me thinking. Isn't this how most women learn to compete, like Cheerleaders? Doesn't this explain in part women's ambivalence about competition? While men are conditioned to compete like Conquerors, women are conditioned to compete like Cheerleaders.

The Cheerleader competes smilingly, submissively, subordinately, attractively, on the sidelines, and for the sake of male players and male fans. She competes only with girls and only for a place on the squad. She competes not to see who is the best but who is the bust-iest. Not to see who is the bravest but who is the most beautiful. Not to see who is the most successful but who is the most sexy. She takes center stage but only for a brief display of bouncing breasts and thrusting hips. When the boys return from the locker room at half-time, the Cheerleader returns to her "natural" place on the periphery.

She uses her voice to chant, to sing, to encourage others, but she rarely says how she feels or who she is or what sort of victory she might want for herself. No matter how she feels, she always smiles. No matter whom she likes, she always flirts.

Cheerleaders are an anachronism, a vestige of an earlier era when men were men and women stayed on the sidelines. Yet they're an archetype that affects us all. Our early training in covert competition and approval seeking pervades women's consciousness.

Kim Irwin cheered at Conestoga High School in Berwyn, Penn-sylvania, in the sixties. When she turned forty-five a few years ago, she realized she "was still trying to live up to a Cheerleader image: happy and bouncy, smiling all the time, having a good figure."

Ann Hopkins's refusal to play the Cheerleader game cost her her job, at least temporarily. Back in 1989, Hopkins, a lawyer, successfully sued her employer, Price Waterhouse, for denying her a partnership. The trial revealed that the male lawyers had told Hopkins she should "take a course at charm school." They had said she could improve her chances at making partner if she would "walk more femininely, talk more femininely, wear makeup, have her hair styled, and wear jewelry."

How much has changed since then? How many women succeed without tempering their competitiveness, toning it down with behav-iors and dress that men consider appropriately feminine? Don't most of us feel pressured to play the Cheerleader game?

Even athletic women can find themselves trapped in the Cheer-leader pose, playing a decorative and supportive role or glancing side-long at their sisters, competing over beauty and boyfriends. Even retired speed skater Bonnie Blair, whose six Olympic medals (includ-ing five gold) are the most won by any U.S. woman in any Summer or Winter Games, has been cast as a Cheerleader. In a recent *Wash-ington Post* article Blair was described as "cheering" for her husband, David Cruikshank, as he competed in the 1996 U.S. Sprint Speed-skating Championships in Milwaukee. In fact she was not cheering but coaching. "I was working with the juniors quite a bit last year, but now I'm working with Dave," she explained. Yet both text and headline misrepresented the situation. WITH HER CAREER ON ICE, BLAIR TURNS TO CHEERLEADER, said the headline.

Cheerleading itself has changed in the past few years, reflecting current confusions and contradictions about how women should com-pete, and for what. Cheerleaders are still sexy, underdressed perform-ers, entertaining the spectators by appearing perky, pretty, and pleasing, but nowadays sometimes cheerleaders cheer for female ath-letes. Some "competitive cheer" squads perform stunts in front of judges. ESPN televises the College Cheerleading and Dance Team National Championship, and younger kids compete in a national high school championship.

Jody Oberfelder, a choreographer for a New York–based feminist performance event called *Wanted: X-Cheerleaders,*[1] feels optimistic that cheerleaders are becoming bolder. While performing in Tampa, she met with a group of African-American girls who had made up such cheers as:

We're bad
we know it
we're here
to show it
and what you see is what you get and you ain't seen nothing yet.

"Their act was so good," says Oberfelder. "They weren't selling their sexuality; they were owning it."

But before you think that cheerleading is liberating girls from stereotypical roles, check out *American Cheerleader,* a magazine for teenage girls. In the April 1997 issue, for instance, articles address "gameday beauty," prom fashions, and hair care hints. In an article titled "Tryout Tales: The Secrets of Your Success," girls are advised: "If you are trying out for the first time, remember to smile and be peppy."

Check out the games girls are playing. A new CD-ROM game for ten- to fifteen-year-olds "features cheerleaders and aspiring actresses chasing males and developing strategies as to how to act to snag a boy."[2]

Also check out how parents are dressing their girls. Little boys, including infants, are often seen wearing NBA and NFL jerseys that sport the names of their heroes on the back. But clothing companies that sell licensed sports apparel report that the fastest-selling items in 1997 were for female toddlers and infants: cheerleading outfits.[3]

Some modern cheerleading squads include boys and men, but the presence of male cheerleaders—who lift and throw the "girls" but never get lifted or thrown—serves only to reinforce the image of women as relatively weak, and as objects of beauty for male enjoyment. One male college cheerleader told sociologist Laurel R. Davis, "I think what a female is there for, really, is to show her flexibility and her beauty . . . the all-American girl, you know, with the smile and everything. And the guy's supposed to smile, but he's supposed to show that masculinity out there, like, you know, he'd throw her up, he'd catch her. He's always stiff. . . . It's always that masculinity and femininity."[4]

Masculinity and femininity. Problematic, aren't they? Neither the "masculine" approach nor the "feminine" approach to competition works very well for women. We don't want to compete "like men" with all their Conquering machismo, nor are most of us comfortable limiting ourselves to the Cheerleader role. We're turned off by competitions that are adversarial and combative, but competing only behind the scenes, and only with girls, and only over beauty and boyfriends no longer feels right either. Fortunately, there is a better way.

Chapter 5

Champions

In *Are We Winning Yet?* I describe what I call the partnership model: "a compassionate, egalitarian approach to sport in which athletes are motivated by love of themselves, of sport, and of each other. Power is understood not as power-over (power as dominance) but as power-to (power as competence). Teammates, coaches, and even opposing players view each other as comrades rather than enemies. Players with disparate ability levels are respected as peers rather than ranked in a hierarchy, and athletes care for each other and their own bodies."[1]

It's a women's way of competing, initiated by pioneering physical educators. A 1953 manual published by the National Association for Girls and Women in Sports lists desirable outcomes for athletic contests: "The participants came to appreciate companionship, experienced growth in desirable personal traits, admired skill in others, and were satisfied with a game well played, regardless of who won."[2]

At a women's sports convention in the early eighties a coach named Betty Menzie proposed: "Sport can be viewed without overemphasis on winning, but with winning being a part of the game. Sport can be a place where all participants can be winners, where losing the contest does not demean or degrade."[3]

Jo Oliver, a professor of kinesiology and health promotion at California State Polytechnic University, Pomona, says through sport, women learn "to understand perseverance and playing as hard as you can against someone and having the utmost respect for that person."

This cooperative, dignified form of competition can extend beyond sports. It can be taken into the workplace, into relationships, even into one's relationship with oneself. It's an alternative to Conquering, an alternative to Cheerleading.

I'm calling it the Champion's way. I use the word "Champion" to describe someone who competes ethically, effectively, and compassionately. She savors the process while striving for results. She respects her opponents and acts in ways that are worthy of her opponents' respect. Perhaps most important, she makes wise decisions about when to compete and when not to compete.

She is not necessarily an athlete and doesn't limit her competitions to sports. But just as my Cheerleader analogy is based on the role of female cheerleaders, so the Champion's way is based on what I have learned from female athletes and what I know about competition from my own athletic experience.

The Champion risks public victory or defeat. She compares herself with others based not on her looks, but on her performance, and based not solely on the final score but on how well she has played the game at hand. Strong and courageous, she exudes a sense of power, openness, and possibility.

The Champion is not a Conqueror. She does not try to slaughter or destroy anyone. She tests herself against rivals and welcomes them, trusting that they will invigorate and motivate her. She finds a way to win without defeating her opponent. She knows she won't win all the time. She acts like a winner anyway: proud, confident, gracious. She acts like a winner even when she doesn't feel like one, not only so she'll impress her rivals, but so that she'll remind herself.

The Champion is not a Cheerleader. She supports her teammates, even cheering for them when she herself is on the bench, but she does not limit herself to a supportive or decorative role. She does not compete for what she wants by acting coquettish or cute. She takes up space with her body and her voice, conveying her own ideas, asserting her own needs, refusing to shrink to meet anyone's approval. She smiles only when she's happy, yells only when she has something to say. She's willing to compete with men.

Buddhists follow an eightfold path that includes "right comprehension that dissipates delusion," "right self-discipline that brings no regret," "right speech that makes for clarity," and "right livelihood that brings no discredit." The Champion's path is what I think of as right competition. Right competition that conquers no one. Right competition that respects all contestants, including the self. Right competition that honors the process as well as the outcome. Right competition that limits women to neither stereotypically male nor stereotypically female ways of competing.

Most of what I know about being a Champion I learned from sports. In sports you get to practice competing. You learn the rules. You identify your opponents. You set goals, practice, persist in the face of disappointment and difficulty. You learn about the delicate balance between wanting to win and accepting that you probably won't. You learn how to love an opponent because she offers you such a fine challenge, but you also learn how to try to defeat her—or him.

I feel like a Champion because my parents treated me like one, expecting me to compete and excel in an honorable fashion. I feel like a Champion because I have competed often, in many ways. If you don't compete, you can't feel like a Champion.

Like most competitors, I've lost more times than I've won. I've been defeated or rejected more times than I've finished first, ahead of the pack. But I've learned to see losses as painful but essential stumbles along an otherwise victorious path. I've learned not to let defeat diminish my core self-concept, my perception of myself as someone who wins. When other writers or public speakers write more beautifully, tell funnier jokes, fly out ahead of me like Gail Devers soaring over the hurdles, they show me what's possible.

This seems to be how it works: You come to think of yourself as a Champion if you are allowed or encouraged to compete; if you come from a culture of Champions; if you are told, "Just do your best"; if your mother or father or spouse walks around the house cheerfully chanting, "If at first you don't succeed, try, try again!"; if you are told that you're okay, that you're good enough—and that you are loved, win or lose.

No one is a Champion all the time. To compete well is rarely easy. Even the best, most well-intentioned competitors lose their balance, lose their perspective, lose their commitment to fairness. Since many jobs depend on bottom-line victories, it's easy for both employers and employees to engage in "minor" ethics violations. Since cheating is so commonplace as to be socially acceptable in many contexts, it's easy for many of us to cheat in subtle, imperceptible ways. Since our society is so greedy for gold, it's easy for athletes to push past ability and into disability, never learning to respect their own physical limits. Even the high school basketball players I coached struggled with competition, devastated by defeat but unwilling to work hard enough to put themselves in a position to win.

I think it's in the striving, in the discomfort, in the intersection between ambition (what you want to do) and reality (what you can do) that one learns to feel like a Champion.

One learns to *act* like a Champion through practice.

Part Two

Five
Useful Ways to
Think About
Competition

Chapter 6

Competition Is a Relationship;
It Requires Compassion

The first time my mother and I competed against each other I was five years old. She was thirty-seven. We swam one lap of our neighbor's pool. She won.

"Ha! Beat you!" she proclaimed.

Mom had been waiting for this day for a long time. Like many women of her generation, Sarah Burton Nelson was born with athletic inclinations and a competitive spirit but little opportunity to express either. She learned to swim before kindergarten and staged competitions with friends but was expected to outgrow such childish games. She acquiesced, limiting herself to lap swimming. Even there she would surreptitiously race against the person in the neighboring lane. Her unabashed enthusiasm for victory ("Ha! Beat you!") often gave her away.

That's why I got to be born. Having failed to find suitable rivals, Mom decided to create some. Her first child, my older sister, Carol, had little interest in sports. Mom's second child, Peter, loved soccer, baseball, crew, and tennis but, because of ear problems, wasn't allowed to swim.

Finally, with me, Mom could stop having kids because I loved all sports, including swimming, and was just as eager to race as she was. I remember that first race, when I was five, with great fondness. We dived into the cold water, and I paddled as fast as I could to the other end of the pool. When I finished, I looked over at Mom and saw her slapping the end of the pool *again*, for emphasis. "Ha! Beat you!"

I was ecstatic too. After all, my mother—dark, curly hair flattened against her head like a cap, eyes red from chlorine—was grinning at me. I had just swum my fastest lap ever. My mom and I were playing together. No one had told me that losing was a bad thing.

Still, I was no dummy. Winning seemed even more fun. So while Mom was busy working, I joined a local swim team. Each summer Mom and I raced and she won. Undeterred, I practiced my breathing, my racing dives, my flip turns. Finally, the year I turned ten, I beat my mom. She disputes this now. "I don't know about that," she says, frowning. "I think you were eleven."

Mom was also my fan. As I saw it, my major competitors were Jean and Joan Spinelli, the twins from the famous swimming Spinelli family in our mini town of Blue Bell, Pennsylvania. Jean had skinny arms as sharp and swift as Osterizer blades; Joan had furious legs that started kicking before she hit the water, like a windup bathtub toy. I didn't stand a chance.

But Mom rooted for me anyway, yelling from the sidelines as if I could hear her underwater. She transported my friends and me to meets all over the county. In those pre–seat belt days she liked to drive fast on Jolly Road so we'd fly out of our seats and scream. She arranged practice time for me during family vacations to the Jersey shore. It made me feel important to skip deep-sea fishing trips with my father and siblings to work out at the Olympic-size Flanders Pool in Ocean City.

At the year-end championships Mom and I ganged up on the Spinelli twins in the mother-daughter relay races. The daughters' lap came first, and Jean or Joan (they alternated years) beat me despite my best efforts. So Mrs. Spinelli dived in while Mom waited impatiently for me. As I touched, I'd look up to see Mom's legs streamlined behind her like the spindly legs of a sandhill crane. I'd feel content, sure she'd catch Mrs. Spinelli and the other mothers. Mom and I were undefeated for six years until adolescence caught up with me and I left swimming for more interesting things, like basketball.

So when I think about competition, I remember the Spinelli twins, who joined me in the showers after the meets, the three of us giggling and whispering until all the hot water ran out. They never considered me a threat and I never begrudged them their speed, though I like to think they swam a little faster when I was splashing near their ankles. I know they inspired me to swim my fastest.

When I think about competition, I remember my six-foot three-inch basketball teammate Heidi Wayment, who rebounded the ball viciously, sharp elbows out. I hated her elbows but loved her audacity and her long, strong hands, mirrors of my own.

When I think about competition, I realize that by introducing me to sports and by never letting me win, my mother—who at fifty-five took up tennis and at sixty tried downhill skiing—taught me about love.

To compete is to connect. To compete is to compare your skills or knowledge or children or clothes with those of someone else. Psychologists call it social comparison theory: Through comparisons with others, people seek to understand themselves and to measure their own success. In this process you get to know the other person: his or her strengths, weaknesses, fears, hopes, dreams. You gain compassion for others. You get to know yourself and gain compassion for yourself.

Usually you improve. In the earliest known experiment on competition, British bike racer E. B. Turner studied bike racers between 1886 and 1889. He confirmed what athletes suspected even then: Racing against a person yielded faster results than racing against the clock. Turner concluded "that the bodily presence of another rider is a stimulus to the racer in arousing the competitive instinct; that another thus can be the means of releasing or freeing nervous energy for him that he cannot of himself release; and further, that the sight of movement in that other by perhaps suggesting a higher rate of speed, is also an inspiration to greater effort."[1]

The bodily presence of other competitors—or spectators—does not have that same effect on everyone. Turner studied only men; women's reactions to competition are sometimes different. He studied only bike racers; people who ride bikes recreationally or compete in other arenas may have a different reaction to competition. He studied only people with histories of public performance; people who are shy might not thrive on having an audience. His work is also more than one hundred years old.

But writer Valerie Miner sounds very much like Turner when she describes her "cooperative competition" with another novelist: "The very presence of the other writer made us try harder—gave us both a permission and a further incentive—to get our work published."[2]

What Turner noticed is important: Competition is a dynamic that happens between people or between teams. It's a connection; it's a comparison; it's a relationship.

A competitive relationship *can* be antagonistic and destructive. It often is, when the winner gloats or cheats or the loser feels defeated, personally or permanently. In these cases, competition destroys intimacy. But must it be antagonistic? No. Competition need not be adversarial or hateful. It does not even have to involve trying to make the other person lose.

Much depends on the attitude of the competitors. Sometimes you like your rivals because they seem competent or kind, because you appreciate that they're challenging you to excel, because they are gently teasing and playing with you. Sometimes you don't like your rivals because their naked ambition reminds you of your own, because they're succeeding where you're failing (or where you haven't even tried yet), or because you perceive competition to be unseemly or threatening.

When competition is confusing, it can be useful to return to my definition—seeking excellence together—and ask yourself: What am I seeking? Joy? Attention? Possessions? Vindication for past defeats?

Am I "together" with my opponents, respecting their abilities and desires as well as my own? Also, am I "together" within myself: moral, wise, mature?

It's also helpful to cultivate compassion for losers. Mary Duquin, a University of Pittsburgh professor who teaches the psychology and sociology of health and the body, acknowledges that "the feeling of the winners is wonderful" but asks her students to imagine "the misery of the people who lose." She reminds her students that "there are a whole bunch of people who seldom win and who have internalized that sense of loss." This is not an easy lesson to convey. "In our culture it's very difficult to develop compassion for people who lose because the mentality of the system is that you probably deserve to lose."

Ideally the loser does not feel miserable—in part *because* of the compassion of the winner. Ideally competition is unifying. The tennis net divides two players, but they are playing *together*. An argument polarizes two women, but they are *talking*. An employer chooses only one of two high school classmates for a summer job, but in the process of applying for the job, both teens clarify their goals and potentially deepen their friendship.

Women who compete with each other are both separate *and* connected. You want to win, but you don't want the other person to suffer. You want the other person to excel, to feel excellent, and to challenge you so that ultimately your winning effort (or your losing effort) means something. You want the other person to do her best because you want her to feel good about her effort too. In a way you're actually cheering for her, hoping she succeeds. Because of your respect for her and your respect for the competitive process, you do your best to succeed also.

In this way opponents become allies, not enemies. Gail Whitaker, associate vice-president of San Francisco State University, refers to opponents as "kindred spirits who serve to bring out each other's best performances."[3]

Sport psychologist and Temple University physical education professor Carole Oglesby asks, "When trying to win, run faster, beat somebody, is that inherently an act of carelessness? I argue that it's not. Your best becomes a standard that potentially lifts everyone around you. That makes questing an ultimate act of care."

Ambition is the desire to succeed. But unlike ambition, which can be solitary and self-motivated, competition is the desire to succeed in concert with someone else who also desires success. It requires relationship, and it requires that both parties be ambitious. Competition means little if all parties are not trying to do well. In an athletic setting, if one person refuses to try hard, the other will often legitimately complain, "You're not even trying!" In a business setting, if one person refuses to try hard while the opponent continues to give her best effort, the competitive relationship will soon cease because the one who is giving the lesser effort will in effect drop out. So competition is a form of cooperation, a way that two or more people or groups of people, agreeing to play by the same rules, challenge each other to succeed.

Female athletes often perceive this connection between competition and cooperation, according to Gloria Solomon, a sport psychology consultant and physical education professor at Texas Christian University. Along with several colleagues, Solomon interviewed five groups of female athletes, from mountain climbers to softball players, and concluded: "The study participants tended to value cooperation regardless of the degree of competitiveness of their physical activity involvement. In many cases cooperation was described as a necessary precursor of competition and . . . competition was valued in large part because it enhanced cooperation."[4]

Solomon elaborates: "They didn't separate the teamwork, the social relations, and the camaraderie from the competitive experience." The women discussed opponents "not as people they were opposed to, but as people they worked in conjunction with in order to have this competitive event. There was a strong valuing of the opponent. Often they were friends off the field."

In the complex game we call life, there's rarely one winner.

There's room for lots of people to succeed. If you help a colleague, then she or he "wins" some spoken or unspoken contest between the two of you, does this detract from your career? It can seem like it. What's often overlooked is how good you can feel about your role as a helper. How you can grow in the process of critiquing your colleague's work. How grateful the colleague will feel for your help. How your friendship might blossom. And that there will be future contests you can win.

Some would say, if you help a colleague, you two are not competing, you're cooperating. I'd say you're cooperating *and* competing. Your success inspires her so she competes to keep up. At another time or in another aspect of your relationship, her success inspires you, so you compete to keep up. If one gets too far ahead to provide a realistic measuring stick, you stop competing, at least in those realms. You set new goals, find new people to challenge you. Meanwhile why not cooperate and compete at the same time?

Because it's scary. It risks damaging the friendship. True. But sometimes we need to see others out there ahead of us in order to imagine what we might achieve. If, to retain a feeling of safety, we compete only with ourselves, we might not imagine how successful we could become. Ideally we set our own goals based on what we think we can achieve, and ideally we think we can achieve a lot. But there's nothing wrong with using others for inspiration along the way. The camaraderie born of cooperation combined with competition can make the journey a lot more fun and less lonely.

Female athletes seem to understand this. "There's nothing like a little competition to bring us all closer together," said an ad in the 1995 National Collegiate Athletic Association Final Four program. "Welcome to the Women's Basketball Finals."

Chris Voelz, the University of Minnesota women's athletic director, says she once competed for a job as athletic administrator at Stanford with another woman, Cheryl Levick. "Often, women think there's only one spot for a woman, and often they're right," says Voelz. "But then they feel like they can't help each other. We decided to do it differently, to share information and compare notes throughout the whole process. We were on the phone constantly. It felt different and refreshing. As friends and colleagues, the process was just as important as the result. We believed that inevitably one of us would be chosen, and the other would have helped her get there.

"When she got the job, I had no regrets. The next year I accepted the job with Minnesota. We still compare notes as we negotiate our contracts, and we laugh about the Stanford job, and the fact that we negotiated that together. It's something we're proud of."

In the game of bridge you don't show your opponent your hand. You don't have to do that while competing for a job either. But you can make conscious decisions about how to compete and how to co-operate with your opponents.

Your rival can become your teammate. She can help you win mother-daughter relay races or larger victories. But even if you don't actually team up, she can help you. If you study your opponent, you'll surely learn something you need to know. Your opponent can become your teacher, guiding you toward persistence or resolve or success. Opponents offer a challenge, an invitation to excellence. That's why you thank them afterward.

To be a successful competitor, you need not seek revenge. You can compete in such a way that beating the other person is far beyond the point. The real challenge, Charles Johnson writes in the novel *The Middle Passage,* is "how to win *without* defeating the other person."[5]

My mother competed with her colleagues and she competed with my father and she competed with her kids, and in her seventies she's only getting stronger, more focused, more successful. Because of Mom's example, I too learned to thrive on competition. It was through this woman—a high achiever, a joyous winner, a hell-bent competi-tor—that I learned to see competition not as a selfish desire to defeat others but as a vehicle for loving the people who join me in this impossible quest for perfection. What better way to get to know some-one than to test your abilities together, to be daring and sweaty and exhausted together?

"If you compare yourself with others," a line in "Desiderata" warns, "you may become vain and bitter, for always there will be greater and lesser persons than yourself." True, this can happen. Yet I have found that by comparing myself with others, I become both self-confident and humble. Through competition I have learned to acknowledge my failures and make allowances for the failures of others. Isn't that what intimacy is all about?

When you compete—when you admit what you want and, in the presence of someone else, strive to obtain it—you expose yourself. Thus competition, like other forms of intimacy, can be terrifying as well as gratifying. Remember how it feels to roll a bowling ball into the gutter? Remember that long walk back to the hard plastic couch where your friends await you, scanning your face for a reaction? Maybe you laugh or shrug to show them: *It's only bowling*. But of course you care. Of course you want strikes, not gutter balls. The more you care, the more bowling (or any activity) holds the potential for satisfaction because there's joy in that unmitigated desire to excel. You want to knock down more pins than the last time you played. You want to knock down more pins than your friend Tammy, who always beats you in poker, and more than your friend Jason, who has an infuriating habit of telling you how to hold the ball. That's competition. And that's the intimacy of it: sharing with your friends those human frailties, that craving, that intensity, that victory or loss.

Try saying this: "I want to succeed." Try saying to a friend: "I want to be as good as you at surfing [or computer programming or mothering]." You might feel terribly vulnerable. What if you fail? What if your friend feels threatened by your ambition? Here's why it can be worth taking that risk: When you're honest about what you want, you open up the possibility of intimacy. You allow others to see who you are, and you allow the light of day to shine on your competitiveness. Then it doesn't seem shameful and secretive. There's nothing wrong with wanting to win.

I offer this vision, this possibility, this true story: mother and child seeking together—swimming, racing, laughing, caring, growing closer and stronger and swifter. And this update: Now Mom races against her grandkids. A few years ago I watched an impromptu race between Mom and my sister's eldest daughter, Teagan. The two swimmers, one seventy and one ten, churned furiously back and forth for two laps of a hotel pool. Teagan won.

"I lost to a ten-year-old!" moaned Mom.

"It's not the first time," I teased mercilessly.

"You were eleven!" she insisted.

"And you were in your forties," I said, more gently now. "I don't know if you've noticed, Mom, but you're not in your forties anymore."

Mom was quiet for a long time. Finally she said, "Don't tell anyone."

Mom and I still race against each other too. I'm faster than I was at five. Because she has been in training—at seventy she started competing in meets—she's faster than she was at thirty-seven. Nevertheless I give her a head start. Fair is fair, and competitions are most exciting when close. We dive in, frantically swimming as fast as we can. If I win, she insists we race again. If she wins, she smacks her hand against the wall, jerks her head up, and yells, "Ha! Beat you!"

I complain that she must have cheated. She splashes me. I dunk her. We laugh a lot. I think: Yes, this is love.

Chapter 7

Competition Is a Process;
It Requires Awareness

In an attempt to attract female viewers, Dick Ebersol, president of
NBC Sports, designed a kinder, gentler coverage of the 1996
Olympics. Rather than focus on rivalries and victories, NBC focused
on personalities, stories, and obstacles the athletes had to overcome.
Rather than focus on athletes' strengths—as is traditionally done in
sports broadcasting—he emphasized their vulnerabilities. In this way,
he hoped, women in the audience would be able to empathize with
the Olympians.

"Men will sit through the Olympics for almost anything," said
Ebersol, "as long as they get to see some winners and some losers.
Women tend to approach this differently. They want to know who
the athletes are, how they got there, what sacrifices they've made.
They want an attachment, a rooting interest."[1] In other words, they
care about the process.

So in what came to be known as the Oprah Olympics, NBC told
us about athletes' troubled pasts: cancer, car accidents, sports accidents, joint problems, financial problems, coaching problems, divorced parents, dead parents. The storytellers were men (only 20
percent of NBC's broadcasters were women), but the heart-wrenching
stories themselves, along with the very notion of sports as story, rather

than sports as battle, were ostensibly female. It was the "up-close and personal" approach taken to overweening extremes, but from NBC's perspective it worked: The Olympic audience was huge, with 50 percent women (and 35 percent men, 15 percent children and teens of both sexes).

Yet Ebersol's answer to Freud's classic question "What do women want?" was not entirely correct. I heard complaints from women who grew tired of seeing more background than foreground, more sad tales of trying times than happy tales of stunning success. Female sports fans were angry that they didn't get to watch, for instance, the entire gold medal soccer and softball games, which the Americans won and which surely would have been shown in their entirety had they featured male Americans. In fact, in the months after the Olympics, what women seemed most impressed with was the fact that so many American women's teams had won. Not *how* they had won but simply *that* they had won. What Ebersol forgot is that women are competitive as well as compassionate. They care about rivalries. They like to win. They identify with female winners. They do care about process, but that's not all they care about.

Ebersol had played what writer George Leonard calls the Dichotomy Game, in which we choose between seemingly mutually exclusive dualities. Win or lose. Cooperate or compete. Focus on how you play the game, or focus on winning. Ebersol acted as if women and men were opposites, as if cooperation and competition were opposites, as if women's interest in sport somehow ended before the ending of the game.

He should have known that for both women and men, the thrill of competition is dependent upon both process and results. Football coaching legend Vince Lombardi was wrong when he said, "Winning isn't everything, it's the only thing." (He later retracted the statement.) But those who say that "how you play the game" is all that matters are wrong too.

Both matter. How you play the game matters, and winning matters.

Process comes first. Young children are baffled when parents ask, "Did you win?" Before they are taught about keeping score and the consequences that can accrue from the final tally, they just care if they got to kick the soccer ball. They remember if Justin or Jamika knocked them down. They're impressed if the coach brings Gatorade or Popsicles.

Later, as adults, these same people forget about the importance of process. They act as if winning were paramount. They badger their kids: "Did you win?"

Somewhere between the innocence of childhood and the pragmatism of adulthood lies this truth: Process and results both matter. If the result is not good—if you want very much to win and don't—you will be disappointed. But if the process is not good—if you cheat, or the other person cheats, or if you are insufficiently challenged, or if you for any reason do not enjoy the actual play or work that constitutes the competition—the victory will be tainted or meaningless.

In this culture, it's obvious that winning matters. "You have to win," tennis pioneer Billie Jean King has said. "Otherwise, no one pays any attention to what you say."

It's harder to remember that process matters too. Marilou Awiakta, a Cherokee/Appalachian poet and the author of *Selu: Seeking the Corn-Mother's Wisdom*, says, "Some leaders in America say flatly, 'It's a competitive society, and we need to teach people to be competitive.' I'd like these leaders to take a deep look at what they're doing. True, society is structured in a competitive way, but society is also deconstructing into drugs, suicide, and despair. It seems to me we're out of balance. It seems to me that competition is harmful when it's in excess. Competition can be positive when it is in harmony, when the focus is on the process and the development, the relationship. When a business competes to improve its product, to improve service to its customer, to attain a reasonable profit, that's good. But when it turns to corporate raiding and inferior merchandising and ignoring the customer or viewing the customer as a sucker, that's wrong."

The process of competing can go like this: You feel envious of your competitors for what they have, what they're doing, how they look or act or achieve. *Webster's* defines "envy" as "painful or resentful awareness of an advantage enjoyed by another joined with a desire to possess the same advantage." So you start disliking the person of whom you're envious. You find yourself criticizing her house, her spouse, whatever she's got that you want. This is a passive, powerless state. You might get stuck there because the next step, competition, feels unfamiliar and scary. Or because you don't understand competition, confusing it with conflict and conquering.

But the process can go like this: You feel envious. You feel awful. Then you deliberately shift into a competitive mode, telling yourself: "I could do that too. I could be that smart, be that successful, have that thing or that quality or that relationship that I so envy in another person." You do your homework. You try your best. You compete.

As it turns out, you might not get what you want. You might not succeed. You might not feel victorious in any way. Competition is like that. You don't always win. But in the effort you improve. At least, when you focus on your own behavior, you stop feeling inadequate, deprived, and one down and you start feeling empowered.

Often the process is the most rewarding part of competition. Stephanie Erickess-Caluya, a Seattle carpenter and former Stanford basketball player, says, "There's a good part in being a little bit competitive, getting this rhythm going when you're working with a partner. You're asking the other person to be their best. You're pushing them. I love that. It's wonderful. It reminds me of basketball.

"On a roof, say, you're figuring out patterns. It's geometry, and it's repetitive. You're doing shingle after shingle. It's a lot about speed. You're bending over at the waist, and it's not your favorite thing to do—no one loves to bend over at the waist—so you want to get it done. It's precise, and you each have a different task. Say your coworker does A, B, then you do C, D. It's like a drill. You do it over and over. A, B, then C, D. I lay down a shingle, my partner shoots [nails] it, I've got the next one laid out, my partner shoots it. You're not talking very much when you're good. The smoother you get, the better it feels. It's fast, you're in a rhythm. It's like the ball goes in the basket, you're delivering it into their hands, just right. It's cooperation. What's competitive about it is you're pushing yourself to max it, and they're pushing too. Someone who's not challenging themselves is a drag to work with.

"What I love is the teamwork, the process, and it's there in the trades. If the process sucks, it doesn't work. But when the team really works together, then I'm happy with the product, whether it's a basket or a countertop or a roof. Because everybody's going *yes*."

Lisa Ryerson, president of Wells College in Aurora, New York, says, "I like victory, and I also like the process of getting to victory. I play the clarinet, and I remember that from a very early age, if the instructor said I could play a level four, I wanted to play level five. You didn't get to a five by wanting to be a five. It wasn't wish magic. It was very hard work, and there was a method to it. Did I need to work on my tone or my fingering? Did I need to practice more? I liked the method. You can obtain knowledge, and work through a process, and get to the goal.

"I attained the college presidency in 1995, when I was thirty-five, sooner than I thought I would. I love setting goals and reaching them. But it's also important to see things through. I can be tempted to say, 'Okay, did that. Where's my next victory?' Instead I'm settling in, committing myself to achieving some things for Wells College. Attending a women's college is not the in thing these days. There are many fine women's colleges vying with us for a limited number of interested students. It's a competition, so of course I love it."

Women who understand competition as a dance, or as a form of intimacy, or as an exquisitely pleasing mutual challenge can have a hard time explaining this to other women. In *The Queen's Gambit*[2] Beth Harmon is a thirteen-year-old chess prodigy who competes in the Kentucky state championship against a handsome young man. Novelist Walter Tevis describes the game:

He moved a knight to the fifth rank, and Beth moved a knight to the fifth rank. He checked with a bishop, and she defended with a pawn. He retreated the bishop. She was feeling light now, and her fingers with the pieces were nimble. Both players began moving fast but easily. She gave a non-threatening check to his king, and he pulled away delicately and began advancing pawns. She stopped that handily with a pin and then feinted on the queenside with a rook. He was undeceived by the feint and, smiling, removed her pin, and on his next move continued the pawn advances. She retreated, hiding her king in a queenside castle. She felt somehow spacious and amused, yet her face remained serious. They continued their dance.

It made her sad in a way when she eventually saw how to beat him. It was after the nineteenth move, and she felt herself resisting it as it opened up in her mind, hating to let go of the pleasant ballet they had danced together.

. . . Beth felt genuinely sorry for him when he resigned, tipping his king over and saying, "Damn!" But he stood up, stretched and smiled down at her. "You're one hell of a chess player, Harmon," he said.

Later a *Life* magazine reporter named Jean Balke comes to Beth's house to interview her. "When I was a girl," the reporter tells Beth, "I was never allowed to be competitive. I used to play with dolls."

Beth says, "Chess isn't always 'competitive.'"

"But you play to win," says Jean Balke.

"Beth wanted to say something about how beautiful chess was sometimes, but she looked at Miss Balke's sharp, inquiring face and couldn't find the words for it."

Competition is discussed so overwhelmingly in terms of winners and losers that it can be hard to find the words to describe the beauty of the dance. It can be hard to remember that athletes enjoy playing games, not just standing on victory stands. In a study by Diane Gill, exercise and sport sciences professor at the University of North Carolina at Greensboro, athletes actually placed more emphasis on performance and less on outcome than nonathletes.[3]

Stanford women's basketball coach Tara VanDerveer has said, "We have to be aware of so many things. You have to work hard not just at winning, but winning the right way. I think we have a responsibility to be role models. I think sportsmanship is important."[4]

Mia Hamm, the soccer star who led the United States to an Olympic gold medal in 1996, talked with me the previous summer, after her team had defeated Norway, which had beaten the United States in the world championship earlier that year. "Everyone wanted to hype this up as a revenge match, but I just wanted to play and have a good time," Hamm said.

"Really?" I said. "You mean, winning wasn't important to you?"

She looked at me as if I were from Jupiter. "That's why we're here," she said. "To win. You get a lot of joy out of winning. Especially when it's done right."

Here's how I finally understood what Mia was saying: She wanted to win but cared about how she won—whether the process felt skillful, whether she felt in tune with her teammates and coach. She set two goals: winning *and* "having a good time." She wanted to win because "that's why we're here"; that's how success is measured in sports. She wanted to have a good time because it's more fun to play in a relaxed sort of way than to be angry and vengeful toward the "enemy" team. This young woman, generally considered the world's best soccer player, also seems to understand that when one sets out to have a good time, winning is more likely to occur.

"Obstacles are what you see when you take your eyes off the goal," some say, and it's a nice adage, but the truth is, we've got to see those obstacles too. A hurdler may have her eye on the end of the track, but if she can't see the hurdles with her peripheral vision, she's not going to jump over them. At the same time, in order to pace herself properly, she does have to focus on the finish line. It's not either/or. She sees both.

Similarly, at the popular goal-setting seminars frequently offered to professionals, something is missing if only goals are discussed. Rather than just ask, "What do you want to achieve?" and, "Where do you want to be in five years?" I think we need to ask, "What do you like to do?" and, "When do you feel fulfilled?"

Once you see competition as something that requires attention to both process and result, you can get beyond several Dichotomy Games. Competition can include enjoying one's experience as well as one's accomplishments. Compassion for one's opponent and compassion for oneself. Desire for victory and acceptance of loss. Awareness of one's goals and awareness of one's limitations. Cooperation with teammates and competition with teammates. Journey and destination.

Linda Bunker, associate dean for academic and student affairs at the University of Virginia, defines herself as a "very competitive" person. But when playing cards with people who don't want to keep score, she says, "I try to be sensitive to their needs and experience."

"You can be a competitive person and do that?" I asked her. What I usually do in that situation is try to convince my friends to do it my way: "Come on, let's keep score, it will be fun!"

But Linda can be both competitive ("let's keep score") and compassionate ("oh, okay, if you don't want to.") At the same time, she adds that most of her friends *do* like to compete, that she tends to choose friends who enjoy the same things she does.

University of Pittsburgh professor Mary Duquin doesn't like competition and generally chooses not to compete. But she does play bridge "because I like the game, and competition is intrinsic to the game," she explains.

Yet throughout a bridge game Duquin remains aware of the process of play and moderates her competitive behavior in response to those around her. "I'm not out to win tooth and nail," she says. "If, for instance, the people I'm playing with are having a lousy evening and don't look real happy, I may choose not to bid the hand aggressively. I might say, 'You haven't played many tonight; go for it.' I then defend as best I can; I don't purposely misplay. There are aggressive players who would rather go down than let the other team make it.

For me, part of a good time is in balanced competition. If the cards are going against one couple all night, it usually won't be terribly fun."

Are there competitive situations in which process is not important? At Wimbledon, for instance, are the tennis players focused only on victory? If so, they won't win. During a competitive event, successful elite athletes focus on hitting a ball, getting to the right court position, responding to the opposition. They're aware of the score, but they're also aware of what's happening on the court—and in their bodies—during each moment of play. It's when athletes focus only on the end result that they injure themselves. Or they injure their integrity through cheating. Or they injure other players through recklessness. They injure their chances of success.

Destroying one's own body or others' bodies in the name of victory is the dominant athletic (and military) model in this society. Some respond by saying we should not compete at all. I'm suggesting that there is an alternative approach: we can compete with others as well as be compassionate for them and for ourselves. It's possible to focus on the self and the other at the same time. It's possible to focus on both the goal and the means to achieve that goal.

It's sort of like lovemaking. You want to please yourself, and you also want to please your partner.[5] You want to achieve a goal, and you also want to enjoy the pleasure en route to that goal. This is possible: You can pay attention to your own desires and to those of your partner. You can move toward a climax and enjoy each moment along the way. This form of lovemaking requires a broader awareness than the more selfish, goal-oriented "just do me" approach. Many, I would guess, consider it more satisfactory.

Like lovemaking, competition need not consist solely of an egotistical drive toward an accomplishment. Like lovemaking, competition can be altruistic and mutual and rewarding for its own sake, long before the final score is tallied. Like lovemaking, competition can be risky and scary and well worth the effort. Like lovemaking, competition is best when its participants are fully conscious, fully aware of each individual moment of joy.

Chapter 8

Competition Is an Opportunity; It Requires a Sense of Humor

A friend called. "I've written a book proposal," she said. "Would you mind if I contacted your agent?"

"Of course not," I replied.

"Okay," she said. "I just wanted to make sure you didn't have any feelings about it."

Feelings? You mean, competitive feelings? Me? Not at all, not until my friend called to tell me that my agent had found her a publisher and that the publisher had offered a gargantuan amount of money for this, her first book. A humongous advance, one larger than the advances I received for my first two books combined. "Congratulations!" I said, with extra enthusiasm to cover my envy. "That's great! You deserve it!"

"Thanks again for telling me about your agent," she said. "I'll take you out to dinner next time I come to town."

We went to dinner, and I let her pay for it. Then I went back to work, writing the best book I could possibly write.

Afew months later another friend called. This was a professor who had asked me many questions over the years about mainstream writing and publishing. I had freely shared what I know. I had also told him about my work in progress, the book that became *The Stronger Women Get, the More Men Love Football: Sexism and the American Culture of Sports*.

"I'm writing a book," he said. "About sexism in sport."

"Oh?" I said. "When will it come out?"

"June," he responded.

"That's when mine's coming out."

"I know," he said. "I thought we could support each other, go on all the talk shows together."

I was furious and told him so. I couldn't argue that he was ripping off my ideas—he had been writing academic books about men's sports and sexism for years—but I told him that his timing was insensitive at best. Even though the books would of course be different because we are different people with different perspectives, from his description I feared they would *sound* the same, and thus his book would detract attention from mine. "This is not something friends do to each other," I said.

My friend listened, explained his reasons for writing his book, and maintained his right to publish whatever he wants, whenever he wants.

My agent and editor told me not to worry about it.

I worried about it. I fumed. I felt betrayed.

Then I got back to work, writing the best book I could possibly write.

In the first case I envied my friend's money. I felt defeated in the writing game: She was winning somehow, and I was losing. I felt this way even though I'm happy with my career, I like the books I've written, and I have "done well" by most authors' standards. I've done well by *my* standards. I had never aspired to earn more money than my friend, never intended to measure my own success in terms of publishing advances. Yet I felt I was losing a contest I hadn't wanted to enter.

In the second case I was angry and scared. The professor was violating an unwritten rule, it seemed to me: If someone is writing a book, that person's friend shouldn't write a similar book, to be published the same month. It's like cheating—except that cheating is cheating only if both participants have agreed to the rules beforehand. We hadn't. My friend didn't perceive himself to be cheating. He thought that all was fair in love, war, and publishing. Ultimately I decided not to let the rift permanently separate us.

When I find competition painful, it's usually because I'm losing. Often I'm losing a game I didn't realize I was playing. The feelings associated with losing—envy, anger, betrayal, fear—are unpleasant at best. It can be easier to let a friendship die than to confront one's own feelings of inadequacy.

But if I pay attention to my feelings, I can learn something. In an essay titled "Competition and Friendship," Drew Hyland notes that by competing with friends, "we find out who we are in the midst of becoming who we are."[1]

When I felt one down to my friend with the huge advance, I finally admitted to myself that making money is important to me. Before that, influenced by the hippie era, a dozen years in the San Francisco Bay Area, and Zen Buddhism, I had claimed not to care about mere dollars. Then my feelings of being one down to my friend smacked me in the face, and suddenly I was free. Why? Because I was admitting the truth, and the truth is liberating. Once I acknowledged that I'd rather make a lot of money than a little bit of money, it didn't sound so awful after all. The realization didn't make me change my priorities, but it helped me see and accept my desires.

If you notice when you're competing, you'll notice what you want. Not a bad thing to be in touch with. Not such a terrible thing, wanting. Not so shameful, wanting what others have. You don't even have to *do* anything about it.

Say you meet a friend's new spouse. You find yourself comparing this spouse with your own spouse or, worse, your lack of spouse. You feel sick. You have a hard time smiling politely. You decide that you don't like the way your friend (or his or her spouse) talks or chews or interrupts.

There is an alternative. You *could* say to yourself, "Oh, this queasy, judgmental feeling must indicate that I'm feeling one down. I probably feel like I'm losing because my own spouse is less witty or intelligent or charming." (Or "because I'm single and lonely.")

If you take the honest path, you've learned something useful: Having a partner, or a charming partner, is important to you. Maybe you've denied this to yourself before. Now that you acknowledge it, you can consider what, if anything, to do about it.

You might miraculously become freer to appreciate your friend's joy. You might notice that you're not lonely after all; that what you crave is not an intimate partner but the social approval that couples seem to enjoy. You might notice that your friend reminds you of your sister, who has always one-upped you socially. When examined, one's competitive feelings can become an important values clarification exercise. Why do you feel competitive with a particular person? Do you feel as if you're losing? Do you want to win? Or do you simply want to achieve your own success? How do you define success? Is your goal worth striving for? Or is it just something you think you should want because everyone else has it?

Most competitive problems, it seems to me, stem from unacknowledged competition. Once acknowledged, competitiveness can be a tool that points you toward action and success. Psychotherapists Luise Eichenbaum and Susie Orbach write: "Feelings of competition are disagreeable, but they are not simply an emotional state of affairs that just have to be grappled with (or applauded.) Competitive feelings are a signpost to other feelings, a defense structure that, uninvestigated, clouds a relationship with difficult and unworkable tensions."[2]

Competition—in oneself or one's loved ones—can be ugly. Admitting it can make you feel exposed and vulnerable, like that moment after you tell someone what you really want and before you receive a response. Some of my least proud moments have occurred in competitive situations. I have taken a friend to a tennis court, said, "Let's just hit a few," then blasted the ball beyond her reach. I have, during a recreational two-on-two volleyball game, refused to pass to my partner so we could win. Competitive work situations have mirrored to me my jealousy and pettiness. It's not pretty.

But it's useful. Gandhi saw his political opponents as teachers. I try to think of my opponents as opportunities, invitations to get to know myself, to grow, to rise to meet a challenge.

"Oh, happy blessed opportunity!" That's what I say when I feel as if I'm losing. I learned the phrase from Zen Buddhist guide Cheri Huber. It's one of five Zen "gratitudes," along with "Oh, happy blessed day!"; "Oh, happy blessed place!"; "Oh, happy blessed time!"; and "Oh, happy blessed path!"

"Oh, happy blessed opportunity!" is my favorite. Among Zen students, the phrase is used ironically, often accompanied by great laughter, in response to crises. Your car breaks down in the middle of rush-hour traffic? Oh, happy blessed opportunity! You've been diagnosed with an incurable disease? Oh, happy blessed opportunity!

The humor comes from the reluctant recognition of this truth: Difficult situations *do* offer opportunities to learn, to develop patience or endurance, to rise above a human tendency to wallow in the mud of self-pity. They offer opportunities to awaken, as Buddhists put it, to that particular moment and all it has to offer.

It's a useful paradigm for competition. Rivalries offer opportunities to assess goals, get in touch with feelings, and deepen relationships. Your best friend is applying for the same job as you? You've just been turned down for a promotion? Your spouse has been acting strangely ever since you started earning more money? Oh, happy blessed opportunities!

Linda Bunker, the prominent sport psychologist from the University of Virginia, developed bone cancer and has used a wheelchair since 1994. "I turn everything into a competition," she says, "even how many strikes it takes to pound a nail into the new wood on my deck. In a sense I compete with everyone who's in my field: to write books, to be asked to do keynote speeches, to learn to play tennis, to drive a car, to work a wheelchair. It's all part of the challenge. I've always thought of competition not necessarily as besting an opponent but as doing better tomorrow than you did yesterday.

"They didn't think I'd live to see Christmas of '94. I've convinced the doctors not to talk about it. You want people to be honest, but that decision to tell someone that they've got three months to live . . . it worked to my advantage because I decided to beat the odds. Many cancer patients take the projected longevity as a sentence rather than a challenge."

When approached with the right attitude, competition can provide opportunities to become self-aware, to deepen friendships, to develop the courage needed to take risks. This is why athletes shake hands after a game. Win or lose, it was an opportunity to grow.

And to laugh. Linda Bunker tells this story: "One time when I lived in Charlottesville, I hit tennis balls with Martina Navratilova. I would have been crazy to compete with her, but I felt like a colossal winner just to be able to rally with her. Then she moved to Texas, and I read an article in which she said that she had to move because nobody in Charlottesville could stand on a court with her." Bunker laughs. "It was good for my humility."

Madelyn Jennings also combines humor and competition. For more than fifteen years, Jennings served as senior vice-president for personnel for the Gannett Company, which publishes USA Today and 122 other newspapers and employs more than forty thousand people. "At staff meetings we have a lot of laughter because afterward you're more creative," she says. "Also because it's fun to laugh." Her advice to women dealing with competitive pressures in the workplace: "Don't lose your sense of how funny the whole thing is. It's all a game. Often, in meetings, when faced with the most serious business matters, some CEO will say, 'Just remember, it's all a game.' They're not being irresponsible. Somehow when you view it that way, you go at it in a stronger fashion, with more creativity and more concern for your colleagues."

"Opponent" and "opportunity" aren't derived from the same Latin root word, but maybe they have a future in common. Maybe we'll come to see opponents as opportunities, not only in some New Age–speak but as a way of life. Our way of thinking is so limited by language and habit it can be difficult when we hear the word "opponent" to hear "opportunity" instead of "enemy," just as it can be difficult when we hear "competition" and "cooperation" to remember that they're not opposites. It can also be difficult in this society, which takes competition so seriously, to adopt a playful approach. "Angels fly because they take themselves lightly," some say. I venture that competitors, like angels, would soar if we were always on the lookout for laughter, if we would continually seek opportunities to lighten up.

Chapter 9

Competition Is a Risk;
It Requires Courage

To compete is to risk failing, looking foolish, feeling disappointed, not living up to your own expectations, not living up to society's expectations of how and where and with whom women "should" compete. To compete is to risk winning and feeling guilty or embarrassed or undeserving or pressured to win again. To compete is to risk learning what you can achieve and what you cannot achieve. To compete is to commit yourself, to say, "I want to win, and I'm willing to try."

Babe (Mildred) Didrikson, the most competitive woman I've ever heard of, unapologetically coveted victory. "I came out here to beat everybody in sight and that's just what I'm going to do," she told the press at the track meet that served as the 1932 U.S. Olympic trials. She kept her word, winning six events and breaking four world records, single-handedly defeating the second-place team, Illinois Athletic Club, which had twenty-two members.[1]

Who says this now: "I came out here to beat everybody in sight and that's just what I'm going to do"? Tiger Woods says it. Michael Jordan says it. People love them for it. But do any women say that? When's the last time you heard a woman say, "I really want to win"? Even tongue in cheek?

Betty Hicks, an outstanding golfer of Didrikson's era, says Babe (who won eighty-two golf tournaments) was "openly, hostilely, aggressively, bitterly, laughingly, jokingly, viciously, and even sometimes lovingly competitive."[2] Babe was adored for this attitude but also hated for it.

"This boldness and willingness to make her presence felt and desires known were qualities that . . . endeared Babe to her fans," writes the San Diego State University women's studies professor Susan Cayleff in her impressive biography *Babe: The Life and Legend of Babe Didrikson Zaharias.* "These traits also aggravated critics who perceived her extreme self-confidence and razzle-dazzle as arrogance." Thus the best female athlete of the first half of the twentieth century was castigated by reporters as "boyish," "mannish," a "girl-boy child," "unfeminine," "unpretty," "not-quite female," and a "Muscle Moll" who "cannot compete with other girls in the very ancient and honored sport of mantrapping."[3]

Reading Cayleff's book, I began to theorize that competition *requires* courage. And boldness and a willingness to make one's presence felt and desires known. It requires courage, I think, for women to admit a craving for success because like Babe, we're likely to be censured for it.

The word "courage" comes from the French *coeur,* for "heart." The courageous person acts from the heart. But courage doesn't mean you're not afraid. Courage is evident when you're afraid and act from the heart anyway. If something doesn't scare you, it doesn't require courage. The difference between a courageous person and a coward is that the courageous person is not paralyzed by her fear. There's increasing support for female Olympians and college athletes, but the working woman who walks into her boss's office and boldly makes her presence felt and desires known might still be called "too aggressive" or worse. She'll need all the courage she can summon.

Even female athletes endure name-calling and criticism if they speak of a desire to win, especially if that desire is not mitigated by feminine gestures and behaviors to soften the lust for victory. Former

Olympic rower Anna Seaton Huntington wrote in *The New York Times:*

> There were many times when I felt a prisoner of the roles socially defined for female athletes. I watched Olympic and college teammates, and high school girls I coached, struggle to put the acceptable surface on their competitive spirits. At every age, racing off against each other for the first boat induced worried and apologetic grimaces and clouds of tension. Unlike the men, we weren't supposed to spout off challenges and insults to vent the discomfort of competing against our teammates.
>
> We're not supposed to express our will to win, to be the best, so we subvert it. Consequently, we can't leave our battles on the water, the court, the field, or the ice. Many times . . . our desire to win brews and fumes and becomes a personal, destructive force.
>
> Women's sports would be heartier and healthier if there were room for athletes . . . to aggressively inflate their egos, to trumpet their desire to win.[4]

In the workplace, women who trumpet their desire to win can be accused of failing in the arena of motherhood. "People ask me, 'How do you balance work and family?' " says Lisa Ryerson, Wells College president and the mother of three young children. "They never ask my husband that. John works full-time at a telecommunications company. What they ask him is 'How does Lisa manage to balance work and family?' " Ryerson laughs. "Or, 'Why would you be married to that sort of woman?' It's very sexist."

For women, says Ryerson, "the perception is, if you want to go off and have a career, you must be a bad mother. Or you must be a workaholic. I say I want both, and I'm going to have both. It *is* a lot of work. But what I'm showing my three daughters is that they too will have many options. I feel so strongly that a lot of happiness for children is seeing the adults around them happy and committed to reaching their goals."

Ryerson admits that mothers who compete in the workplace face a very real risk of failure. "If you want to be a good juggler, you've got to risk dropping some balls. Women have to have the space to drop balls—in our careers and as mothers. I'm public about my own mistakes. It becomes a teachable moment for others."

To compete is also to risk being wounded by Conquerors, who play by different rules. The Cherokee/Appalachian poet Marilou Awiakta says, "In a highly competitive society, where win or destroy is the central mode, a person who is cooperative and respectful of others must be wary. As a parent, it's difficult to teach children how to deal with competition because on the one hand, you want them to be caring, and on the other hand, you don't want them to get their throats cut. My husband and I tried to raise our three children to strive for excellence and to keep in mind contributing to the whole. But we also had to teach them to be realistic in dealing with people who have the opposite philosophy, who use and consume. Those people can't be permitted to take advantage of those who want to share."

Competitors also face economic and other work-related risks. Madelyn Jennings, the former senior officer for Gannett, says that during her career, "I took some jobs that my best friends and advisers thought I shouldn't have taken. I endured some jobs that were quite boring because they represented a piece of experience I needed to move to the next step. One time I accepted a four-level demotion, which took me back to the factory floor, so I could get the labor relations experience I needed to be considered for much bigger jobs."

Simone de Beauvoir theorized that the women least likely to take competitive risks are those who have no sports experience. When a woman has been denied access to sports, this "leads to a more general timidity: she has no faith in a force she has not experienced in her body; she does not dare to be enterprising, to revolt, to invent," she writes. "Let her swim, climb mountain peaks, pilot an airplane, battle against the elements, take risks, go out for adventure, and she will not feel before the world that timidity which I have referred to. . . ."[5]

Hypothesizing that Beauvoir might be right—that athletes might be more courageous, more assertive, and better risk takers than non-athletes—I asked the women and girls on my survey to respond to this statement derived from Cayleff's description of Didrikson: "I am a bold person, willing to make my presence felt and desires known."

Of the athletes, 78 percent answered "true." Only 58 percent of the nonathletes answered "true." Women who had never played sports were the least likely (48 percent) to see themselves as bold and assertive.

I also compared the self-defined competitive women (those who answered "true" to "I think of myself as a competitive person") with the noncompetitive women (those who answered "false"). The pattern was similar: Of the competitive woman, 78 percent answered "true" to the "bold" question; only 54 percent of the noncompetitive women did.

What do these results indicate? If competitive and athletic women tend to think of themselves as more courageous than noncompetitive and nonathletic women, is that because competitive experiences teach people to be brave and outspoken? Can any person, if offered a constructive competitive experience, develop the willingness to make her presence felt and desires known? Or are competitive and athletic women courageous first, before competing?

I don't know. Maybe the chicken and egg develop simultaneously. Maybe female athletes are more likely to describe themselves on an anonymous survey as "willing to make their presence felt and desires known" than they actually are to open their mouths and say, as Huntington's rowers wouldn't say, "I want to win."

But there does seem to be a correlation among athleticism, competitiveness, and courage. It seems to me that courage is cumulative: The more courageously one behaves, the more willing one becomes to take additional risks. By taking a risk, you learn that you're the kind of person who takes risks. By risking and surviving, you learn that risk doesn't kill you. Gradually you develop the confidence to put yourself in increasingly challenging competitive arenas. One of those arenas where competitive behaviors can be practiced is sports.

Athletes learn to take public risks. They might find themselves announcing "I want to win" on national television or they might play a softball game in front of a few family members. Either way, they're being watched. Either way, they're committed. People are waiting to see how they do.

For women who have been culturally conditioned to be Cheerleaders—to please others at the expense of their own desires—an audience can be inhibiting. But athletes get practice performing under pressure.

When I coached high school basketball a few years ago, I was surprised at how nervous the players were before the games. "Hey," I wanted to say, "this is only high school basketball! It's not the Olympics or anything. It's not even the play-offs." I wondered if the kids were feeling too much pressure to perform well or to win. Then I realized that the games, while "only high school basketball" to me, were the most challenging level of basketball they had ever played. It was natural for the athletes to feel nervous; it was a good sign, even, that they cared intensely about their performance. Their fear was not a problem but an opportunity to practice feeling afraid and acting anyway. It was an opportunity to practice taking a risk, competing in public in front of parents and friends. I think it's through practicing risk taking in these relatively safe settings that we become brave. Athletes transform nervous energy into something usable and productive, a heightened state of alertness and anticipation. They feel afraid but call that fear "getting psyched up." Afterward, if they fail or disappoint themselves, they can minimize the endeavor as "not that important after all" or "only high school basketball." Meanwhile they're developing courage.

That courage will come in handy later, when the athletes assert themselves in the world beyond sports. The Japanese, oriented toward group harmony, have a saying, "The nail that sticks up will be hammered down." Despite our individualistic society, American women who "stick up" are also likely to be hammered down. Or at the very least they are likely to spawn jealousy and anger in others. Junko Tabei, the first woman to climb Mount Everest (in 1975), still climbs, and she now encourages women to "be the nail that sticks up."[6] This is what sports teach women: to stick up, to stand up, to be outspoken and outstanding.

If you are a nail that sticks up, if you are a bold, outspoken, competitive woman, you will have opponents. In sports we welcome opponents because they galvanize us. In other realms opponents can feel a lot less welcome. But competitive women must expect them and learn to deal with them.

In the early years Babe Didrikson didn't care about her critics. "She has the cold indifference to what people think or say about her that is essential to a champion," one reporter wrote admiringly. "Even on the links, no heckler can disturb her."

But over time the derisive comments "wounded Babe deeply," says Cayleff, "and helped precipitate her fierce public rejection of all things 'masculine.'"

In the 1930s the previously androgynous Babe began adorning herself with hats, dresses, girdles, lipstick, perfume, and nail polish. The former all-American basketball player and Olympic track and field star actually suggested that women should limit their activities to golf and swimming. She denied ever having boxed and claimed, "My sports career began with golf." Notes Cayleff, "Denial of this magnitude hints at immense distress and severe personal pain."

But the camouflage worked. In newspaper reports, "Babe's successful ascension to femininity [was] hailed as an applaudable accomplishment," writes Cayleff.

So Babe compromised, as so many of us do. Her capitulation brings to mind strong feminist friends of mine who, in the presence of a husband or potential husband, suddenly transmogrify into coy, dependent gigglers. How many of us really are bold people, willing to make our presences felt and desires known? Under which circumstances? How many of us can boast of a "cold indifference to what people think or say" about us that just might be essential to competitive success?

My favorite story about Didrikson involves her girdle. She could hit a ball 250 yards, an impressive feat even for the professional women on tour today, who use far better equipment than Babe's. Her skill shocked the crowds in the forties and fifties. One time a reporter asked her how she could hit the ball that far.

"I just loosen my girdle," she said, "and let her fly!"

Few women wear girdles anymore, but there are so many ways we constrain ourselves, hold ourselves back, acquiesce to the pressures to be Cheerleader-like: feminine, dainty, decorative, weak, and not threatening to men. It takes courage—doesn't it?—to name our passions and ambitions, to say, "I want to win," to loosen those girdles and let 'er fly.

Chapter 10

Competition Is a Feminist Issue;
It Requires Understanding

The second-wave feminist movement in the United States began with a statement about competition. Robin Morgan, who later edited the groundbreaking anthology *Sisterhood Is Powerful*, brought several busloads of women to Atlantic City, New Jersey, on September 7, 1968, to protest the annual Miss America Pageant. While the beauty contest was being conducted inside, protesters on the boardwalk held placards saying that women should not be "judged like animals in a fair." They set up a "Freedom Trash Can" into which they tossed symbols of female oppression: stenographer's pads, hair rollers, high heels, and copies of *Playboy*. In a gesture that erroneously became known as bra burning but actually included no fires, they also discarded brassieres.

The implied statement about competition was this: Women must stop competing with each other over how our bodies look. We refuse to compete with other women on the basis of something so superficial as appearance. We refuse to compete with each other for male approval. We resent being judged like animals. Beauty contests—Miss America plus Miss Kentucky plus Miss Universe plus Ms. Senior America plus all the daily unofficial ways women feel compelled to compete with each other over physical appearance—are contests women did not create, rituals that demean us, games in which most of us feel like losers. We will not compete in that arena anymore. Good-bye to all that.

The earliest feminist writings addressed competition by exposing the fallacy of male superiority. In 1739 "Sophia, a Person of Quality" published one of the first feminist documents: "Woman Not Inferior to Man: or, whole and modest Vindication of the Natural Right of the Fair Sex to a perfect Equality of Power, Dignity and Esteem with the Men." In 1792 Mary Wollstonecraft wrote *A Vindication of the Rights of Woman*, generally considered the first feminist text; in it she says that men invented the notion of a "superior sex" and then created political and educational institutions to bolster that claim. And in one of the most influential feminist books of all time, French author Simone de Beauvoir called women the second sex, describing in a brilliant 745-page book of that name how men treat women as "other," as anatomically or intellectually inferior or as morally superior but never as equal human beings.

Feminism throughout the ages has emerged from this awareness: Women should not be treated as other, second, deficient, or losers in a power struggle with men. Refusing to be subordinate, submissive, subservient, subjugated, or sub anything else, women have demanded equal rights. That has always been the feminist rallying cry: equality. Not meaning "exactly the same," but meaning "the same access, the same resources and responsibilities." Equal citizenship, political participation, legal rights, education, work opportunities, pay, access to public speech, child care responsibilities, birth control responsibilities, sports opportunities. Equal rights not to be raped or sexually harassed; equal rights to get divorced, to wear comfortable clothing, to hold public office, to love and marry whomever we choose. Feminists have tried to create families in which neither the husband nor the wife rules. A society in which women are free to live alone or with other women, without having to negotiate whether a man is going to be on top.

In other words, women want everything men have—except their

dominance over the "opposite" sex. Women have never wanted to reverse roles, have never said that we alone should rule, as men alone ruled for so many years. Women haven't tried to reign supreme while others below retreat in fear or shame. We haven't wanted to succeed while men fail. That's never been what women meant by equal rights. "We do not wish to have power over men, but over ourselves," explains Wollstonecraft.

That women want equality but not dominance seems a difficult concept for many men to grasp. It's outside their framework of hierarchical thinking, Deborah Tannen suggests. To many men, if you're not one up, you must be one down. In most American sports—the pervasive metaphor for so much of life—a game cannot end in a tie. There must be a winner and a loser. Naturally most men would rather win than lose.

Meanwhile, feminists have rejected the entire hierarchical system, developing an ethical position that opposes competition. The thinking goes like this: Women are tired of being losers. Competition, because it produces winners and losers, is bad for women. "One up" *and* "one down" are negative. Competition is negative because it seems to be about one-upmanship, a word for which there is no feminine or gender-neutral form. You can't engage in one-upwomanship even if you tried. Nor has one-uppersonship caught on.

Many feminists also reject competition for this reason: Feminism is rooted in an ideology of solidarity among women. Feminists obtained power and perspective by working together, often in deliberately nonhierarchical, leaderless (sometimes called leader-full) collectives that encouraged participation, respect, consensus. In consciousness-raising groups, women talked honestly with each other, using words like "sexism" to name what had previously seemed like individual complaints. At battered women's shelters, rape crisis centers, and alternative health care centers, women worked together to serve other women, especially those who were poor or otherwise disadvantaged. At political rallies, women joined their voices into a chorus to make themselves heard.

None of these activities involved overt competition. Female athletes have long enjoyed competition as a form of sisterhood, but most feminists didn't understand sports, and many were suspicious of their competitive aspects. Competition became a dirty word, synonymous with Conquering, and to this day most feminists use it that way.

"I think this society is structured in an ugly, competitive way," says sociologist Barrie Thorne.[1]

A competitive system "keeps self-esteem low," writes Gloria Steinem in *Revolution from Within*.[2]

Competition between women is "friendship's ugliest ringworm," says Letty Cottin Pogrebin in *Among Friends*.[3]

"The sisterhood that is necessary for the making of feminist revolution can be achieved only when all women disengage themselves from the hostility, jealousy, and competition with one another that has kept us vulnerable, weak, and unable to envision new realities," states bell hooks in *Ain't I a Woman?*[4]

Audre Lorde says in *Sister Outsider*: "Black women have been taught to view each other as always suspect, heartless competitors for the scarce male, the all-important prize that could legitimize our existence."[5]

"Patriarchy thrives by keeping women divided, setting them up to compete with each other," write the authors of *Mother-Daughter Revolution: From Betrayal to Power*. Their own ambitions thwarted, mothers often feel jealous about their daughters' greater freedoms, and these feelings "inhibit authentic connection between mother and daughter and guide a mother to act in ways that will feel competitive and hateful to a daughter."[6]

Most feminists who have not criticized competition have ignored it. In *Women's Ways of Knowing*, Mary Field Belenky and her co-authors make no mention of competition as a way to know other women (or men). In *Women Who Run with the Wolves*, Clarissa Pinkola Estes offers no competitive female archetype. Classic feminist utopias such as Marge Piercy's *Woman on the Edge of Time*, Dorothy

Bryant's *The Kin of Ata Are Waiting for You*, Sally Gearhart's *The Wanderground*, and Joanna Russ's *The Female Man* portray worlds in which women do not compete with each other or (when men are present) with men.

In *Herland*, one of the first feminist utopias, published in 1915, Charlotte Perkins Gilman describes the women of Herland: "They were sisters, and as they grew, they grew together—not by competition, but by united action." When male visitors to Herland describe "the advantages of competition: how it developed fine qualities; that without it there would be no 'stimulus to industry,' " the Herlanders are baffled.

"Do you mean, for instance, that no mother would work for her children without the stimulus of competition?"

No, the men admit. But the world's work was different, the men contend, and "had to be done by men, and required the competitive element."

The Herlanders think the men are crazy.

Some of the women and girls who wrote comments in my survey would have made good Herlanders. "Give up the idea of competition—it's dualist, patriarchal thinking," a thirty-two-year-old wrote.

"Women need to stop being divisive and competitive amongst themselves socially," said a twenty-seven-year-old. "The energy could be used more productively. Women need to support one another."

A fourteen-year-old girl added: "I think women who are competitive are witchy. Most need to mellow down and not be so competitive!"

Being "competitive" is a "masculine" trait on the Bem Sex Role Inventory, which asks people to indicate on a seven-point scale how well each of sixty items describes them. "Aggressive," "assertive," "independent," "self-reliant," and "athletic" are some of the other traditionally masculine adjectives. Traditionally feminine adjectives include "yielding," "shy," "affectionate," and "compassionate."

When Cornell University psychologist Sandra Bem created the still-popular inventory in the seventies, she proposed a radical perspective: Healthy people employ both traditionally masculine and traditionally feminine behaviors. She called these people androgynous. She made it clear that her scale's "masculine" and "feminine" adjectives were based on stereotypical ideals and in no way reflected her own ideas about how men and women should behave. Yet many still consider competitiveness a male trait.

In my survey I asked women if they agreed or disagreed (on a five-point scale) with the sentence "If a man is called competitive, he's generally being praised." More than half (60 percent) agreed. Only 42 percent believed that "If a woman is called competitive, she's generally being praised." So the word "competitive" is applied differently to men and women.

Maybe it's good news that more than 40 percent of women and girls heard "competitive" as a positive word for women. On the other hand, 90 percent of the sample thought that "learning to win and lose are essential skills in today's society." Most (65 percent) agreed that "competitive women tend to be successful." So female competitiveness is essential, they seemed to be saying, but, compared with male competitiveness, unpopular.

Even Roseanne has noticed, as she said in the last episode of her television show, "Neither winning nor losing count the same for women as they do for men."

The irony is this: Feminism itself is a competition—not to wrest power out of the hands of men and into the hands of women, but to win equality. Feminism offers this competitive challenge to male superiority: You men are wrong to think you're superior, to give yourselves superior status and privilege. We women are right to believe we're as capable and smart as you, to demand equal rights and responsibilities and respect.

Most feminist gains begin with competition. Before ever competing in the games themselves, female athletes had to compete for the right to play sports. Before achieving success in medicine or law or government, women had to compete with men who didn't want them to participate.

Many feminist victories have been won through legislative votes in the democratic (competitive) system. In fact the enfranchisement of women was itself a political victory for women, the result of women and male teammates pressuring the all-male Congress with rallies, hunger strikes, and an effective media campaign.

Eleanor Smeal, president of the Feminist Majority Foundation, former president of NOW, and a longtime political activist, seems to be thinking as a Champion, not a Conqueror, when she describes herself as very competitive. "When I compete, it's not personal," she explains. "The life and well-being of half the population is at stake. It affects millions of people."

Asked to name some of the ways she has successfully competed for women's rights, Smeal mentions the introduction of gender-neutral want ads, the integration of girls into Little League, and the passage of landmark legislation, including the Pregnancy Discrimination Act, the Equal Credit Act, the Civil Rights Restoration Act, the Violence Against Women Act, and the Freedom of Access to Clinic Entrances Act. "Probably the most important victory is just that we've raised people's consciousness that something is wrong when women are discriminated against," says Smeal. "That consciousness raising is probably the greatest achievement of the last thirty years."

Smeal also tallies her losses. Her most agonizing defeat was the Equal Rights Amendment. "I put a huge amount of my own life into that," she recalls. "I worked nonstop from 1972 to 1982, often twenty hours a day. We lost by six votes nationwide. It's still unbelievable to me that the largest and oldest democracy in the world failed to vote for full equal citizenship for half its public. When we lost the ERA, we lost equal military opportunities, Social Security, pension plans. We lost a big boost in wages and other employment opportunities. It set us back for the rest of the century."

But because Smeal sees feminism in terms of competition, she knows that no defeat is forever. She turned the ERA loss into a victory by discovering the gender gap. Her 1984 book *How and Why Women Will Elect the Next President* correctly predicted that women's votes would become decisive in presidential politics. "We then used the power of the women's vote to fuel the political victories of the 1980s and 1990s," Smeal says. "We're still only eleven percent of Congress and twenty-three percent of state legislatures, but when we lost the ERA, we realized, *Look, we're losing because it's all men voting for this.* Then we took steps to change that."

Feminists have not been wrong to shun the kinds of competition that have hurt women. But we have been remiss in not imagining how competition could suit our needs. Feminism is about women defining ourselves, choosing for ourselves if we should compete, and how, and with whom. It's about women having power over ourselves. It's about women freeing ourselves from social conditioning that would have us compete only with women or only, in the Cheerleader's way, for "feminine" goals. As women gradually win equal rights, we are winning not only the right to compete as free human beings but also the right to rewrite the rules, defining competition according to our own values.

The primary training ground for such lessons in competition? Sport.

Part Three

How Sports
Are Changing
Women

Chapter 11

Female Athletes Get Comfortable with Competition

S upreme Court Justice Sandra Day O'Connor has not spent much time shooting free throws, so when handed a new leather basketball one day in December 1995, she held it tentatively, like a pumpkin. Earlier in the day she had called the Supreme Court gymnasium "the highest court in the land," making a joke. Now she was serious, staring at the basket, concentrating.

"Go ahead and shoot," said Lisa Leslie, the six-foot-five-inch national basketball team member who had just given O'Connor a lesson. Leslie and the U.S. team were touring the country that pre-Olympic year, and O'Connor had invited them to stop by.

O'Connor heaved the orange squash at the basket. It banked off the backboard, nicked the rim, then splatted into the middle of the net. Leslie gave a yelp. O'Connor laughed in glee. They slapped high five, but that wasn't enough. O'Connor made the rounds, slapping high five with other smiling Olympians: Ruthie Bolton, Sheryl Swoopes, Jennifer Azzi. "This is awesome," said Rebecca Lobo, the former Connecticut all-American.

O'Connor, who regularly attends aerobics classes, had invited Leslie and her teammates to the court—and to the Supreme Court itself—"because what you're doing is important," she told them. Referring to Justice Ruth Bader Ginsburg, O'Connor said: "I can't tell you how happy I was when she got to the Court. It makes a night-and-day difference to have women on the bench."

A night-and-day difference.

Night: only men deciding what justice is, only men shooting hoops.

Day: women on the legal bench, on the sports bench, on the legal court, on the sports court. Together. A team. Taking shots, teaching each other, offering high fives.

"When you play, when you win the gold medal, you aren't just playing for yourself, you aren't just winning the medal for yourselves," Representative Patsy Mink, a Hawaii Democrat and a coauthor of Title IX (the federal law that prohibits sex discrimination in educational institutions), had told the players earlier that day at a congressional luncheon in their honor. "You're winning it for thousands of little girls across the country who want to do what you're doing."

Lisa Leslie agreed. "I know that when I put on that uniform, it's almost like . . . Wonder Woman. You . . . kind of transform, you recognize that you're representing your country—especially the little girls who hopefully will follow in our footsteps."[1]

Teresa Edwards, en route to winning her unprecedented third Olympic gold medal in basketball in 1996, said, "Little girls need big girls to look up to." Later the fledgling American Basketball League printed T-shirts saying, "Little girls have dreams too." It was a nod to Edwards's statement, a response to the Olympic male basketball players' Dream Team, and a sentiment echoed by many other 1996 gold medalists.

Soccer star Mia Hamm said that maybe her team's Olympic victory "will help start a league, give girls who want to play soccer something to look forward to."[2]

Softball player and physician Dot Richardson, who hit two homers en route to her gold, said: "We did it for all the people who played before and are playing now. And for those who are going to play in the future."[3]

Amy Van Dyken, who won four gold medals in swimming, said, "Hopefully we have shown that women can do whatever men can do—and probably do it better. Growing up, we didn't have as many role models as the boys did. Girls need to understand it's cool to be athletic."[4]

It's definitely cool to be athletic. Female athletes know it, and the mainstream culture is catching on. In *The Washington Post*'s annual list of what's in and out, "women playing basketball" was in for 1996. "Women playing hard to get" was out.

Yet American women did not achieve their unprecedented success in 1996 because little girls had big girls to look up to. They were successful because of Title IX. They were successful because after athletic directors had dragged their feet about enforcing the law for the first decade, and after the Supreme Court had weakened the law with the *Grove City* decision in 1984, feminist activists lobbied Congress to pass the 1988 Civil Rights Restoration Act (opposed by the male-dominated National Collegiate Athletic Association and enacted over President Reagan's veto), which confirmed that Title IX applies to athletic programs. American Olympians were successful because, twenty-four years after the passage of Title IX, schools and universities were finally giving women a chance to compete.

Discrimination remains the norm: Men receive two thirds of all athletic scholarships and almost two thirds of all athletic opportunities; men are paid more than women for coaching women's and men's teams; men coach more than half of all women's teams, while women coach less than one percent of men's teams. But in response to frequent lawsuits, high schools and universities are gradually (albeit begrudgingly) coming into compliance with the law.

As Representative Mink noted, female athletes don't win just for themselves. They're not just entertaining, not just demonstrating physical competence. Not just playing games. They're showing women how to compete. Giving them permission to compete. Competing with as much intensity and desire as men, but with less hostility and less crime and fewer complaints over contracts. They're competing in public, setting a precedent, demonstrating this fact: Women can be Champions.

Ask a woman about competition, and in all likelihood she'll think you're asking about sports. She won't think right away about competitive tensions in her marriage or about the guy at work who tries to take credit for her ideas. She'll think about whether as a child she belted baseballs over the fence or whether as an adult she enjoys rowing or running fast, until she breathes in heavy, happy gasps. Sports are the arena in which we first hear the word "competition." It's where we form our ideas about who gets to play, what winning means, what's fair. It's the place where competing is permitted, required, part of the game.

Naomi Wolf writes in *Fire with Fire*: "Girls . . . have competitive and territorial impulses toward other girls and women. But since we lack rituals to contain open conflict, we remain reluctant to explore this minefield in sisterhood's garden."[5]

Now, more than ever, we do have "rituals to contain open conflict." They are called sports. The female athlete has become "the rule, not the exception," notes Women's Sports Foundation executive director Donna Lopiano. In 1971 only one out of every twenty-seven girls played high school sports. In 1996 that figure was one in three. Through sports, girls are becoming familiar with the emotional and physical challenges of competing. Rivals and teammates who share victories, defeats, hard work, and much open conflict often become friends. They push each other to excel, not simply by supporting each other in the context of "equality" but by demonstrating their strengths and challenging each other to improve. "Go ahead and shoot," they say.

In 1990 Stanford University women's basketball coach Tara VanDerveer knew her team had the talent to win the national championship but sensed that her young players didn't believe they could. She consulted Stanford swimming coach Richard Quick, whose team had won two national titles. His advice: "The players have to get comfortable with the idea of being national champs."

VanDerveer posted a sign on the locker-room door: 1990 NATIONAL CHAMPIONS: GET COMFORTABLE WITH IT.

"It stayed on the door all year," recalls VanDerveer. "Some people said, 'Isn't that cocky? With the opposing teams walking by and seeing it?' I said, 'No, it's just our goal.'" The team won the championship. Two years later they won again. Four years after that it was Van-Derveer who coached the national team to the Olympic gold medal.

These days more girls and women than ever before are getting comfortable with victory and the supreme, focused effort that competition requires. Through their daily struggle to win competitions with each other, to win the respect of the general public, and to win the right to compete, they have figured out some things about competition. They know it's okay—important, even—to win. They know it's okay to lose. They know it's scary to enter a race, and thrilling. They know it can be dangerous, but also fun, to defeat boys and men.

"Women start . . . from a position in which they have been dominated," writes Jean Baker Miller in *Toward a New Psychology of Women*. "To move out of that position requires a power base from which to make even the first step."[6]

That power base is the athletic arena. Sports fundamentally influence our competitive attitudes. As girls we learn the joys of wrestling and running, or we learn that the social censure for athletic excellence outweighs the thrills. We become intimately acquainted with the physical rewards of actually throwing ourselves into contests, or we are deprived of such visceral knowledge. We mature into women who are willing to compete in nonsports arenas, or we associate all competitions with our early athletic failures. According to the Women's Sports Foundation, female high school athletes are more likely than nonathletic girls to score well on achievement tests, to perceive themselves as popular, to attend college, to avoid drugs and pregnancy, to see themselves as leaders, and to make progress toward bachelor's degrees.[7] Female athletes score higher than nonathletes in self-esteem, self-confidence, optimism, and positive body image.

In my survey, 93 percent of athletes answered "true" to "I think of myself as a competitive person." Only 52 percent of nonathletes did. This finding was consistent with other research, such as that of University of North Carolina, Greensboro, psychology professor Diane Gill, who surveyed college students and found that "competitiveness clearly differentiated athletes and nonathletes." (This was true for both women and men. The differences between athletes and nonathletes were greater than the gender differences.)[8]

Athletes also enjoy competing with peers: Of the athletes in my survey, 80 percent said they "have enjoyed competing with friends or lovers." Only 50 percent of the nonathletes concurred.

Athletes expect success. They are more likely to "expect to win or have a sense of success" when faced with a new competitive situation (67 percent versus 49 percent). They more often report having a positive feeling when comparing their achievements with those of others (52 percent versus 36 percent).

And an athlete was more likely than a nonathlete to describe herself as "a bold person, willing to make my presence felt and desires known" (78 percent of athletes; 58 percent of nonathletes).

College varsity athletes were the most comfortable with competition, often more comfortable than Olympic and professional athletes. College athletes were the most likely to define themselves as competitive (95 percent did so) and the least likely to say they were uncomfortable with competition (only 16 percent did so). Along with pros and Olympians, they were the most likely to have enjoyed competing with a loved one[9] and the most likely to feel positive when comparing their achievements with those of others.[10] Along with community league athletes, college varsity athletes were the most likely to think of themselves as "bold . . . willing to make [their] presence felt and desires known."[11]

Nonathletes were more likely to be uncomfortable with competition (52 percent of nonathletes; 17 percent of athletes), to avoid competitive situations (45 percent of nonathletes; 12 percent of athletes), and to believe friends shouldn't compete (37 percent of nonathletes; 25 percent of athletes).

But nonathletes were just as likely as athletes to believe that "learning to win and lose are essential skills in today's society" (90 percent of all respondents). They were equally likely to agree that "competitive women tend to be successful" (65 percent of all respondents). More than half of both groups (59 percent overall) thought that "Often, women can compete without being cutthroat about it."

Although nonathletes were clearly less comfortable with competition, about half of them described themselves as competitive (52 percent), half said they'd enjoyed competing with friends and lovers (50 percent), and about half stated that in a new situation they expect to win (49 percent). So it seems you can learn to be a Champion without sports. Most nonathletes (67 percent) also answered "true" to "If I had/have a daughter, I'd want her to play competitive sports." (So did 95 percent of athletes.) Even nonathletic women seem to believe that sports can offer girls valuable lessons.

Why do athletes see things so differently from nonathletes? Do sports actually give women the confidence to compete and the skills to compete well? Or is it simply a matter of self-selection: Competitive people pursue sports, while noncompetitive people avoid them? Maybe athletes seek sports precisely because they enjoy the intensity or camaraderie of competition. Or they enjoy winning and win often either because they're talented or because they're motivated to win, so they try harder. Or maybe somehow they don't mind the losing too much.

Maybe nonathletes avoid sports because of their discomfort with any sorts of comparisons between people. Maybe they weren't taught to play or didn't learn quickly. Or they may have lost often and felt frustrated and inadequate and resentful, not only of sports but of any competitive endeavor.

Early childhood experiences with sports were strongly associated with later decisions about whether or not to be athletic. While 64 percent of the athletes reported having had "very positive" experiences in sports as children, only 18 percent of nonathletes said this was true for them. In interviews nonathletic women confirm this: They say they didn't feel coordinated or successful; they were chosen last for teams; they felt like failures. Why continue in sports? Of course it made sense to drop out.

Girls or women might choose sports because they're interested in competition or willing to give it a try, but athletes aren't born good competitors any more than they're born knowing how to ski. Learning to compete well is an acquired skill. Good competitors immerse themselves in competitive situations, gleaning all they can from the cornucopia of lessons available there.

Sports offer a relatively safe place to try on competitive behaviors for size: how to set goals, how to work well with other people, how to persevere despite setbacks, how to handle failure and success. They offer essential training in competition not because they comprise a black-and-white world where there are clear winners and losers, but because they represent a complex world in which your teammate is, during practice, also your rival. Your rival is, in the heat of a match, also your ally, because you've agreed to play by the same rules, and she's pushing you to do your best.

Athletes learn when to compete and when not to. Six-foot three-inch pro beach volleyball player Gabrielle Reece credits sports for teaching her to "be aggressive and competitive." She recently quit her lucrative job as a fashion model because her muscular physique and height made her feel out of place in "a universe where everything is so small." She now decries the traditional ways women compete—over whose "legs are longer" and who has "nicer hair"—as "completely ludicrous."[12]

Athletes learn what's required to win. That you don't always win. That there's always another game. That it's okay to compete against your friend. That it can be difficult to compete against your friend. That it would be foolish to let a man win. And that if you win—

especially in competitions with men—you may be either praised or penalized.

Athletes learn that coaches don't necessarily have your best interests in mind. That winning can be seductive and, like any seducer, potentially bad for your health. That some people cheat.

Athletes seem more likely than nonathletes to believe that sports teach these valuable life lessons in teamwork and assertiveness and defeat and rising to the challenge. In a Women's Sports Foundation survey, 93 percent of almost seventeen hundred female athletes agreed that girls who participate in sports are better able to compete successfully later in life. In my survey, about 70 percent of self-described athletes agreed that "girls who play sports become women who can compete at work." Only 41 percent of nonathletes agreed.

Many of America's most powerful women are athletes. Attorney General Janet Reno grew up sailing and scuba diving and now enjoys early-morning walks. Former Representative Susan Molinari of New York exercises on a home ski machine. Former governor Joan Finney of Kansas golfs, bikes, and works out on a stair climber. Senator Barbara Boxer of California runs. Senator Patty Murray of Washington (the "mom in tennis shoes") was a competitive gymnast in high school and a recreational softball player in college, where she majored in recreation.[13] Senator Carol Moseley-Braun of Illinois was a high school basketball player and college gymnast.

Donna Shalala, U.S. secretary of health and human services, played first base in the Cleveland Pigtail Girls softball league. Her coach, then college student George Steinbrenner, said Shalala was "one of the toughest competitors that I have ever seen, male or female, and that seems to have carried her all the way through her distinguished life. She was never afraid of anyone or anything."[14]

According to a study by University of Virginia psychology professor Linda Bunker, 86 percent of the women holding key positions in Fortune 500 companies participated in sports when they were young and 80 percent said they would have been described by others as tomboys.[15] In another study, adult women who played sports demonstrated higher competence at work than nonathletes.[16]

Amy Miller, owner and founder of Amy's Ice Cream, a two-million-dollar company based in Austin, Texas, is also a boxer. She started boxing for exercise, competed in a professional tournament in 1991, and felt pressured to begin a pro career. But protective head-gear, which is mandatory in amateur boxing, is prohibited in professional boxing, and "the risks of professional boxing were so physical and so immediate that I was able to listen to my gut rather than to my supporters' cries for more," she says. "I wasn't avoiding a challenge. I was taking measured risks I felt would best lead me toward *my* idea of success. That was a lesson I needed to apply to my business." As a result, she resisted pressure to open new ice-cream stores and increase sales, which "seemed the only measure of success" to some of her colleagues. Instead she decided to grow the business slowly, a strategy she thinks of as "the George Foreman approach to business: pick your battles, be true to your beliefs, and win in the long run."[17]

So do sports really teach women to compete well off the field? Not necessarily. Do we have a nation of men—former Little Leaguers—who now selflessly cooperate in the quest for common victory at work? No.

Nor do women necessarily take their sports lessons to work—or home—with them. A woman may refuse to allow anyone to push her around on an ice hockey rink but feel unable to stand her ground when her husband yells at her. One of the most aggressive basketball players I know told me she can be reduced to tears by an unscrupulous auto mechanic. "In that domain I'm a total wimp," she admits.

If skills and values don't transfer automatically, how do they transfer? Rationally. Athletes who deliberately, thoughtfully apply what they learn in the sports world to the rest of their lives are able to benefit from the myriad character-building sports lessons, according to social scientists. Those who fail to make conscious connections between, for instance, sports flexibility and real-world flexibility or between sports risk taking and real-world risk taking in effect waste their sports lessons on the playing fields.

"Sports were where I learned respect for the rights of others, even when I wanted to defeat them," says House Democrat Carrie Meek of Florida. "I learned that being behind didn't necessarily mean losing—there's always a chance to come back and win."[18]

New Jersey Governor Christine T. Whitman has been riding horses since age four. When sitting atop a nine-hundred-pound animal, she says, "You can't use brute force or impose your will by sheer strength, so you have to learn to be persuasive."[19]

"The same things that make you great in sports—repetition, concentration, accepting blame for errors, belief in perfection—make you great in business," says the Women's Sports Foundation's Lopiano.[20]

Kathryn Tucker, a lawyer who recently argued in front of the Supreme Court for the right of the terminally ill to physician-assisted suicide, said of the experience that "it takes a certain fearlessness. I think back on all my years whitewater kayaking. Any loss of aggression will cause you to falter, and faltering can mean disaster."[21]

Stacy Sunny plays third base for the Colorado Silver Bullets and also works as a field production supervisor for the television program *Rescue 911*. "It's one big stress," she says of the show. "You've got nine days to get everything together. It's a competition against time. I love the adrenaline and intensity. It teaches you discipline."

Sports Illustrated senior writer Johnette Howard threw the javelin at her suburban Pittsburgh high school and was undefeated for three years. One day another girl threw the javelin fifteen feet farther than Howard's best. "I threw it three feet beyond that," recalls Howard with pride. "I always do better when I'm against a good opponent." Nowadays Howard finds it "stimulating" rather than intimidating to spend time with more successful writers. "If someone is better, I like to talk to them. All I care about is writing well."

Sports can also help women cope with adversity in their personal lives. AnnMaria Rousey (then AnnMaria Burns), who won the judo world championships in 1984, was the first American to win a world championship in that sport. "I have had five knee operations and for many years did not have what anyone else would consider a life. Yet I got to stand on that podium while 'The Star-Spangled Banner' played and know that no one else on this planet could claim to be better than me," says Rousey. "It was worth it all and more, and I would do it again in a heartbeat. It is not just the thrill of victory that stays with you, but the strength that comes from meeting what everyone around you thought was an impossible goal. When my husband died a few months ago, I sat in my house and thought, *I cannot do this. I cannot go to the funeral and see him lying there. I cannot raise three small children by myself. I just can't go on.* Then I thought, *Of course I can. If I can win the world championship, I can do this.* We get a lot more from winning than a collection of medals."

When twenty-year-old American Lindsay Davenport won the 1996 Olympic gold medal in tennis, she said, "These Olympics, probably more than any before, are showing a lot of little girls it's okay to sweat, it's okay to play hard, it's okay to be an athlete."[22]

Shannon MacMillan, the twenty-one-year-old who scored the winning goal against Norway in overtime, said, "I hope what we've done at the Olympics, getting to the gold medal game and getting these crowds [more than sixty-four thousand] will help women's soccer. I know the U.S. women's teams here have done well and it means a lot to all of us."[23]

Tara VanDerveer, told by a reporter that she was the only female coach in the entire twelve-team Olympic basketball field, said, "I am? Then I hope I'm a good example for women out there who are watching."[24]

Washington Post columnist Michael Wilbon heard what the chorus of Olympians were saying. "Female athletes are playing for something so much more fundamentally important, like self-respect and inclusion and self-confidence—if not for themselves then for the young girls who in this culture still don't necessarily receive encouragement to compete," he wrote.[25]

Athletes are teaching girls to embrace victory. Athletes are the ones who think of themselves as competitive, who expect to win, who describe themselves as bold, willing to make their presence felt and desires known. They know that it's okay for friends to compete with one another, and they admit that they compete with friends, family members, classmates, and colleagues as well as themselves.

When Chris Evert was inducted into the International Tennis Hall of Fame in 1995, she said, "I'm often asked what I think I'll be remembered for. I hope it's that I helped the notion that it's okay for a woman to be athletic, to be tough, to be competitive. It's always been okay for men to be those things, but it's not until the last twenty years or so that it's been okay for a woman to be those things."

Evert won eighteen major championships and at least one grand slam tournament every year for thirteen years in a row, from 1974 to 1986. She added: "I'd like to say to little girls all over the world: 'Pursue your dream.' I wasn't the best athlete. I wasn't the fastest or the quickest. But I wanted it badly enough to make it happen."

Some newspapers quoted only this part of her speech: that she wasn't the fastest or the quickest. They omitted the part where she said it's okay for a woman to be athletic, tough, competitive.

Didn't matter. There are millions of young Chris Everts now, millions of aspiring Mia Hamms, millions of little Lisa Leslies.

Jen Rizzotti, who led her University of Connecticut basketball team to a national championship in 1995, was named the nation's outstanding collegiate woman athlete the next year, and now plays professionally for the New England Blizzard, says bluntly, "I'm extremely competitive in everything I do. If I'm good, that's why."

Water skiing champion Camille Duvall says, "Being competitive is good. It's healthy for women. Unfortunately you get labeled: You're aggressive, you're a bitch. But we women athletes, there's this huge sisterhood. We support each other."

Stephanie White, the high school basketball player who in 1995 averaged the most points per game (36.6), was asked by a USA Today reporter to describe herself in one word.

"Competitive," she said.[26]

Chapter 12

Female Athletes Learn
to Compete with Men

When people list the benefits of sports—strengthening the heart, lungs, and muscles; preventing osteoporosis and depression; enhancing self-esteem and self-discipline—they routinely fail to mention one of the greatest benefits to women: Sports teach women to compete with men. The way sports are structured, one could get the opposite impression: that women don't compete with men; that the two genders are justifiably segregated; that because women are "naturally" inferior to men, women "should" compete only with other women.

Athletes know better. Virtually any female athlete who has kicked a soccer ball or dedicated herself to any pursuit of physical excellence eventually compares her skills with those of the boys in her school or on her block and notices this: She's better. She might not be better than all of them, but she's swifter and stronger and more agile than some of them. It's fun to compete against boys, she discovers, either because those particular boys are friends and competing with friends is fun or because she's been told that boys are better and she's proving that they're not or just because the boys happen to be there, like mountains: another challenge.

Later, when a girl grows up, she'll take this knowledge with her:

She can compete with boys and men. She can win. It's okay; it's fun; it's possible. She understands this possibility viscerally, in her muscles and bones and ligaments, because she learned it there, with her own body, in the sports arena.

"Pool has steeled my nerves, given me a poker face, and taught me to handle confrontation head-on," says movie executive Laura Friedman, a semipro billiards player who usually competes against men. "I've learned about people. And believe me, the sharks in the pool room aren't all that different from the sharks in the movie business."[1]

But women are not "supposed" to compete with men; at least that's what many of us were taught. Linda Brock-Nelson, a retired Phoenix car dealer, recalls that as a child she hunted, fished, and "could climb trees faster than guys," but these talents did not make her popular in Oklahoma, Texas, and Mississippi, where she grew up in the forties and fifties. "It was not appropriate for women to win. You were taught not to let your husband know how smart you were, or he might not like you."

Feminist activist and author Eleanor Smeal remembers that a college roommate warned her not to beat her date in Ping-Pong or she'd never get married. "I'm supposed to purposely lose?" responded Smeal. "I'm not going to throw a Ping-Pong match! Why would I want to marry a weak person who would have to win all the time?" But this was a typical message in the fifties and sixties, Smeal recalls. "Women were told that in school too. You weren't supposed to compete for grades, or you wouldn't find a man. If a girl was called a brain—and that's the kind of girl I was, though I also loved all sorts of sports—you weren't supposed to be popular."

Nowadays girls still get harassed for beating boys and still get warned not to wound male egos. But millions of girls also go ahead and enjoy competing, openly and aggressively. Catherine Etzel, of Berkeley, California, told me in a letter:

My select soccer team this spring is playing in a boys' league,
meaning we play only boys' teams. My coach believes that we
will become a stronger team by playing against boys because
they are naturally faster and more aggressive. When we return
to playing against girls next fall, we will be better. When my
coach first explained this to me, I was quick to argue, stating
that girls are just as fast as boys, and just as aggressive. I kept
saying, as I do about anything, that girls are just as good as
guys. But I have unwillingly learned that in some aspects of
soccer boys have the advantage. Boys do not pass as much as
we do; they hog the ball ten times more. Yet they are very
quick dribblers and can often get by us on offense. These are
just some of our advantages, and theirs, and because they are
different, we can learn from each other. We can learn to be
quicker on our feet on defense, and they can learn to pass.

Catherine and I began corresponding after she wrote me a pre-
cocious and insightful letter about my first two books, which she had
read for an eighth-grade paper. In my response I told her about this
book. "Funny you should mention that," she wrote back. "I've just
been giving the subject of competition a lot of thought." Part of the
fun of competing with boys, Catherine says, is exceeding male expectations.

I enjoy showing boys that we can hold our own and play just as
rough as them. In my game just yesterday I took this boy down
while he was dribbling. The best part about it was that he looked
so confident that he was going to get by me, and when I ended
up with the ball, I didn't even have to look down at his face to
know he was embarrassed that a girl had stolen the ball from
him. The next time he tried to get past me it was more difficult
for me to steal the ball, but yet again I emerged with it. We
didn't win that game, but I felt good for having played well.

CBS sportscaster Mary Carillo learned a different sort of lesson through tennis. One of her childhood opponents, John McEnroe, eventually attained the world's number one ranking. Mary played professionally herself, and the two teamed up to win one grand slam, but beginning when she was ten and he was eight and they were playing at the same private club in Queens, New York, "he could always beat me," she remembers. "So I knew what it was to be outplayed, out-talented. I knew someone who was great at something. I would practice more hours than John, yet he could borrow a racket and still beat me. I learned that some people are very gifted and will always be better than you. It made it very clear to me that I didn't have to be the best in order to succeed."

Ironically, Carillo did become the best tennis broadcaster—despite the efforts of a relatively new sportscaster to supersede her. The newcomer, a man who has claimed that women are unqualified to comment on men's sports: John McEnroe.

The highest-paid female sportscaster is Robin Roberts, a former Southeastern Louisiana University basketball star who in 1995 signed a six-year $3.9 million contract to anchor sports broadcasts for ESPN and ABC. Sportscasting is a "very competitive field," says Roberts. "There are very few on-air positions. You have to compete with men." But you don't have to act like those men. "I work with some guys who are sarcastic, really take shots at people. I'm more considerate. I'm the kinder, gentler type."

Competing with men means refusing to accept second-class status, Roberts says. "I am very aggressive about preparing, making myself ready. If two people are vying for airtime, I'm not going to be demure. I'll pipe up to make sure I have equal time with my partner. To be where I am right now, I've had to walk into the managing editor's office and say, 'I want to work on NFL prime time.' He might be considering Joe Blow, but I can't cower in fear. I can't say, 'As a woman, I'm just so grateful to be here.'"

Mary Jo Kane learned from sports not to be intimidated by men. "When I give a paper at a conference and some man tries to rip me to shreds because of my feminist analysis, I feel like I can win," says Kane, an associate professor of sport sociology and the director of the Tucker Center for Research on Girls and Women in Sport at the University of Minnesota. "Sport has taught me not to back down. I'm also unafraid to confront men verbally in any kind of street encounter."

As a child Kane "played football, basketball, and baseball—always against boys. It made me not the least bit uncomfortable with competition, with challenging and beating boys and men. That has contributed enormously to whatever professional successes I've had."

Women can succeed without sport experience, Kane acknowledges, but "a lot of women are successful in male fields because of sport. To push yourself beyond what you think you can do, you have to be dogged. You need endurance. You need to test yourself, maintain your composure, think quickly on your feet. You need to experience winning. If women are defeated, in part it's because they've had so few competitive experiences."

Women also have fewer "degrees of freedom," notes Kane. "One misstep and you're hammered, you're gone, especially if you're a threat to men. Whereas men can fail and fail and fail and always get yet another opportunity."

Kane cautions women not to "shrink in the presence of men, especially husbands and boyfriends. You're cheating yourself by not allowing yourself to be the best you can be and also by remaining with someone who would be insecure about your success."

Linda Brock-Nelson has also learned to compete with men. She opened an auto dealership in 1969, shortly after her husband left her for another woman. She ended up raising their four children alone. "I've scared off a lot of guys," she says. "I was often smarter. I figured if they couldn't handle it, they were not the right guy for me." (She is now married to my father.) When Brock-Nelson opened the dealership, she ran into "a lot of resistance, a lot of chauvinism. The banks were unwilling to talk about financing unless my father agreed, which he didn't. So I found a male business partner, but the banks demanded that he own more than fifty percent. I refused that."

By 1979, when her partner retired, she had a successful business and a good relationship with the banks. She also had a bachelor's degree in business and a master's in counseling. "Any guy with half of that would have done fine," she says. But manufacturers put her on probation and insisted that she hire a male general manager. She refused that demand as well. "In the business world there's no value in being the weaker sex," she notes wryly. In 1995, Linda's final year in business, she employed two hundred people and sold eighty million dollars' worth of BMWs, Dodges, Oldsmobiles, and Volkswagens.

Linda was the only female golfer in the Phoenix Open pro-am in 1990. She was heading for the women's tee when she was told she'd have to play from the men's, just like everyone else. "I had a miserable day," she recalls. "You had to carry the drive over the desert to get to the fairway, and I couldn't do it. After that I started playing from the men's tees. I didn't want to be embarrassed again. Now I play from the men's tees all the time. It's much more companionable. When I outdrive men, it's sometimes more than their egos can take, and they drop out at the turn. I can hit it one hundred eighty to two hundred yards—if there's a tail wind and a little downhill. Guys can hit it farther, but it doesn't go straight."

Women fear their own power, strength, and ability, says Brock-Nelson. "They're afraid to push themselves. They don't want to improve because they might outgrow their husbands. They feel fragile or think men are fragile. They think in terms of fragility: Who's going to get hurt feelings? They think: *If I really give it my best, other people might get their feelings hurt, and they won't like me.* It's the fear of not being popular. We've got to get over that."

Chapter 13

Even Athletes Are Ambivalent
About Competition

E ven serious female athletes get confused about competition. David W. Armstrong III, a research scientist who spends his spare
time training women in outrigger canoeing, marathon canoeing,
Olympic kayaking, and Chinese dragon boat racing, has observed a
profound ambivalence in the women he coaches. Armstrong compiled
the following list of "purely unscientific observations" from his five
years of experience coaching more than two hundred women. He
submitted them to an Internet women's sports list humbly, as "just
one man's observation," noting that members of the National Capital
Area Women's Paddling Association tend to be white-collar working
women: lawyers, engineers, scientists, professors, technicians, and
teachers. I reprint them here with his permission:

1. Generally the women are not married or in relationships.

2. If they become involved in a relationship with a man,
   participation suffers.

3. If the man is the stronger figure in the relationship,
   participation with the team is always limited and eventually
   terminates.

4. When a young paddler is married, she is generally the stronger part of the relationship and the man acquiesces to her desire to participate on the team.

5. The married women usually don't have children. Those who do have children are married to husbands who enjoy child care responsibilities and are involved with their children. Or, the women are older and their children are adults.

6. Few are involved in same sex relationships. These relationships do not affect performance, and do not cause any difficulties for the team.

7. Most women believe that they will fail *before* they try.

8. Fifty percent of the women view any goal that the coach sets as unachievable by them. The other fifty percent get in the weight room or paddle the "erg" or do the pull-ups and try to succeed.

9. Participants are not particularly self-motivated to train. They prefer the team environment.

10. They want an authority figure to lead them.

11. The coach spends a great deal of time assuring individuals that they will succeed and achieve the goals for the team.

12. More than half the women are anxious about the changes in their physiques, particularly their upper body as their muscles develop.

13. More than a few women stop participating at the point when they reach mastery of the sport. Many stop if they begin to lose weight and gain muscle definition.

14. The women form cooperative and supportive bonds within the team.

15. Most of the participants dislike performance standards (for pull-ups, weight-lifting, etc.) that compare individual team members.

Armstrong's observations will sound familiar to coaches, social scientists, and athletic trainers. Husbands and boyfriends often undermine women's competitive efforts. Women lack confidence, fear failure, dislike competing with teammates. Women worry that their muscles are too big and train primarily to lose weight. They want to win but feel ambivalent about it.

Gordon Bakoulis, a New York marathoner who coaches elite runners, complains, "The women I coach are too nice. One will follow another the whole race, then not pass her. I'll ask her afterward, 'Why didn't you pass her?' She'll say, 'Oh, she worked so hard . . .'"

Gordon tries to tell them what it means to be a Champion. "Winning is not about beating someone else," she explains, "or being mean. It's getting the best out of yourself. Don't be afraid to be a winner."

The women don't get it, she says. "I feel like I'm in the Stone Age."

Kathy Delaney-Smith, Harvard women's basketball coach and an avid recreational tennis player, admits that sometimes she "lets up" when playing tennis with men. "One time another coach challenged me to a match, but when we got out on the court, it was clear I was much better, and he was going to be humiliated. So I let up. Then I lost! I'll never forget that. I swore I'd never do it again. But I have. I still do it. There are times when I've played my husband in tennis, and I've let him win points so he feels better. It makes me sick; it's a part of my personality that I don't like."

Linda DiVall, president of a polling firm called American Viewpoint, once beat Dan Quayle in a longest-drive golf contest at the Republican Governors Association meeting. "It was probably about a 230-yard drive," she recalls. When she realized the previous longest drive had been by Quayle, she thought, *What would my mother want me to do?* She hesitated "for about 2.5 nanoseconds," then crossed out "The Vice President" and wrote her own name.[1]

Ambivalence seems strongest in women over forty, who are less likely than younger women to have athletic backgrounds. According to my research, slightly older athletes (average age, forty-three) are less likely than college athletes to see themselves as competitive, more likely to say, "Competitive situations tend to make me uncomfortable,"[2] and more likely to say that they tend to avoid competitive situations.[3] (I made these comparisons by surveying Armstrong's paddlers and combining those responses with responses from members of the Claremont [California] Older Women's Soccer league [COWS] to form a group of "slightly older" female athletes. The COWS have been playing soccer together since 1980. The flyer announcing the league asked, "Do you sometimes feel the need to kick something very, very hard?"[4]) Since these "slightly older" pre–Title IX athletes did not benefit from early sports training, it makes sense that they'd embrace competition less wholeheartedly than younger women.

But even some young women who have played sports throughout their lives agonize over competitive issues. Olympic soccer star Michelle Akers says, "I struggled with competition as a kid. What was proper and what was not? Should I want to win? Should I run over everyone to win? Is it okay to be better than everybody else, boys included? I didn't want to step up and away from the crowd. I sensed criticism, mostly from the girls. I didn't fit in. If you're very good, it means you're different from your peers."

At twenty-three, Akers found herself playing on a pro team in Sweden. If she didn't score, the team didn't win. "I came to understand that it's okay to be the best. Now I'm past caring what people think. When I speak to girls and boys, I say: 'You decide who you want to be. Don't let anyone else define you.'"

But Akers has also struggled with this question: How can you be an aggressive, competitive athlete and still be a Christian? Through her religious studies, she has concluded that "God wants us to use our talents and our gifts to glorify Him. He wants us to be our best, but to compete fairly. There's lots of things in the Bible about pressing on toward the goal or winning the prize or competing with all your heart." She adds laughingly, "I think as long as I'm playing within the rules and playing fair, I can run somebody over to get the ball."

Some college athletes also seem ambivalent about competition. They loathe competing against teammates in practice and worry incessantly about team harmony. Sarah Glass, a Harvard rower, told me, "It's almost as if in order to be a 'good' team, the women I know feel like we all have to like each other and be friends outside of the boat as well." This perceived need to be friends was detrimental to her 1996 team's performance, said Glass.

College coaches also complain that this fierce need for friendship interferes with a team's competitive goals. Sanya Tyler, Howard University basketball coach, says, "Some of my players have competitive urges, but they don't come to fruition. Their desire to be liked and accepted is greater than their desire to do the job." Pointing to two of her players, she says, "This one and that one won't play hard against each other. They're roommates and buddies. One will achieve everything, and one will achieve nothing."

"How do you teach competitiveness?" I ask.

"It's very difficult to get across," she says. "I try not to let them get so close."

Marymount University women's basketball coach Bill Finney believes that competitive sports can train young women to be successful in life and reminds his athletes of this during the most grueling parts of practice. "Why are we doing these push-ups?" he'll yell. "To make ourselves better people!" the athletes must respond. Not better basketball players, better people. Yet Finney too is frustrated that many of his players will compete against each other only reluctantly.

"How do you teach competitiveness?" I ask him.

"I try to recruit for it," he answers. "If a girl isn't comfortable with competition in high school, it's hard to teach it to her at this level. You've got to find the kids who want to be the best. But even then, they're going to become angry with their teammates sometimes, and their relationships are going to become strained. That's a big problem, because women care so much about their relationships. I try to explain what we're doing: working to put the best team on the court, and that we need the competition to do that."

Young athletes seem to be increasingly comfortable with competition. The middle school and high school girls in my survey were more likely than older women to define themselves as both athletic and competitive. "To me, a strong, smart, healthy girl should be the example of popularity, not a skinny, weak, clueless-about-life girl," says Catherine Etzel, an avid soccer and lacrosse player from Berkeley High School. "I strive to be confident, intelligent, and strong in sports as well as in academics. To me winning isn't everything, but I love to win, and I don't care whether it is considered popular or not."

But Catherine observes that even some of her athletic peers struggle with competition, in and out of sports. "Most girls I know are not as competitive as myself. I know a few girls who, when working in groups in class, act as if they don't know a thing when they're around boys. Either that, or they act like knowing anything is a waste of time, stupid, and uncool. I see classmates deliberately lose to a guy, in sports and in class."

Sarah Rogan, a high school track, soccer, and basketball player at Georgetown Day School in Washington, D.C., loves to compete. She took the SATs in seventh grade and scored 1,020. "That's higher than some eleventh-graders," she notes. "That's something I can feel good about. When I'm in eleventh grade, I would like to get a perfect sixteen hundred. I know that's hard. I tend to set really high goals for myself."

Her friends and family tell her she's too competitive. "I can see their point, but that's just the way that I am," Sarah responds. "I turn everything into a competition. I compare tests I took last year to the same tests my younger sister's taking now. If she's better, then I'm upset. She hates it, and my mother hates it. I don't like it, but I can't really do anything about it."

In seventh grade Sarah developed a painful academic rivalry with a good friend. "In history, if she'd say, 'What'd you get on the test?' and I'd say, 'Ninety-seven,' then she'd be, like, 'I got a ninety-eight.

I'm so much better.' It was a compliment in a way; she sees me as a smart person. But I was hurt that it was so important to her to be better than me.

"In eighth grade it got worse. We'd get into mini-arguments. She'd say, 'How come you never come to dances or sleepovers? You should for once skip a soccer practice.' She doesn't understand that at the level I'm playing I can't do that. She practices two hours a day at flute, but she doesn't try to understand my commitment to soccer. On Valentine's Day we had a fight, and she said, 'I don't care about your fucking grades.' I was really hurt. I found myself almost hoping she moves to Hawaii. I think that with this girlfriend, competitiveness went too far. It came between us. I hope we can still be friends."

Sue Schaffer, Sarah's mother, has a doctorate in business administration and teaches students at George Washington University how to function effectively in groups. "In the right place and time, competition is great," says Schaffer. "But when you lose sight of your moral and ethical framework, it's very bad."

A former competitive swimmer, Sue encourages Sarah to be less competitive. "It's detrimental to her," says Sue. "If she gets an A minus, she doesn't feel successful. She can't stand it when she thinks someone in the class is doing better. I'm trying to instill in Sarah a sense of 'I'm okay.' If a person feels good about herself, that gives her the tools she'll need not to succumb to some of the negative pressures of competition."

Anne Collins, a counseling psychologist from Washington, D.C., says that sports offer girls an opportunity to be with other girls "who are seeking mastery and control, instead of just inclusion, which is the recess dynamic." Collins has supported her daughter's interest in soccer because "there's great pleasure in using your body in an efficient and instrumental way" and because "there are few opportunities for a girl to be physically aggressive and be applauded. I figure this training will serve her well on the subway later in life."

However, "mastery still hurts girls socially," Collins notes. "It's not cool to be better than your friends. If you hurt a friend's feelings by outdoing her, the next day there will be consequences."

Even Catherine Etzel has struggled with competition and friendships, especially in early adolescence, a notoriously difficult time for girls. During kickball games in elementary school, she recalls, "whenever an out was called, I was always up in some guy's face arguing with him about the call, sometimes even if I knew he was right. I guess I felt that since no other girls were making the effort to question anything, I should double my voice power, and I certainly did."

In seventh grade "there was a major switch. Now it was not accepted at all for girls to play knockout on the [basketball] courts with the guys, or football in the driveway. Girls were just supposed to sit around and talk. I had changed schools, so I really needed to make friends, and at the beginning I did what I needed to do to make them. I know that sounds horrible, and believe me, I'm not proud of it, but middle school is a rough time, and people can be cruel."

Catherine kept playing soccer, though, and found it to be a "refuge, the only place I could go where I felt I belonged. Out on the field no one cared who your friends were or what you wore. All they cared about was if you could play, and I sure could."

In eighth grade, Catherine says, "my confidence as well as my individuality came back. I gave up on pleasing people and focused on the things I enjoyed: school, sports. I reevaluated my friends and changed my whole outlook on life. My parents noticed a significant change in my attitude and were proud of my transition."

Girls and women have a long history of contradiction and conflict about what competition is and should be. Men have argued that female athletes become unattractive, infertile, and masculine. Female physical educators and coaches have also, paradoxically, been wary of competition. In the 1920s the Women's Division of the National Amateur Athletic Federation maintained that competition would "harm the nervous system, encourage rowdiness, and lead to injury and exploitation." Between about 1920 and 1960, female coaches sponsored athletic events that combined teams from different schools in order to curb any competitive tendencies.

They sought to provide sports opportunities without the pitfalls of men's sports: corruption, commercialism, the pressure to compete when injured, the exclusive focus on victory. They created some competitive environments but asserted that a young woman's future role as wife and mother was "of far greater importance than any championship she may ever win through competition."[5] They enforced this strict rule: Never compete with boys.

Meanwhile, working women in the thirties, forties, and fifties were playing basketball and running track in highly competitive industrial sports leagues that offered monetary rewards, promoted individual stars, and emphasized winning. The male organizers of these leagues believed that athletic competition boosted worker morale and improved efficiency and harmony in the workplace.

In the late fifties, female physical educators began to change their anticompetition stance. "People want to talk about competition," announced Anna Espenschade of the National Joint Committee on Extramural Sports for College Women. "Many . . . were taught that it is bad, but they cannot always justify this viewpoint from their own observation or experience."

In the 1960s, the Division for Girls' and Women's Sports began advocating competition and for the first time endorsed the Olympics, admitting that it had inadvertently "perpetuated the myth of women being weaker, nonathletic, noncompetitive creatures."[6]

In the seventies, eighties, and nineties, women's sports opportunities expanded tremendously, mostly because of the passage and gradual enforcement of Title IX, increased media exposure, and increased corporate support. Nowadays there is much less talk about if women should compete and more agreement that they should get the chance.

But the story of our people—female people—includes this complex history: women's desire to participate, to achieve, to win; male taboos against female competition; male support for female competition; and women's own ambivalence about it. Just as childhood experiences influence us long after we're grown, our collective history of competitive contradictions and controversies continues to exert its influence even now, when teams of openly aggressive, obviously competitive women play sports on television and in front of millions of adoring fans.

So when women compete, even at the Olympic level, we sometimes hear echoes of "You can't because you're a girl." Or "Always let the boy win." Or "The way to play smart is to play dumb." When women run, this history runs along behind us, tapping us on the shoulder. Are we competitive? Do we want to be? Why? How? With whom? Is winning unattractive? Unfeminine? We ask the same questions our foremothers asked: Should we compete as the men compete? If not, then how? Should we compete with men? If so, then how? Will competitiveness make us unattractive to men? If so, does this matter? Does it imply that men should adjust or that women should?

The lesbian stereotype further complicates women's ambivalence about competition. The myth that "all female athletes are lesbians" is false, but there is some truth in it. In the 1940s, 1950s, and 1960s, a disproportionate number of female athletes probably *were* lesbians. Heterosexual women tended to avoid baseball, basketball, and other "masculine" pursuits lest they be branded unwomanly. Or they tried to play sports but were forbidden by their husbands (who in those days exercised stricter control over their wives' activities). Or they played sports but only in skirts, only while smiling, and only against other women.

In a way, lesbians were freer. Not wanting to attract men, they did not have to adhere so rigidly to "appropriate" feminine behavior. Not beholden to husbands, they were more likely than heterosexual women to pursue the pleasures of sports. No data exist to prove this assertion because very few lesbians were out of the closet. But there are many indications, including firsthand accounts from the women themselves, that some of the best athletes and coaches in the middle decades of this century were lesbians. Some of the women who played in the All-American Girls Baseball League, which existed from 1943 to 1954, have told me that they and many of their teammates were lesbians. Many of the women who played on the Ladies Professional Golf Association in its early days were lesbians. Physical education and coaching also seemed to attract a disproportionate number of lesbians, perhaps because lesbians were more likely than married women to work outside the home and teaching was one of the few career opportunities available to women.

Billie Jean King and Martina Navratilova, both of whom had a tremendous impact on the development of women's sports, are lesbians. Some of today's best athletes are lesbians. Softball, basketball, rugby, bowling, swimming, running, and other sports leagues remain important elements of gay social life. But there seem to be fewer lesbians in sports today—proportionately—than ever before. Because most sports—especially at the recreational level—are no longer considered masculine and because most husbands no longer have the social or economic power to insist that wives stay home, heterosexual women now flock to the playing fields too. Ironically, it is because lesbian athletes risked social censure that sports have now become more socially acceptable for all women.

According to my survey, lesbians, bisexual women, and straight women are equally likely to think of themselves as athletes. "There's been a sea change in society's definition of what's appropriate for a woman, and now 'athlete' is included in that," explains Pat Griffin, associate professor of social justice education at the University of Massachusetts, Amherst, and the nation's leading authority on homophobia in sports.

However, lesbians in my survey were more likely than straight women to describe themselves as "bold . . . willing to make [their] presence felt and desires known."[7] They were also more likely to have competed at high levels of sports, perhaps in part because of that assertiveness. Consequently 61 percent of lesbians but only 42 percent of bisexuals and 37 percent of heterosexuals had competed at the college varsity level, while 6 percent of lesbians, 4 percent of bisexuals, and 1 percent of straight women had participated at the Olympic or professional level. So while "athlete" is equally claimed by straight, gay, and bisexual women, "highly competitive athlete" is still disproportionately claimed by those bold lesbians.

"That doesn't surprise me," says Griffin. Heterosexual women respond to cultural pressures not to claim the spotlight and not to intimidate men, she says, but lesbians by definition care less about men's opinions of how women should behave. To wit: Cannondale, the cycling manufacturer, features downhill mountain biking world champion Missy Giove, one of the few professional athletes who are openly lesbian, in ads that say, "Some women worry about catching a man. . . . Others simply pass them."

Taking sports seriously jeopardizes straight women's relationships with men, canoe and kayak coach Armstrong noted. Griffin says this is "because unfortunately it still takes a special man to be in a relationship with a woman who's strong and independent and whose athletic prowess and achievements may overshadow his." Heterosexual women also drop out of competitive sports because "the higher you go in sport, the more likely you are to be associated with the lesbian label, and they're terrified of that."

Joli Sandoz, adjunct professor of literature at Evergreen State College in Olympia, Washington, has spent more than five years gathering and analyzing women's sports literature (written by women) from 1895 to the present.[8] She notes that since the eighties the most serious and complex women's sports literature has had lesbian themes. "Either it was written by a lesbian, it's about lesbian-heterosexual tension, or it's about the pain and struggle of being lesbian in a homophobic environment," she says. For instance Lucy Jane Bledsoe, author of *Sweat* and *Working Parts,* writes about the lesbian label "as a scare tactic to keep women in their place. This is what you'll become if you don't follow society's definition of feminine, if you don't do sport in moderation, if you don't compete the way we'd like you to."

Sandoz calls this lesbian trend in sports literature "interesting and probably significant. My guess is that lesbians in sports are used to taking risks, so they're the people who are exploring the precipices of sexism, and part of sexism in sports is homophobia."

Women's sports writing has changed in the past hundred years, Sandoz says, and this change "reflects societal attitudes." In the early years an athlete was typically confronted by "the boyfriend or the newspaper reporter who didn't approve." From about 1920 through 1970 an athlete was typically a "white middle-class educator" for whom "moderation and social acceptance were more important than competitive skill and aggression." Much literature for young women still preaches this "social acceptance" theme, according to Sandoz.

In the 1980s and 1990s authors began to portray "a more matter-of-fact" approach to competition. "Competition exists; it is accepted; it is a part of people's lives," she notes. "There's still opposition, but it's not given much time in the books."

In these modern stories authors "are also envisioning what's possible," says Sandoz, such as a professional women's ice hockey league. Unlike earlier stories, which tended to focus on "your basic high school team," contemporary stories feature female champions "on pretty heroic terms." Sandoz mentions Jenifer Levin, who in *The Sea of Light* and *Water Dancer* created athletes who play heroic roles, "showing that one can rise above one's circumstances, can accomplish, can contribute to society."

Sandoz says modern women's sports fiction asks: "Can women display what we have: our talents, our discipline, our skills? And can we be accepted for our strengths?"

Good questions for real-life competitive arenas as well.

Part Four

Why

Competition Is

Complicated

Chapter 14

"I'm Not Competitive, But . . ."

When a friend failed to get a job she wanted, she told me defiantly, "I will not let this defeat me!"

"I know you won't," I said. "You're a winner."

"Well, I'm not into winning," she responded.

"I'm not trying to win," other women tell me, or "This is not a win-lose thing." Playing cards one evening with a group of friends after dinner, someone suggested, "Since we're all women, we won't keep score, right?"

Cordelia Anderson, a consultant from Minneapolis, recently wrote a book about the beneficial effects of sports for children. She noted that sports can improve health and fitness, develop a sense of competence, and allow children to experience the joy of winning. Three female friends read a draft of the manuscript. All told her the same thing: "Take out the word 'winning.' It's negative."

What's the matter with victory? Can women not enjoy triumph? Isn't there a way to climb a victory stand without stomping on the backs of the losers?

Maybe that's part of it: We know what it's like to lose. Women know all about power plays and ritualized quests for dominance. We know the sting of defeat. Women were born losers, born disappointments, born with bodies that Sigmund Freud called defective and that, at least in China, are still sufficiently disappointing that female infanticide is common. Many women *feel* inferior. Researchers say women evaluate their own abilities as lesser than men do, and many see their own gender as inferior.[1]

Nevertheless, women do not like to lose. We do not like to lose out, to feel like losers, to finish second, to be second-class citizens, the second sex. We don't like walking a step behind, starting out in second place, winning only beauty contests, receiving only booby prizes. We do not appreciate Powder Puff football, girls' push-ups, six-dribble basketball. When being looked down on, talked down to, condescended to, patronized, we notice.

Women are tired of being subordinate but don't want to subordinate anyone else. To be female is to know what it's like to be one down, but to be female is also to be compassionate for others. So we won't compete. Won't play that game.

Psychoanalyst Jean Baker Miller notes in *Toward a New Psychology of Women* that subordinate people always develop "personal psychological characteristics that are pleasing to the dominant group." These characteristics include submissiveness, passivity, docility, dependency, weakness, and helplessness.[2]

They do not include competitiveness.

Women want to win without losing anyone's approval or affection. Competing for professional success might mean leaving a respected colleague behind. Competing with a female friend might feel like betrayal. Competing with a husband might result in divorce. Even competing within a structured sports setting can send women spiraling downward into a morass of ambivalence: If I win, how will my opponent feel? Do I really want to win? Can I? Is winning okay? Is losing failure? "Competing successfully" can become an oxymoron, an impossible dream.

For many women, competition seems to represent an elaborate web of relationships and contingencies and potential wounds. Acquainted with exclusion and defeat, women want to win but are unwilling to risk more loss. They want to win but worry that their opponents might be devastated. They want to win but don't want to be punished for being pushy. They want to win but have grown accustomed to second-sex status and now believe they can't win. They want to win but can't help noticing that even female athletes who win Olympic gold medals usually cannot win popularity contests unless they are fourteen years old or grow long fingernails or smile a lot or have husbands who remain in charge as coaches.

Regardless of what Nike says, women can't "just do it." Susan Greendorfer, a sport sociologist from the University of Illinois at Urbana-Champaign, has been criticized simply for trying to improve the skills of her softball teammates. "I think if women are unskilled, we should teach them," she explains. "But I've been told, 'Why would you teach them, only so they could win? That's too competitive.' "

While many men (and athletic women) would find that exchange ludicrous, such debates (are you trying to win? If so, is that okay?) do rage on softball fields—and in workplaces—all over the country.

Sometimes, in their eagerness to be cooperative and helpful, women relinquish their own rights to victory. Temple University sport psychologist Carole Oglesby, a former member of a nationally ranked softball team, laments: "Until recently I was hesitant to compete, both in sports and professionally. I used to say, 'Winning and losing don't mean that much to me; if they mean so much to you, then you go ahead and win.' It seemed it was a bigger deal to others. But actually it was a bigger deal to me. I wish I'd known how to just go for it and win."

When women say, "I don't like to compete," or, "I'm not into winning," some mean, "I don't believe that winning is the only thing." Others mean, "I don't like to lose." Still others mean, "I don't like conflict." Or "I'm afraid to find out what I can or can't do." Or "I'm afraid to deal with your feelings about winning or losing." Or "I'm afraid to deal with my own."

Or "I'm afraid I'll be punished if I win." Grace Park, a Korean teenager now living in Scottsdale, Arizona, won three state golf titles for her high school, dominates the girls' junior ranks, and during one contest drove golf balls farther than every pro except Laura Davies. "I enter every tournament to win," she says, sounding very much like Tiger Woods. Then she says something I hear exclusively from women: "But I don't want to stand out too much."

We say, "Everybody loves a winner," but do we mean female winners? We cheer for female athletes—as long as they are playing sports that have become acceptable for women. But when women compete against men, when women openly express a desire to win, or when they merely insist on equality, we call them driven, overbearing, militant, domineering, arrogant, ambitious, abrasive, too competitive, lesbian, bitch. Why is Hillary Rodham Clinton a bitch? Why is prosecutor Marcia Clark a bitch? Roseanne? Barbra Streisand? Barbara Walters? These women are smart. They're ambitious. They're competitive.

So women say, "I'm not competing," "I don't want to compete," and the ever-popular "I'm competitive, but only with myself." With the second half of that sentence they soften the first. "I'm competing," they seem to be saying, "but not with you, and not with anyone else who might feel threatened by or critical of that competitiveness."

It reminds me of celibate gay priests. Women who compete only with themselves are as safe and nonthreatening as priests who admit they're gay but agree to be celibate. The Catholic Church permits priests to be openly gay as long as they don't involve anyone else in their sexuality. Similarly, women seem to think it's okay to be competitive as long as they don't involve anyone else in those competitions.

Competition is complicated. There are good reasons why women avoid it. But avoiding it doesn't make it any easier to function in a competitive society. It just makes losing inevitable. Competition gets easier when it's understood, when we can be honest with ourselves about our feelings and our desires, and when we comprehend the cultural context in which we find ourselves.

Chapter 15

Family Games, Cultural Games

Each family plays its own games by its own rules. Each family keeps score in its own way. Usually with little overt conversation, each family defines for itself what competition is, and who should engage in it, and how.

In my family we're competitors, all of us. We're ambitious. We're driven, aggressive, compulsive, obsessive. Mom, Dad, Carol, Peter, and I, we're a Type A family, never resting and never satisfied. We want to win. If we do win, we immediately seek more difficult challenges. If we don't win, we want to compete again. And again. And again.

Assembled for vacations, we play games: baseball or golf or freeze tag or capture the flag. We always keep score. When we play charades, we time the number of seconds it takes each team to guess the answer.

Anything—even tossing trash into the trash can—can become a contest. Cardboard tubes that hold wrapping paper are transformed into swords as soon as the paper is gone. We chase each other, high-stepping over beds and couches and behind the Christmas tree, waving our swords. "Ha! Got you!" We complain: "No fair! Start over! I wasn't ready!"

Over dinner we discuss our work: Who is succeeding and by what measure? You're doing well, but well enough? Are you the very best? Not yet? Why not? What will get you from here to there? Do you want some advice?

It can be exhausting to be around us. I find it exhausting myself.

But this is who we are, how we are. We were born to be players, participants, performers, contestants, never spectators. When my sister, brother, and I were growing up, every activity was a race, a game. See that tree? Race you to the highest branch. What are your grades? Mine are better. Our daily language was the language of challenge: Let's pick teams. You be it. Heads or tails? Last one there's a rotten egg! On your mark, get set, go! No cheating!

My brother, Peter, is two years older than I. We played all the sports we could find plus games of our own invention: Tree Seek, Witch Piggle-Wiggle. Riding our bikes to a friend's house, we'd cycle as fast as our feet could churn the pedals, then leap off and watch the bikes teeter away while we stumbled to the front door, breathless. On rainy days we played Ping-Pong in Pete's bedroom, a converted attic. Or we went bowling. Or we knocked down toy soldiers with marbles. Or we conducted hamster races, betting on whose hamster would first make its way through the elaborate mazes we constructed out of building blocks.

Our sister, Carol, two years older than Pete, joined us sometimes, belting baseballs over the willow tree that marked home run territory. She developed expertise on the unicycle, which she could ride forward and backward and turn in jerky figure eights, her arms flailing for balance. Otherwise Carol felt uncoordinated—"klutzy," she said. She couldn't run fast. But she excelled at intellectual games. While Dad drove the car during trips to visit our grandparents, we would play word games like Password and Ghost. Mom, a physician, had no compunction about using medical terms—"osteoarthritis," "electrocardiogram"—in order to assure victory. Intrigued by medicine's jargon, Carol became the first to defeat Mom.

I can trace my competitive cravings to the influence of all these people: Peter, who became a founding partner of a successful Los Angeles entertainment law firm; Carol, who became a successful Philadelphia trial lawyer with her own firm; Dad, now a retired hospital president and impressive golfer who, after my parents' divorce, married an extremely competitive car dealer; and Mom, a swimmer and psychiatrist who, after divorce, married a very competitive social worker. As the baby of the family I've spent my life scrambling to keep up with all of them.

That's the rub. In my family one can never win *enough*. There's always the next goal, the next challenge, the next competitor, waiting around the bend.

Throughout elementary school my siblings received straight As on their report cards. My report cards would contain all As and one B. I mentioned this to a therapist one time, who found the pattern amusing. "Always? All As and one B?" she asked. She interpreted the B as a subtle form of rebellion. I had seen it as a subtle form of failure.

At Stanford I continued to receive As and Bs—or passes, for pass/no pass classes. I avoided the most difficult courses—even when the subject matter interested me—for fear of "failing" with lower grades.

I have written two books. The first won a national award and dozens of laudatory reviews. The second received a tidal wave of media attention and more than a hundred good reviews. Both books have enabled me to make a living as an author and public speaker. *But what if none of my books ever make the best-seller lists?* I have worried.

Recently I tried to explain my feelings of inadequacy to my brother. This is a guy who once told me that he's good at everything he does. We were about eight and ten years old at the time, and we were talking about swimming. Because of persistent ear problems, Pete wasn't allowed to swim. "But if I could swim, I know I'd be good at it," he said.

"How do you know?" I asked, suspicious.

"Because I'm good at everything I do," he said.

Had I been more cynical, I could have laughed at his arrogance.

Instead I took it as a challenge. Am I good at everything I do? If not, why not?

Pete and I have always been friends, so I thought it might be useful to tell him about my perception that I never succeed *enough*. I thought he might say something helpful.

"*Stronger Women . . .* is selling well," I told him soon after the book was published. "The reviews are positive—except the ones written by football fans—and I'm receiving a lot of letters, and I've been on more radio and television shows than I could possibly count, and I'm pleased with the book itself; I think it's a good book. Yet I've been feeling inadequate recently because it's not on the *New York Times* best-seller list."

"How many have sold?" he asked.

"All but two thousand of the first printing," I said. I kept talking, hoping my rapid-fire words would deter him from the criticism I sensed looming. "We sold excerpts to four national magazines plus the *New York Times* syndicate. It's on one distributor's best-seller list. The publisher is happy. They're negotiating paperback rights with other publishers; it's coming out in audiotape soon and will also be published in England. Plus I'm receiving an award from a women's sports organization next month."

"What about those other two thousand?" Peter asked.

"Pete!" I said, laughing. "That's just what I was talking about! I feel like it's never enough! There's always that question: What about the other two thousand?"

He laughed too—he got it—but quickly his laughter ended, and he asked without irony, "What about the paperback deal? How well will you do on that?"

Now I felt exasperated. "Don't you see what that sort of it's-never-enough thinking does to us?" I pleaded.

"Makes us successful," he responded seriously.

"And unsatisfied," I added. "Remember when you won your first sailing race last month? You were happy, but only for a week, because you lost the next race. How much do you have to win before you're satisfied?"

"Everything," he said without reservation. "Isn't that always the goal? To win it all?"

There's always a catch. You win accolades at school, but your sister resents you for it. You win your parents' affection, but along comes a younger sibling with whom you must share not only that affection but your toys. You feel pretty but not as pretty as your mother. You feel prettier than your mother but not as smart. You win today but lose tomorrow. You learn from your family how to win, then face a world that resents female winners.

From our families we learn to relish rivalries or avoid them or merely cope. Our coping strategies may be effective or ineffective, but they begin when a sibling says, "My hamster's bigger than yours," or, "I got more dolls for Christmas," or, "Daddy likes you more," and you respond somehow, however you can. In our families we learn that competition is humiliating or hilarious, frustrating or fun. Or all of these, on different occasions. In our families we come to believe we are basically winners or basically losers or basically unable to compete.

As girls we hear that competition is essential for success, or that *not* competing is essential for success. We hear that contests are important or evil or unwinnable. We see mothers competing with their friends over whose children are the smartest or most attractive or the lightest-skinned. We see sisters competing with brothers over who washes dishes. We compete with those sisters and brothers for our parents' attention and love. Our parents compete with neighbors over whose deck is bigger or who does the most for the community. Our parents compete with each other, openly or surreptitiously, over who controls the children, who drives the car, who makes more money, and who's right. They tell us not to compete with boys, not to "emasculate" men, or to "do your very best at everything, no matter what." To a large extent, these early lessons determine how we will compete in the larger world.

Fathers play a crucial role in defining competition for women, according to psychologists. High levels of "father supportiveness" contribute to producing women who are competitive and aggressive in positive ways. Lack of paternal support yields unassertive, passive, and dependent daughters.[1]

But how many girls experience high levels of father supportiveness? Even today, when men are supposedly more involved than ever in child rearing, how many minutes a day does each father spend interacting with his children? In 22 percent of American families with children under eighteen there is no man present at all.[2]

Sometimes mothers support their daughters to be healthy competitors. If mothers play sports, their daughters are likely to play sports too.[3] But most experts assume that mothers and daughters are unhealthy rivals for male attention. According to the authors of *Mother-Daughter Revolution*, mothers and daughters "become smiling competitors. Who will be more attractive? Who is more popular? Who will get the attention of the man in the house or other interesting men?"[4]

When daughters fail or seem reluctant to compete, Mom gets blamed. She has held her daughter back, some psychologists say, because of her own fear of being surpassed and superfluous.

But why is male attention so important to mothers and daughters? Why do so many mothers feel surpassed and superfluous? Destructive rivalries between mothers and daughters can often be traced to sexist environments, where male attention is valued more than female attention and mothers have not had a chance to feel successful in their own right. A recent Canadian study examined 102 adolescent girls' perceptions of their relationships with their mothers. The daughters who had good relationships with their mothers tended to see themselves and their mothers as feminist. Some of the girls who had poor relationships with their mothers pointed to their mothers' lack of feminism to explain the problems between them. Their mothers were urging the girls to capitulate to traditional female roles and, in the girls' minds, trying to limit their sexuality and their freedom.[5]

Sometimes daughters use their mothers' failures as a motivation, Judith Arcana reports in *Our Mother's Daughters*. About half the women she interviewed competed with their mothers "to bypass them, to best them, to succeed where they had failed—we will be the exceptional women; we will not be the degraded creature, woman."[6] But such competitions exact a price: a tendency to feel superior to other women.

A girl's first and most enduring experience of competition is usually with her sisters and brothers. Though generally considered by parents to be annoying at best, sibling rivalry is understood by child development specialists to offer essential training in competitive skills. Says Jane Greer in *Adult Sibling Rivalry: Understanding the Legacy of Childhood*:

> Sisters and brothers not only vie for their parents' physical care but for their love, attention, approval, intellectual stimulation, and guidance. Such competition is simply part of being human. Sibling rivalry does not mean that children are too aggressive or demanding, or that parents are insufficiently nurturing. . . . Sibling rivalry isn't an intrinsically negative force. It's a way for children to learn assertiveness; it's also a testing ground for coping with the wider world; it even provides a setting for sisters and brothers to master cooperation. Sibling rivalry is in essence a survival mechanism—a means by which children try to obtain a fair share of parental resources.[7]

Still, it can hurt. "When I play tennis with my brother, he never admits it when I hit a good shot," complained Monica Seles in 1996. Monica rallies with her brother all the time; he is her hitting partner.

"The most painful matches I had to play as a pro were against my sister [Jeanne]," Chris Evert said upon retirement. "I played her three times, and I just wanted to throw up. I didn't want to lose to her, but I also didn't want to see her lose. I hated the way I was, but it showed how much I wanted to win."[8]

To avoid such conflicted feelings, siblings (especially those close in age) often compete only in separate arenas, one excelling at school while the other studies painting, one practicing karate while the other skates. It's called the principle of competitive exclusion, according to Frank Sulloway, author of *Born to Rebel: Birth Order, Family Dynamics, and Creative Lives*. This biological rule says that "no two species can coexist in the same habitat if their ecological niches are identical."[9]

The creation of "occupied zones" diminishes "envy, jealousy, and rivalry, thus reducing the risk of conflict," says Greer. "Yet the cost is often great in restricting [one's] personal and professional development."[10]

Sibling rivalries can also be enriching. Wells College president Lisa Ryerson comes from a family of six children: five girls, then a boy. She was the fourth girl. "We were highly competitive in every arena: academics, athletics, and music too," recalls Ryerson. "We had a family band with all eight of us singing and dancing and playing instruments. We were loving and supportive but pushed one another to achieve success. It would be unacceptable if you knew that a sister could get an A and she was doing B work. You'd say, 'What are you going to do to get the A?' And you'd compete: 'I got an A. Can you get an A?' But if you didn't get an A you still wanted her to get that A. You didn't sit back and say, 'I hope she bombs.'"

In junior high and high school Lisa and her younger sister competed on the debate team. "It became very important for us. We did a lot of research and work. There were boys who didn't want to compete against us, who would say negative things about 'those competitive Marsh sisters.' I can't remember how we responded to them. Except that we went ahead and won. Stood up and grabbed the trophy."

As adults Ryerson and her siblings "continue to support each other, wanting each other to achieve, pushing and nudging each other along," says Lisa. "Because most of us are women, we ask, 'Are you being paid what you should be paid?' There might be some resentment of who gets paid more or that sort of thing. I bet there is. That's human nature. But there's a lot of pride. I perceive our competitiveness to be a very healthy dynamic."

Birth order plays a major role in how we compete. Barbara Hackman Franklin, one of the first women to graduate from the Harvard Business School and now the owner of Franklin Associates, a management consulting firm in Washington, D.C., found in her research that the majority of women attending Harvard Business School were firstborn. From this she developed a "son theory": that fathers often raise eldest daughters as if they were sons, giving them special attention and encouragement.[11]

Middle children are less likely to be high achievers. They may feel unable to keep up with older siblings, surpassed by younger ones, and overlooked by parents, who naturally focus more attention on the firstborn—who arrived first—and the last born, who needs more attention when young.

The last born has her own set of competitive challenges. The late Erma Bombeck, in one of her rare serious columns, said that third children in families with three kids "learn a lot about competition and loneliness." They notice that the world was created for pairs and quadruples, Bombeck wrote. From cars to place settings to hotel beds, humans are expected to group themselves in twos or fours. In a family of five, the third child feels extra, extraneous, squeezed in. She learns not to take up too much space, not to demand too much.

"Sibling rivalry is unquestionably the most powerful dynamic among sisters and brothers while they are growing up," says Greer. "Fully as significant, however, and often more damaging, is the fact that sibling rivalry lives on long after childhood."[12] Grown siblings compete over who's got the best house, the nicest children, the fanciest clothes, the most prestigious job, or, still, the closest relationship to Mom or Dad.

A thirty-eight-year-old graphic designer and professional singer (I'll call her Mimi) told me that as the youngest of five siblings she "could never be as good because they were older," so she "stopped trying" to compete. As an adult Mimi feels uneasy about competition in general and wonders if she's "not competitive enough" at work. When she was promoted recently, it was "almost against my wishes," she says. "I'd rather feel successful where I am than have to try hard to keep up."

Her unacknowledged competition with one of her sisters—another singer, a forty-six-year-old with a husband and a son—persists. Mimi and her female lover had a "wedding" ceremony a few years ago. Then last year Mimi gave birth to a child. Mimi says her sister was "fine with my being gay" in part because "my sister thought, *Well, she'll never have the real thing—wedding, social support, presents, everything.* Then we did. And now we have a child. So she's not winning anymore."

How does Mimi know that these things upset her sister? I ask.

"Little barbs she'll make," says Mimi. "And when I was pregnant, she kept saying that some women get their figures back afterward, but in our family, we don't. But then I did. And she still hasn't. So now she's losing."

Could it be that Mimi herself is competitive? I ask.

"I'm not, but she is," she responds without irony, adding: "Plus, I have an album out, and she doesn't."

"How does it make you feel to be 'winning?'" I ask.

"Bad," she says, "because she takes it out on me."

Like many women, Mimi still feels victimized by her older sister's competitiveness. She's unable to see that she too is still competing. As the youngest child she's tired of the "loser" role and of trying to keep up. She tried to drop out of competing and believes she has. But she also senses that maybe she's "not competitive enough" at work, unwilling to take risks because of her fear of feeling like a failure—or getting punished for success—yet again.

Competitions with nonrelatives can also be rooted in sibling rivalries. The first writer of whom I felt envious was Jay McInerny. I had never met him, and still haven't. But when his first book, *Bright Lights, Big City*, became a best-seller, I suddenly felt angry and inferior. I hadn't published much yet, and Jay was only two years older (we both were in our twenties). I perceived him to be "winning." It struck me as odd because I hadn't felt the least bit envious of other writers. Why was I feeling diminished by this stranger's success?

Later, as I began to study competition, I remembered that Jay had attended Williams College with my brother. Somehow I had merged the two, and perhaps subconsciously I felt as if my brother were beating me at writing, my own game. Once I made that connection, I stopped resenting Jay McInerny and started enjoying his books more.

This phenomenon is known as displacement, "an unconscious psychological defense mechanism that is employed to transfer emotions toward a different person or situation. Angry, hostile, and resentful feelings are commonly displaced toward a safer and less threatening person or situation," says Greer.[13]

Greer defines "the Invisible Sibling" as "someone other than a sibling whose presence in your life evokes old feelings of siblinghood, some of which may be positive (love, appreciation, admiration) and some negative (dislike, hatred, contempt)." The Invisible Sibling is "a means by which you attempt to deal with the legacies of your sibling relationships." It can be "either a creative or destructive force."[14]

The problem with Invisible Siblings, says Greer, is their invisibility. "You don't see any sibling conflict either because you've stopped dealing with your sister or brother directly or because you've cut back considerably on your involvement with her or him. All you're aware of is that you're having real problems with some other significant person in your life."[15]

Invisible Parents loom as well. Luise Eichenbaum and Susie Orbach write in *Between Women*, "Almost all women unconsciously transfer a version of their hopes and restrictions of their own mother-daughter relationship to their current relationship. Women . . . project onto [their friends and colleagues] a whole range of emotions that reflect the legacy of their relationships with their mothers."[16]

So if you find yourself in a power struggle with some person at work (or at home) and he or she is driving you crazy, you've probably been through this before, years ago. Your parents or siblings probably acted the same way, refusing to acknowledge when you were right or offering unwanted advice or bragging about the ways they were "winning." That doesn't mean that this person in your present workplace or home isn't acting like a jerk—he or she may be—but tracing it to the ways your family competed can help you understand what's going on.

From our families we learn what kinds of competition are considered appropriate for girls and women of our particular ethnic, racial, and religious backgrounds. Janet Gray, editor of *She Wields a Pen,* says, "I grew up in a Quaker community in Southern California. Quakers are not anticompetitive per se, but there was always an emphasis on collaboration, on collectivities. I was a middle child and the only one out of three daughters who was an academic achiever. My parents tried to convey that three sisters are supposed to be equal. You don't want to stand out too much."

As an instructor at Princeton University, Gray feels "very uncomfortable with the grading system," she says. "I'm uncomfortable with reinforcing a sort of anxious competition. My dream class would have no grades, small enough that I could give a thorough discursive evaluation. But this is impossible to feed into a computer system. So I spend a lot of time writing comments, talking with students, encouraging people to do collaborative projects."

Native Americans also tend to value collaboration. Often "tribal members either avoid competition or redefine competitive situations

white women.) Muñoz says Hispanic people tend to assume that success is transferable: "If you can be successful in one area, you can be successful in another area. So success in sports will help you succeed in life. But in reality, because family is so important, the girls are still expected to baby-sit, to cook, to help at home. So they're not necessarily staying after school to play sports." This also helps explain why a large percentage of my Latina respondents (31 percent) identified themselves as *former* athletes. They had early sports experience but then stopped participating, perhaps because of family responsibilities.

The African-American women who filled out my survey were among the least likely to define themselves as athletes (only 51 percent did so, compared with 76 percent of white women) and to want their daughters to play sports.[19] They were also the least likely to believe that "girls who play sports become women who can compete at work" (only 34 percent of black women agreed, compared with 79 percent of Hispanic women).

These findings are consistent with other research. Though some of our country's greatest female athletes are black, African-American girls on the whole receive less encouragement to play sports and have less access to sports than white girls. According to a Women's Sports Foundation study, the parents of black girls are more likely than those of white girls to believe sports are more important for boys than for girls. African-American girls are more likely than others to believe that "boys make fun of girls who play sports." Black girls also have fewer financial resources for lessons, equipment, and transportation.[20]

My African-American survey respondents were the least likely to believe that "Competitive women tend to be successful." (Only 27 percent of African-American women agreed, compared with 93 percent of Hispanic women.) Ruth L. Hall, president (collective coordinator) of the Association for Women in Psychology and associate professor of psychology at the College of New Jersey, says these results make sense in light of how black women perceive the intractable power of racism. "In general, black women think that because of racism, it doesn't matter how competitive you are, or whether you play sports or not," says Hall, who is African-American. "Black men think basketball is going to get them out of poverty, but black women don't necessarily think like that. Meritocracy is a dead issue. Success is achieved by who you know, connections, contacts. By being competitive, you might learn how to handle failure better, but it won't necessarily make you a success."

Connie Todd, program director of the Foster Grandparent Program of Washington, D.C., says, "Black women have always had to be competitive. We've had less access to money, information, technology. And we've always perceived ourselves to be in position where men were less able to provide for us. Therefore we've had to compete more, but then we've been stereotyped as too strong. So we have attained certain things because we're strong and driven, but we've also been punished."

African-Americans were much less likely than the other cultural and racial groups to believe that "often, women can compete without being cutthroat about it." (Only 28 percent of African-American women agreed, compared with 55 percent of Asian-American women, 56 percent of Hispanic women, and 70 percent of European-American women.)

Hall comments that black women are unlikely to believe that anything less than cutthroat competition would be effective. Given the double oppression of sexism and racism, "you have to go all out or you're not going to achieve anything," says Hall.

If you want to understand your feelings about competition, take a look at what messages you received from your family, your community, your religious teachings, and your culture. Remember what was said or implied about competing with men, with women, with people of other races or ethnic backgrounds. Look at your role in the family; remember how your parents competed, or didn't, with each other. The better you understand your own family games, the better you'll understand the ways you compete and refuse to compete in the larger world.

Chapter 16

Beauty Contests

Women first voted in 1920. The next year, the Miss America Pageant was born. So, we won one, then lost one. We won the right to participate in the political process, then we lost some momentum toward full personhood.

By the 1990s, the institution that pits female "beauties" against one another had expanded in scope to include local, regional, national, and international contests, and in age to include babies. Girls between the ages of two months and ten years now compete in Pretty Little Princess, Lil' Darling, Universal Miss Supreme Beauty, Hollywood Babe, and hundreds of other annual pageants. Talent is not necessary, organizers tell parents. Instead girls are judged on beauty, charm, and personality as they smile, wave, and blow kisses.

Murder victim JonBenet Ramsey, the girl whose body was found in her Boulder, Colorado, home, focused national attention on a pint-size version of our national obsession with beauty contests. JonBenet, who wore false eyelashes and high heels to create an image that was eerily adult, had been the reigning Little Miss Colorado. She was six.

Even those of us who do not enter official contests tend to compete silently, secretly, agonizingly. "Every day in the life of a woman is a walking Miss America Contest," artist Wendy Bantam has said.[1]

This is the primary way women compete: through our physical appearance. "The preservation of youthful beauty is one of the few intense preoccupations and competitive drives that society fully expects of its women," writes Susan Brownmiller in *Femininity*, "even as it holds them in disdain for being such a narcissistic lot."[2]

The beauty contest begins at birth. "She's going to be a real beauty," parents say. Or they quietly worry about her lack of beauty. A girl may compete at soccer or softball or baseball, but she will also be encouraged to compete in uniquely female games: over jewelry and clothing and fingernails, over boyfriends and husbands, over how attractive her own children are. A new video game by Nintendo (makers of Game Boy) features Barbie "navigating a mall maze to meet Ken for a date."[3] In a *Washington Post* review of girls' games, the reporter concludes, "There is the occasional reference to a career, or being smart, but the overriding theme of these . . . games is that a girl should be pretty, plot how to get, keep, or trade a boyfriend, go shopping, gossip, paint her toenails and her face, and kiss kiss kiss."[4] These are the competitive strategies a girl will "need," apparently, to win a boy.

If a girl does feel pretty—even if the fairy-tale mirror tells her she's the fairest of them all—she is likely to doubt her inner beauty, to doubt if the boys can see past her breasts and lips and eyelashes, to wonder if they "only want her for her body." The pretty young woman will believe that she can't win.

Women who are perceived to be ugly or fat may, paradoxically, have better chances at the sort of success that leads to self-esteem. Though barred from jobs that require female (but not male) beauty and scarred by cruel remarks, women who "can't compete" in the beauty game may give themselves permission to compete openly in other arenas. In fact, refusing to compete in the beauty game may be one of the most liberating things a women can do.

In a Nicole Hollander cartoon, Sylvia is asked, "What would the world be like with no men?"

"A lot of fat, happy women," Sylvia responds.

This is funny because it points to a truth: "A lot" of us engage in semistarvation or compulsive exercise or surgery in a frantic and obsessive desire to please men. This misguided beauty contest is generally based on weight or lack of it. "I was anorexic and bulimic, but almost all of us are," 1997 Miss Universe Alicia Machado of Venezuela told Knight-Ridder. By "almost all of us" she seems to have meant official beauty contestants, not women. But these "winning" women are the ones who, for many of the rest of us, still define how women should look.

"I always check to make sure I'm the thinnest woman at a party," a Washington lawyer admits.

"You have to be the thinnest?" I ask. She's a runner; she's thin.

"Not the thinnest, but not the fattest," she replies.

"Have you ever been the fattest woman at a party?" I ask dubiously.

"It's hard to tell," she says. "I've got that typical distortion. I look in a mirror, and I always look fat."

This woman competes with men in road races and bike races. She likes sprinting or cycling past men or, if she's ahead, increasing her speed to "make sure they can't catch up." But she's reluctant to compete with women in sports, and she dropped out of a predominantly male running club when other women joined. "Were they faster?" I ask.

"Well, yes," she responds.

"And thinner?"

"To be honest, that was it," she admits.

It is socially acceptable for two women, observing a third woman, to say that on the basis of that woman's looks, they hate her. "Beauty thinking urges women to approach one another as possible adversaries," Naomi Wolf writes in *The Beauty Myth*. "Women tend to resent each other if they look too 'good' and dismiss one another if they look too 'bad'. So women rarely benefit from the experience that makes men's clubs and organizations hold together: The solidarity of belonging to a group whose members might not be personal friends outside, but who are united in an interest, agenda, or world view."[5]

Girls and women who make continual comparisons with each other over physical appearance are likely to feel like losers. A 1995 Melpomene Institute study of 150 American and Mexican girls aged eleven to seventeen found that girls who scored high on a body image test did not compare their appearances with those of others. Girls with low body image scores "almost always" did.

In my survey, more than half (56 percent) of the women and girls said they always or frequently compare themselves with female friends or family in regard to size, fat, and weight. Almost half (48 percent) said they always or frequently compare themselves with female friends or family in terms of physical attractiveness. Nearly 40 percent said they always or frequently compare themselves with female friends or family in terms of clothing. Yet only 23 percent made such comparisons regarding work or school.

The women least likely to compare themselves with others on the basis of physical attractiveness, weight, or clothing were lesbians.[6] Since lesbians are by definition less interested in attracting men than are straight or bisexual women, it makes sense that they would be less likely to compare or compete with other women over anything to do with physical appearance. Predictably, lesbians were also far less likely to say they always or frequently compare themselves with female friends or family "regarding popularity with men."[7] (Lesbians and straight women were equally likely to say they compare themselves with female friends or family "regarding popularity with women.")

Of the various racial and ethnic groups, African-American women were the least likely to compare themselves with other women on the basis of physical attractiveness or size, fat, and weight.[8] These results concur with other research showing that black women have better body images than do white women. In one study, 50 percent of black girls and only 21 percent of white girls said, "I like the way I look." Another study found that women are more dissatisfied with their appearance than they were ten years ago, but that black women are less dissatisfied than white women.[9]

The College of New Jersey psychology professor Ruth L. Hall explains: "If you look at *Essence* or *Ebony*, you see a greater variety in size, hair, skin features; there's a broader spectrum of acceptable physical types. Not that racism doesn't enter into it. There's still internalized oppression every day. Big butts, big noses, skin color, and hair texture are still major issues. But among black women there's a term, FBI—for fat, black, and intelligent. There's an acceptance that we're not going to look like white women, and we appreciate who we are."

In newspapers the word "competition" appears often with "women" in stories about beauty. Increasingly the way women (especially white, heterosexual women) "compete" for jobs and promotions and power is not through enforcing antidiscrimination laws but by hiring surgeons to cut and reshape their skin and fat and bones. Face-lifts, facial liposuctions, and eyelid surgeries increased 150 percent between 1988 and 1993, according to the American Academy of Facial and Plastic Reconstructive Surgery. Once a desperate technique of the old to look younger, now more than 40 percent of these surgeries are done on people between the ages of thirty and forty-nine, primarily women. These women report wanting to look youthful so they can "compete" or "stay competitive" with younger women in the workplace. Repeated surgeries are often "necessary," but eventually nature wins. Eventually, with age, all women become losers in the beauty game.

In some ways we learn early to be losers, to hide our aspirations under veneers of vulnerability and charm. Nancy Friday, in "The Age of Beauty," describes a turning point at a yacht club one evening when as a preteen she learned "the loser's agony of defeat." She saw her friends "happy in the arms of desirable boys" and decided she needed a mask, "a new face that belied the intelligent leader inside." Friday's authentic self, a girl "so full of words waiting to be spoken and skills to be mastered . . . had to be pushed down like an ugly jack-in-the-box," she writes. "No boy was going to take a package like me."

Friday says she did "what most women still do: I swallowed my anger, choked on it. I bowed my head, in part to be shorter, but also, like a cornered cow, to signal I had given up. By morning I had buried and mourned my 11-year-old self, the leader, the actress, the tree climber, and had become an ardent beauty student."[10]

The beauty student learns that in order to win love, she must create an appearance and a demeanor that is pleasing to boys and men. She learns to be small, quiet. She learns to lose because in the nonsensical, topsy-turvy world of female beauty, winning is losing. Did you lose? Congratulations. Did you gain? Too bad. We must become ever, endlessly smaller, less than we are. According to *The New York Times,* people (mostly women) spend thirty-three billion dollars each year on diet and weight loss remedies.

The closer we get to equality in the workplace, the more pressure we feel to be small, dainty, and decorative. The stronger women get, the thinner we're supposed to be.

How does this pressure to lose affect our desire to win? How does it relate to our desire to gain, to acquire, to win prizes or accolades or jobs or money? We do want those things, but we equate *them* with losing. If I lose weight, I will win friends, promotions, self-esteem. Losing must come first, and because it never really does, not forever—there's always that extra five pounds, or one pound, or the potential for that weight to come back—many of us become so obsessed with losing we forget all about the winning that might happen later. Or we fixate in the opposite way: If we win awards and promotions, we will suffer by losing friends.

In 1995 the Miss America Pageant asked the American people to vote on this issue: Should the contestants parade in bathing suits? More than a million voted (most in favor of the suits) with paid phone calls. In 1996 pageant officials asked the American public to vote again, this time for the winner. *Washington Post* writer Roxanne Roberts opened her article about the voting this way: "Forget the Republicans and Democrats. Here's an election that will really stir passionate debate: Should you vote for the cute blonde in the sequined evening gown? Or the perky brunette in the red swimsuit?"[11] Female competition is still reduced to this: cute blondes versus perky brunettes.

It is in part because of this unnatural beauty contest, because of the pain and futility and humiliation of it all, that many women reject competition itself. They've been there, done that, didn't like it. "Let's stop competing with other women," they say, remembering skimpy cheerleading outfits and excruciating high heels.

Okay. Let's stop competing *in this way*. Let's notice our tendencies to compete like this and refuse to. Beauty should not be a contest. We must find a way to stop feeling like losers, despite our imperfect facial features and our body fat percentage. Foster Grandparent administrator Connie Todd says defiantly, "I'm overweight. I like to call it thick. A lot of overweight women won't put themselves forward. They could be in the arena, participating, but their tremendous insecurity holds them back. They're reluctant to say 'I'm the best' if other people are going to say to them, 'How can you say you're the best when you can't even control what you put in your mouth?' I've made a conscious decision to keep doing what I do. I say: Don't let your weight make you wait. It means I move forward even though some people may have prejudice about that."

Todd does not compete with other women over weight or clothes or beauty. She competes at work in spite of discrimination against her—as an African-American, as a woman, and as someone who is "overweight." She keeps moving forward, not letting the beauty game get her down.

Chapter 17

Catfights

Women can't compete. They don't have the right stuff. They aren't qualified. They compete over the wrong things—trivial things like clothes—unlike men, who compete over important things, like whether the Dallas Cowboys win. This is the rap on women: They don't compete well. Women "are their own worst enemies." They "don't know how to be team players." They "don't support each other." They "stab each other in the back." They claw; they scratch; they screech. They're catty and gossipy. They don't share information. They "can't leave the competition on the playing field."

When applied to women, the word "competitive" tends to connote individual conflict in traditional feminine pursuits: who's got the best husband, the smartest kids, the nicest house, the thinnest body. The kinds of competitions, in other words, in which Cheerleaders engage.

Rarely (except in sports) do we imagine that women can marshal their competitive energies toward achieving a goal. Or that competition between women, or between women and men, can serve as a catalyst for success or even for intimacy.

Members of the media are part of the problem. They trivialize and demean female competition. During the past two presidential campaigns, *Family Circle* staged a cookie contest between the Democratic and Republican contenders for the role of First Lady. Hillary Rodham Clinton defeated Barbara Bush in the 1992 bake-off, which was created after Clinton was criticized for saying in defense of her career, "I suppose I could have stayed home and baked cookies." Four years later, recipes for Clinton's chocolate chip cookies and Elizabeth Dole's pecan roll cookies appeared in the September issue of the magazine. Readers could vote on their favorite.

Isn't that cute? Fun? In keeping with family values, in which powerful female lawyers compete over cookie recipes while men run the country?

According to the media, women who aren't competing cutely in cookie contests are competing ruthlessly in "catfights," a term used only in reference to women, a term that implies something wild and absurd about female competition, and a term that distracts people from the fact that women also compete with men. Barbara Walters, the weekly host of *20/20* and the first woman to coanchor the news (with Harry Reasoner in 1976), has objected to industry rumors that she and *PrimeTime Live* anchor Diane Sawyer have a long-standing rivalry. Such talk is "an offensive anachronism" that depicts her and women in general as "raging cats at each other's throats," she says.

ABC's *Good Morning America* anchor Joan Lunden made a similar complaint in response to published reports of tension between her and news reader Elizabeth Vargas. "It saddens me that people want to see some kind of catfight," said Lunden.[1]

Yet television news is unquestionably a competitive industry where ratings rule. Celebrities such as Colin Powell, Christopher Reeve, and Christopher Darden, all of whom appeared on *20/20*, are often asked to grant exclusive interviews. When pressed, Barbara Walters admits that her producers do compete for these guests and that ratings are important. But she explains: "What I like least is the competition—not when it's my friend. I don't like it, and I know Diane doesn't like it."[2]

I hear these contradictory statements all the time. Women feel angry that their competitiveness is used against them. They deny that they compete. Then they admit it—but maintain that it's a necessary evil.

The catfight is a "staple of American pop culture . . . like female mud wrestling or Jell-O wrestling," writes Susan J. Douglas in her marvelous book *Where the Girls Are*. "In its purest form, it features two women, one usually a traditional wife (blond), the other a grasping, craven careerist (brunette), who slug it out on a veranda, in a lily pond, or during a mud slide. Usually they fight over men or children. Sometimes, as in *The Turning Point*, they just hit each other with their little purses."[3]

Catfights serve an important function in a male-dominated culture. They shrink women's appetites to palatable proportions: all women want to win is male attention. All women care about is hairdos. All women focus on is defeating other women.

Hence the public obsession with Nancy Kerrigan's knee. "Had Kerrigan been attacked by a bad man, as it initially appeared she was, the story would have been dramatic, but commonplace," notes Melanie Thernstrom in an essay titled "The Glass Slipper." "The extraordinary public fascination lay in the revelation that behind the bad man lies a jealous woman—a wicked stepsister, a rival."[4]

The Kerrigan-Harding saga was popular, Thernstrom writes, "because it appeared to be a blow to feminism." This is another function of the catfight: It frames women as silly enemies instead of powerful allies. Even the debate about the Equal Rights Amendment, Douglas notes, was portrayed as a bitter contest between women: feminists versus traditional homemakers. In fact the struggle was between women who wanted to see the ERA pass and the largely male Congress, which didn't. That's how catfights work: They divert attention from women's actual efforts to win political or legal victories and instead create silly caricatures of clawed creatures baring their fangs.

Yet isn't it true that women feel uncomfortable about openly competitive peers? That they criticize women who know what they want and go for it? Author and college instructor Janet Gray says, "When I hear the word 'competitive,' I think of a friend of mine. She's very driven. She finished her Ph.D. faster than most people. She got two job offers, which is unheard of. A lot of the women who entered grad school at the same time didn't like her. They thought she was unbearable to be around. She's very aggressive about establishing a place for herself. She got to know all the people in her field. Schmoozing. Taking risks. The other women said, 'She's pushy; she's competitive; she will make us look bad.' "

Isn't it true that women are catty? That they compete in ugly, vicious, sneaky ways? "Within the context of traditional femininity, women learn to win through shrewdness, not directly," says Temple University sport psychology professor Carole Oglesby. "Not the honorable, aboveboard, play-by-the-rules way."

"I hope you're going to write about women undermining each other, stabbing each other in the back, being each other's worst enemies," says a friend when I mention this book. Women say that a lot: that women don't support each other the way they should. Women seem angry about that. They're not angry about men undermining them, excluding them, discriminating against them. Or, rather, they're angry about that too. But male opponents are to be expected, accommodated, forgiven. When women compete with each other, it somehow seems misguided, unfair.

San Francisco attorney Flo Kennedy has given this phenomenon a name, horizontal hostility. Unable to get access to people in power, women (and other oppressed groups) vent their rage and frustration on each other.

Sometimes women even compete to see who's losing. The writer Audre Lorde coined the term "Oppression Derby" to describe an informal contest engaged in by poor, Latina, African-American, disabled, and lesbian women to determine who's the most oppressed.

Sometimes women compete over husbands, boyfriends, or babies because they don't have other ways to measure their achievements. Linda Villarosa, executive editor of *Essence* magazine, is an avid athlete and a lesbian mother who enjoys competition at work and in sports but chooses not to compete with other mothers. She speculates that traditional women without much work or sports experience are more likely to compete in indirect, unsatisfying ways. "I think it's really funny how straight women friends of mine are so competitive with other mothers," says Villarosa. "I don't feel that at all. My neighbor came over, and her son, Sam, is a little younger than my daughter, Kali, and my friend said, 'Oh, Sam is doing XYZ!' Kali was only doing X and Y, and I didn't think, *Oh, no! Something's wrong!*"

Another friend of Linda's agonizes over her child's development and accuses mothers with faster-developing children of competing with *her*. "I challenge her on it," says Villarosa. "It seems inappropriate to be projecting a negative competitiveness onto other women. My friend works at home, so she doesn't have a lot of competition within the work arena. And she had never been an athlete. When you've been an athlete, you understand what competition is and what it isn't. A lot of women my age haven't been athletes, so they didn't get to exercise their competitive spirit. They end up being competitive inappropriately."

Women also mimic male behavior. "Some successful women feel they have to adopt certain characteristics of our male counterparts," observes Wells College president Lisa Ryerson. "They use condescending language toward other women. There's an attitude of 'Frankly, dammit, I clawed to get here, and you'd better claw too.' I don't like that. It's not women-friendly. It's machismo, and it's so hurtful to women. Women will never achieve if we don't help them achieve. But the problem is not really that women don't support each other; it's that *people* don't support women. Are there women who aren't supportive? I do see that. But are there men who aren't supportive? I see that more."

The problem with the catfight stereotype, notes Ryerson, is that it separates women from each other. "Separated, we're not as powerful. If the problem is that women don't support each other, then it's not seen as a problem of male behavior, of society taking women seriously. It's women's fault."

Sportscaster Robin Roberts sees women moving beyond the catfight mentality. "Some women in the past have been each other's worst critics. Instead of supporting one another, we've torn each other down. We've acted like the men: nitpicking and jealous. Now we're more of a sorority. It's tough enough out there anyway. When I signed my new contract, the first person who called to congratulate me was [sportscaster] Leslie Visser. Then [sportscaster] Andrea Kramer called.

"If I do well, it's easier for Leslie and Andrea and Mary Carillo and [sportscaster] Hannah Storm. If one of us does well, it's not such a big deal then, a woman talking about football or men's basketball. We don't root for each other to fail."

But they do compete. They compete with each other and with their male colleagues. The catfight undermines the power of sister-hood, but sisterhood is not just about support. It's about urging each other to succeed and trusting that success need not ruin relationships. The problem with catfights is not that they portray women competing with each other—women *do* compete with each other—but that they trivialize and ridicule such competitions. They render female com-petitiveness laughable—unlike male competitions, which are depicted as serious and important.

In truth women can compete honorably and fairly and in arenas that matter, just as men can. Competition can be empowering and unifying as women strive to achieve while also helping other women (or men) achieve. Competition can also be, at times, good, clean fun, as women or men compete over cookies or pumpkins or pies. But it's not true that women have only three options: loyal sisterhood, down and dirty catfights, or cookie bake-offs. It's not that we need to stop depicting women as competitors; we need to start depicting female competition, both with other women and with men, honestly.

Chapter 18

"I Won, but I'm Sorry": The Femininity Game

When Sylvia Plath's husband, Ted Hughes, published his first book of poems, Sylvia wrote to her mother: "I am so happy that HIS book is accepted FIRST. It will make it so much easier for me when mine is accepted. . . ."

After Sylvia killed herself, her mother published a collection of Sylvia's letters. In her explanatory notes, Aurelia Plath commented that from the time she was very young, Sylvia "catered to the male of any age so as to bolster his sense of superiority." In seventh grade, Aurelia Plath noted, Sylvia was pleased to finish second in a spelling contest. "It was nicer, she felt, to have a boy first."[1]

How many women still collude in the myth of male superiority, believing it's "nicer" when boys and men finish first? How many of us achieve but only in a lesser, smaller, feminine way, a manner consciously or unconsciously designed to be as nonthreatening as possible?

Since I'm tall, women often talk to me about height. Short women tell me, "I've always wanted to be tall—but not as tall as *you*!" I find this amusing, but also curious. Why not? Why not be six-two?

Tall women tell me that they won't wear heels because they don't want to appear taller than their husbands or boyfriends, even by an inch.

What are these women telling me—and their male companions? Why do women regulate their height in relation to men's height? Why is it still rare to see a woman who is taller than her husband?

Here's what I think is going on: Women want to be tall enough to feel elegant and attractive, like models. They want to feel respected and looked up to. But they don't want to be so tall that their height threatens men. They want to win—to achieve, to reach new heights—but without exceeding male heights.

In an ad for Sports and Fitness Health Clubs in Washington, D.C., a photo of a svelte young woman is accompanied by the caption "We Cut Judy Down to Size." This image of women (small, thin, a little muscle tone, but no powerful bulk or weight or height) and this belief about women (the smaller the better; they deserve to be cut down to size; there is some small size that is best for women) predominates in American culture, especially European-American culture, today.

From an early age, girls get indoctrinated into the rules of heterosexuality, including this one: Boys "should" be taller. Because the average girl matures before the average boy, many women have had a childhood experience of feeling "too tall." Even in a heterosexual friendship, both a man and a woman can feel uncomfortable if she is much taller than he is.

Height is valued in men and is often used as a metaphor for growth and success. Winners are said to tower over the opposition, to be huge, large, imposing, of great stature. Winners are "giants among men."

Among women, height is less often used as a positive metaphor. We want to be tall but not towering, impressive but not imposing. We want to look men in the eye but are careful not to look down at them lest that make them uncomfortable. We're very concerned with male comfort and with male size. We're so concerned that we're even willing to shrink ourselves, appearing smaller and weaker and quieter and shorter and less successful than we really are.

How can you win if you're female? Can you just do it?

No, you have to play the femininity game.

Femininity by definition is not large, not imposing, not competitive. Feminine women are not ruthless, not aggressive, not victorious. It's not feminine to have a killer instinct, to want with all your heart and soul to win—not tennis matches or elected offices or feminist victories, such as abortion rights. It's not feminine to know exactly what you want, then to go for it.

Femininity is about appearing beautiful and vulnerable and small. It's about winning male approval. It's about winning a husband. That's a feminine woman's ultimate achievement, her victory, her gold medal. In the film *Muriel's Wedding,* a young Australian believes that marriage will mean she "is worth something" and fixates on her dream, compulsively trying on wedding dresses, inventing a fiancé, and eventually settling for a bogus marriage with a South African swimmer who needs Australian citizenship to compete in the Olympics. "All my life I've wanted to win," he tells her.

"Me too," she responds.

Femininity is also about accommodating the interests of men. One of those male interests is feeling bigger than and stronger than and superior to women, not "emasculated" by them.

Obviously femininity is unhealthy. It would be unhealthy for men to act passive, dainty, obsessed with their physical appearance, and dedicated to bolstering the sense of superiority in the other gender, so it's unhealthy for women too. These days some women are redefining femininity as strong, as athletic, as however a female happens to be, so that "feminine" becomes synonymous with "female." Other women reject both feminine and masculine terms and stereotypes, selecting from the entire range of human behaviors instead of limiting themselves to the "gender-appropriate" ones. These women smile only when they're happy, act angry when they're angry, dress how they want to. They cling to their self-respect and dignity like a life raft.

But most female winners play the femininity game to some extent, using femininity as a defense, a shield against accusations such as "bitch," "man hater," "lesbian." Feminine behavior and attire mitigate against the affront of female victory, soften the hard edges of winning. Women who want to win without losing male approval temper their victories with beauty, with softness, with smallness, with smiles.

Sports scholar Jan Felshin first named this phenomenon in 1974.[2] She called it "apologetic" behavior, explaining that in order to avoid criticism for engaging in the "masculine" endeavor of sport, female athletes appear feminine (through dress and hairstyles), act feminine (through ladylike comportment beyond the playing fields), and extol feminine values (by prioritizing marriage and motherhood over championships).

An apologetic is a defense, a way to seek approval. It's offered by way of excuse or apology: I'm sorry. My dictionary says it's a way to acknowledge fault or failure regretfully, to be contrite. In this case, paradoxically, the fault or the failure is striving for victory in a society in which women are not supposed to win.

The female apologetic has a long history in sports. At each of the AAU basketball championships in the 1950s, one of the players was crowned beauty queen. (This still happens at Russian women's ice hockey tournaments.) Athletes in the All-American Girls Baseball League of the 1940s and 1950s slid into base wearing skirts. In the 1960s tennis players began wearing frilly panties under their short dresses. In 1979 professional basketball players with the California Dreams were sent to John Robert Powers's charm school.

Makeup, jewelry, dress, and demeanor were often dictated by the male coaches and owners in these leagues, but to some extent the players played along, understanding the trade-off: In order to be "allowed" to compete, they had to demonstrate that they were, despite their "masculine" strivings, real ("feminine") women.

Today both men and women wear earrings, notes Felshin, "but the media is still selling heterosexism and 'feminine' beauty. And if you listen carefully, in almost every interview" female athletes still express apologetic behavior through feminine dress, behavior, and values.

Steffi Graf, for instance, posed in bikinis for the 1997 *Sports Illustrated* swimsuit issue. A Coca-Cola commercial aired during the Olympics showed quick images of female athletes interspersed with the words "Their bodies are so strong and yet so feminine." In a Sears commercial Olympic basketball players apply lipstick, paint their toenails, rock babies, lounge in bed, and pose and dance in their underwear. Lisa Leslie, who later starred in the Women's National Basketball Association, says, "Everybody's allowed to be themselves. Me, for example, I'm very feminine."

In an Avon commercial Jackie Joyner-Kersee is shown running on a beach while the camera lingers on her buttocks and breasts. She tells us that she can bench-press 150 pounds and brags that she can jump farther than "all but one hundred and twenty-eight men." Then she says: "And I have red toenails." Words flash on the screen: "Just another Avon lady."

In a 1996 *Newsweek* article featuring female Olympians, Lisa Leslie ran on a beach in a bikini and teammate Sheryl Swoopes wore some sort of tight white bra and shorts. Soccer player Carla Overbeck, perhaps impersonating an animal, crouched bizarrely, clad only in what appeared to be a leopard-patterned slip. Whatever happened to action photos? Whatever happened to clothes?

Tennis player Mary Pierce wore a fitted black dress with a low-cut neckline at a recent French Open. When she walked onto the court, the fans whistled. *France-Soir* reported that Pierce's dress "made more of a sensation than her victory."

Graf, Mary Pierce, Monica Seles, and Mary Joe Fernandez all have played in dresses. They are "so much more comfortable" than skirts, Fernandez explained. "You don't have to worry about the skirt coming up or the skirt being too tight. It's cooler, and it's so feminine."

"When I put on a dress I feel different—more feminine, more elegant, more ladylike—and that's nice," added Australia's Nicole

Bradtke: "We're in a sport where we're throwing ourselves around, so it's a real asset to the game to be able to look pretty at the same time."

"Strong is sexy!" promise the women's magazines. And "Beauty is Power!" Athletes have become gorgeous, flirtatious, elegant, angelic, darling, and—the skating commentators' favorite term—"vulnerable." Some think this is good news, proof that femininity and sports are compatible. "There doesn't have to be such a complete division between "You're beautiful and sexy" and "you're athletic and strong," says Linda Hanley, a pro beach volleyball player who also appeared in a bikini in the 1997 *Sports Illustrated* swimsuit issue.

But aren't the strongest women in the world being downgraded to pretty playthings for male enjoyment? Isn't female victory being depicted as pleasing rather than powerful? Sexy ladies aren't Champions, are they? Doesn't "The lady is a champ" sound a wee bit condescending? Or at least confused? Listen to this contradictory comparison by Frank Deford in *Newsweek*'s June 10, 1996, cover story: "They aren't bad at it, the ladies. They can throw like a boy."

Athletes and advertisers reassure viewers that women who compete are still willing to play the femininity game, to be Cheerleaders. Don't worry about us, the commercials imply. We're winners, but we'll still look pretty for you. We're acting in ways that only men used to act, but we'll still act the way you want women to act. We're not threatening. We're not lesbians. We're not ugly, not bad marriage material. We're strong but feminine. Linguists note that the word "but" negates the part of the sentence that precedes it.

Some recent media descriptions emphasize female power in an unambiguous way. WOMEN MUSCLE IN, *The New York Times Magazine* proclaimed in a headline. The *Washington Post* wrote, AT OLYMPICS WOMEN SHOW THEIR STRENGTH.

A new genre of commercials protests that female athletes are *not* Cheerleaders, and don't have to be. Olympic and pro basketball star Dawn Staley says in a Nike commercial that she plays basketball "for the competitiveness" of it. "I need some place to release it. It just builds up, and sports is a great outlet for it. I started out playing with the guys. I wasn't always accepted. You get criticized, like: 'You need to be in the kitchen. Go put on a skirt.' I just got mad and angry and went out to show them that I belong here as much as they do."

But if they're not Cheerleaders, just what women are is still in question. Many ads offer only a pseudofeminist message. In a promotional commercial for a televised basketball tournament, players aggressively shoot, rebound, block shots, and steal balls. Then one walks toward the camera, wiping her sweaty face with a towel. "Who says you always have to act like a lady?" she asks. As a stray ball comes bouncing toward the camera, a voice concludes: "State Farm is proud to present the 1996 Women's Basketball Tip-Off Classic—from a safe distance, that is."

What's the point here? What or whom is State Farm maintaining a safe distance *from*? Are female athletes so competitive that they're scary? To whom?

Other commercials tell us that women can compete like Conquerors. A Nike ad called "Wolves" shows girls leaping and spiking volleyballs while a voice says, "They are not sisters. They are not classmates. They are not friends. They are not even the girls' team. They are a pack of wolves. Tend to your sheep." Though the athletes look serious, the message sounds absurd. When I show this commercial to audiences, they laugh. Still, the images do depict the power of the players: their intensity, their ability to hammer the ball almost through the floor. The script gives the players (and viewers) permission not to be ladylike, not to worry about whether their toenails are red.

In a commercial for the pro basketball team that was originally called the Richmond Rage, female athletes could be seen playing roughly, bodies hitting each other hard. Maurice Chevalier sang, "Thank heaven for little girls." The tag line: "Thank heaven they're on our side."

So we're not ladies, not friends, not even the girls' team. We're scary little girls? We're dangerous wolves? Isn't there some way to conceive of female athletes who are neither meek supplicants nor rapacious animals? Neither Cheerleaders nor Conquerors?

And doesn't all this talk about girls and ladies simply focus our attention on femaleness, femininity, and ladylike behavior? The lady issue is always there in the equation, something to redefine, to rebel against. It's always present, like sneakers, so every time you hear the word "athlete" you also hear the word "lady"—or "feminine," or "unfeminine." It reminds me of a Coors magazine ad from the eighties that featured a photo of Olympic track star Valerie Brisco-Hooks. "Funny, she doesn't look like the weaker sex," said the type. You could see her impressive muscles. Clearly the intent of the ad was to contrast an old stereotype with the reality of female strength and ability. But Brisco-Hooks was seated, her legs twisted pretzel style, arms covering her chest. In that position she didn't look very strong or able. In the line "Funny, she doesn't look like the weaker sex," the most eye-catching words are "funny," "look," "weaker," and "sex." Looking at the pretzel that is Valerie, you begin to think that she looks funny. You think about weakness. You think about sex.

When she was young, Nancy Kerrigan wanted to play ice hockey with her older brothers. Her mother told her, "You're a girl. Do girl things."

Figure skating is a girl thing. Athletes in sequins and "sheer illusion sleeves" glide and dance, their tiny skirts flapping in the breeze. They achieve, but without touching or pushing anyone else. They win, but without visible signs of sweat. They compete, but not directly. Their success is measured not by confrontation with an opponent or even by a clock or a scoreboard. Rather, they are judged as beauty contestants are judged, by a panel of people who interpret the success of the routines. Prettiness is mandatory. Petite and groomed and gracious, figure skaters—like cheerleaders, gymnasts, and aerobic dancers—camouflage their competitiveness with niceness and prettiness until it no longer seems male or aggressive or unseemly.

The most popular sport for high school and college women to play is basketball. More than a million fans shelled out an average of $15 per ticket in 1997, the inaugural summer of the Women's National Basketball Association. But the most televised women's sport is figure skating. In 1995, revenue from skating shows and competitions topped six hundred million dollars. In the seven months between October 1996 and March 1997, ABC, CBS, NBC, Fox, ESPN, TBS, and USA dedicated 162.5 hours of programming to figure skating, half of it in prime time. Kerrigan earns up to three hundred thousand dollars for a single performance. National champion Michelle Kwan pocketed a million dollars in 1996.[3]

Nearly 75 percent of the viewers of televised skating are women. The average age is between twenty-five and forty-five years old, with a household income of more than fifty thousand dollars.[4] What are these women watching? What are they seeing? What's the appeal?

Like golf, tennis, and gymnastics, figure skating is an individual sport favored by white people from the upper classes. The skaters wear cosmetics, frozen smiles, and revealing dresses. Behind the scenes they lift weights and sweat like any serious athlete, but figure skating seems more dance than sport, more grace than guts, more art than athleticism. Figure skating allows women to compete like Champions while dressed like Cheerleaders.

In women's figure skating, smiling is part of "artistic expression." In the final round, if the competitors are of equal merit, artistry weighs more heavily than technique.[5] Midori Ito, the best jumper in the history of women's skating, explained a weak showing at the 1995 world championships this way: "I wasn't 100 percent satisfied. . . . I probably wasn't smiling enough today in my performance. That could have been one of the problems with the competition."[6]

At the 1988 Olympics, Debi Thomas wore a black unitard similar to an outfit her friend Brian Boitano used to wear. The Lycra accentuated her muscular thighs and looked more appropriate on her, somehow, than any four-inch skirt ever did. But she received poor marks for artistic impression, and soon afterward the International

Skating Union rewrote the women's rules to outlaw unitards. Like pants, unitards are not girl things.

The media portray female figure skaters as "little girl dancers" or "fairy tale princesses" (NBC commentator John Tesh); as "elegant" (Dick Button); as "little angels" (Peggy Fleming); as "ice beauties" and "ladies who lutz" (*People* magazine). Commentators frame skaters as small, young, and decorative creatures, not superwomen but fairy-tale figments of someone's imagination.

After Kerrigan was assaulted by a member of Tonya Harding's entourage, she was featured on a *Sports Illustrated* cover crying, "Why me?" When she recovered to win a silver medal at the Olympics that year, she became "America's sweetheart," and rich to boot. But the princess turned pumpkin shortly after midnight, as soon as the ball was over and she stopped smiling and started speaking. Growing impatient during the Olympic medal ceremony while everyone waited for Oksana Baiul, Kerrigan grumbled, "Oh, give me a break, she's just going to cry out there again. What's the difference?"[7] Later, asked whether she should have won, she complained, "I was so perfect. . . . I was flawless. . . ." Kerrigan's popularity took another nosedive when, surrounded by Mickey Mouse characters during a tour of Disney World, she observed, "This is so corny. . . ."

What were Kerrigan's crimes? That she felt too old to cavort with cartoon characters. Isn't she? That she expressed anger and disappointment—even bitterness and bad sportsmanship—about losing the gold. But wasn't she supposed to want to win? What happens to baseball players who, disappointed about losses, hit each other or spit on umpires? What happens to basketball players and football players and hockey players who fight? Men can't tumble from a princess palace because we don't expect them to be princesses in the first place, only athletes.

Americans fell out of love with Kerrigan not because they couldn't adore an athlete who lacked grace in defeat but because they couldn't adore a female athlete who lacked grace in defeat. They couldn't abide a Miss America who, instead of prettily waving her white gloves from atop the float, honestly commented on the absurdity of the situation. As soon as Kerrigan proved herself to be less than a charming princess, the applause stopped. Three years later she claimed implausibly in *Sports Illustrated Women/Sport*, "I never cared that much about winning."

African-American women's sports teams have traditionally "placed more value on racial uplift and African-American achievement than on white middle-class views of femininity," says historian Mary Jo Festle, author of *Playing Nice: Politics and Apologies in Women's Sports*. Sprinter Wilma Rudolph was embraced as a hero in the black community. For some she was as important a symbol of achievement as Joe Louis or Muhammad Ali. Dancer Gregory Hines has spoken movingly of her influence on him when he was young. Her three Olympic victories in 1960, he says, gave him hope. Althea Gibson, who integrated tennis, was compared in the press with Jackie Robinson, who integrated baseball. Even after she had lost in the finals of the national indoor championship in 1950, Gibson was welcomed home by a parade, a marching band, and the president of Florida A&M University. "Obviously, they all felt that what I had done was important not just to me but to all Negroes," Gibson stated.[8]

Black leader and sports historian Edwin B. Henderson said in 1951: "There are those who condemn strenuous athletic contests for women, who fear women will lose some of their charm and possibly what is more important, health. But so long as women of other races and nations engage in these sports with no proven evidence of detriment, our girls have reason and right to compete. Victory in physical contests, as with high rating in mental or spiritual measurements, helped kill off the Nazi-inspired doctrine of inferiority."[9]

So black female athletes have long represented something beyond themselves, something that black men sought too: equal rights. Until Billie Jean King came along, white female athletes were not perceived to be representing anyone but themselves. Yet black women have also faced pressure to apologize, to compensate, to prove their femininity, and still do. Willye White, who competed in five consecutive Olympics, from 1956 through 1972, describes herself as a tomboy and an outcast, explaining that sports were "not acceptable in American society."[10]

Ed Temple, the legendary coach of the Tennessee State Tigerbelles, the team that produced Wilma Rudolph, Wyomia Tyus, Willye White, Madeline Manning, and countless other champions, enforced a dress code and stressed that his athletes should be "young ladies first, track girls second." Florence Griffith Joyner, Gail Devers, and other track stars of the modern era dedicate considerable attention to portraying a feminine appearance. Basketball star Lisa Leslie received more attention for being a model than for leading the Americans to Olympic victory.

Female politicians, lawyers, and businesswomen of all ethnic backgrounds also play the femininity game. Like tennis players in short dresses, working women seem to believe it's an asset to look pretty (but not too pretty) while throwing themselves around. The female apologetic is alive and well in corporate boardrooms, where women say, "I'm sorry, maybe someone else already stated this idea, but . . ." and smile while they say it.

When Newt Gingrich's mother revealed on television that he had referred to Hillary Rodham Clinton as a bitch, how did the First Lady respond? She donned a pink suit and met with female reporters to ask how she could "soften her image." She seemed to think that her competitiveness was the problem and femininity the solution.

So if you want to be a winner and you're female, you'll feel pressured to play by special, female rules. Like men, you'll have to be smart and industrious, but in addition, you'll have to be "like women": kind, nurturing, accommodating, nonthreatening, placating, pretty, and small. You'll have to smile. And not act angry. And wear skirts. Nail polish and makeup help too.

One thirty-two-year-old writer and downhill skier who asked not to be identified told me the following story: "I love male approval. Most women skiers do. We talk about it often. There's only one thing more satisfying than one of the top male skiers saying, 'Wow, you are a great skier. You rip. You're awesome.' And that is the satisfaction of skiing the world's most challenging terrain with total mastery, fluidity, and joy! And it's so fun leaving 99 percent of the world's guys in the dust! Whoops! [she laughed]. I try not to gloat.

"Lately I've learned something useful. If I kick guys' butts and lord it over them, they don't like me. If, however, I kick guys' butts, then act 'like a girl,' there is no problem. And I do mean girl, not woman. A girl is someone who leaves men feeling like men. More than anything, she's nonthreatening.

"The same is true in business. Men seem to have a really difficult time feeling like they're man enough. I don't know why. I was raised to just be a person, but when I act like a person, men are put off. So I have to play a game, catering to men's egos, couching things in an appealing sort of package. Acting like a girl.

"As a writer I handle my own contracts. If I negotiate a contract to my satisfaction and also manage to leave the editor feeling 'like a man,' like he is the one who is dominant or in control, then I get more assignments. It's crazy, but if I am going to 'win' in a negotiation, then my goals are better served if I also flirt, wear sexy clothes, or consciously cave in on a point because then the man feels like *he* won—or simply feels like a man."

The rules are different, this woman observes, for men. "I know hugely successful men who behave in ways that are demeaning, disenfranchising, brutal, and just plain obnoxious. They do things that no woman could ever do and still have a career. They get called assholes, but people still respect them and do business with them. Women who do none of those things but simply walk through the world with confidence get called bitches. The ways of men are so weird to me, but I am learning that I have to accommodate those weird ways if I am going to be empowered in the material world.

"What I'm doing is manipulating them. I don't think 'manipulate' is inherently a bad word. It's useful. I don't think I'm selling myself out. My business interest is furthered if I take the sting out of it by acting like a girl. Hugging them, for instance, instead of shaking hands. Wearing high heels. Wearing form-fitting clothing.

"Some might say this way of being is pathological, a symptom of codependency or dysfunction. But I'm not trying to make them think I want to have sex, and indeed I don't have sex with my business associates. I don't crimp my power. I don't act weak or defer to men or accept lower wages or act helpless. I'm just lightening up. It's like my Ninja disguise."

Despite this woman's purported success, I don't endorse this as a strategy, collectively or individually. As long as we disguise ourselves in order to placate men, we're not going to win equal rights or respect. The femininity game has not been successful for female athletes, and it hasn't worked for Hillary Rodham Clinton or other politicians.

Notes Carolyn Heilbrun: "I have learned that however hard women try to win the admiration and support of male power, they never succeed."[11]

Chapter 19

Do Women Care Too Much?
Female Friendships

If you don't care about your opponent, competing against her will be uncomplicated by your affection for her, your desire to please her, your need to stay close. If you do care about your opponent, competing against her might be difficult. You might worry that she'll be disappointed by defeat. You might worry that she will be so disappointed that she'll stop liking you. You might feel embarrassed by your own desire for victory, or humiliated by your own loss. You might concern yourself with any of a thousand potential problems in the relationship, distracting you from the task at hand.

This problem—caring so much about one's opponent that the caring interferes with one's own goals—seems a stumbling block for many female competitors. It confuses women, inhibits women, compels them to retreat from competitive arenas altogether. For women, "excelling, being different, and fighting are threats to rapport," Georgetown University linguist and author Deborah Tannen has noted.[1]

Women are supposed to be sugar and spice, everything nice. We're the professional, familial, biological nurturers, seemingly designed and obviously indoctrinated to care for others. It's our role, our received identity. We're supposed to be good, considerate, compassionate, empathic, generous, thoughtful. We're supposed to define ourselves in relation: wife, mother, daughter, friend. We're supposed to be friends with everyone. We're supposed to put others first, not crowd them out so we can be first ourselves.

Along with Tannen, feminist theorists Carolyn Heilbrun, Carol Gilligan, Nancy Chodorow, Jean Baker Miller, and others have documented this female tendency toward connection, affiliation, bonding. Gilligan says that in contrast with boys, who as adolescents develop independence and individuation, teenage girls retain strong relationships, apparently needing collaboration and connection as well as autonomy. She calls it a "fusion of identity and intimacy."[2]

Miller writes that in a male-dominated society, "women's sense of self becomes very much organized around being able to make and then to maintain affiliations and relationships. Eventually, for many women the threat of disruption of connections is perceived not just as a loss of a relationship but as something closer to a total loss of self."[3]

Female definitions of success tend to reflect this fusion of intimacy and identity, this urgent desire to maintain affiliation, this dread of separation. Women often define success not in terms of individual achievement but in terms of the mutual development of a family, team, or group. A successful marriage, children who are doing well socially and academically, a business deal in which no one feels ripped off or overly compromised: These are typical female victories.

At a birthday party recently I talked with two friends who swim together. "Who's faster?" I asked mischievously. I suspected the question might make them uncomfortable, but I asked in the interests of research—and breaking taboos. They looked at each other nervously. "I'm faster when we don't use fins, and Nancy's faster when we do," explained Fern at last. It was a response that seemed to satisfy both of them. Competitive swimmers do not use fins in meets, so the idea that one friend is faster *with fins* is sort of like saying one's faster if you swim one-armed; it's irrelevant to any standard test of speed. But they've made it important because it balances the relationship.

I've heard other friends engage in similar efforts to establish parity even when one is far more accomplished than the other. "I'm better at making money, but she's a more patient mom." "I'm better at landscaping the yard; she's better at maintenance." This pattern fits with Tannen's work about conversation: Women try to include, to support, to create a space where everyone feels successful.

Even highly competitive athletes sometimes prefer not to bask in the limelight alone. Ski champion Picabo Street has said that competing against her teammates is "really really hard. If I had my way, we'd all be standing on the podium together, tied for first place."[4]

At the 1984 Olympics in Los Angeles, Nancy Hogshead and Carrie Steinseifer tied for the gold medal in the hundred meter race, the first double gold in Olympic swimming history. "It was more fun that way," says Hogshead, who left the games with three golds and one silver. "We got to know each other better. It gave me a chance to share the victory."

What happens when everyone can't win, when one person's success prevents another from achieving the same goal, at least right then? Given the choice between winning and being loved (why is it that women, but not men, perceive themselves to be faced with this choice?), many women would rather be loved.

A professional clarinetist I know says she has always hated music competitions. "I didn't want to win, to be number one, because then everyone would hate you. You'd lose all your friends. Being number two was okay."

"Success in itself is frightening," says Ellen Wessel, president, co-owner, and cofounder of Moving Comfort, the women's athletic apparel company. "It makes you feel you'll be alone. Women won't trust you as much. You won't be on their level."

Penelope Saunders manages a program at the AIDS Council of South Australia. "I find it hard to be treated differently from the others in the project," she says. "I get more pay, more prestige, and everybody calls me the boss! I rebel against working in this hierarchy. There are three other workers in my team, all women, and we negotiate and reach sensible solutions. I sometimes find myself at a loss to describe my work, and I find myself saying things like I 'look after' a health education project. I think this is because Australians are not supposed to boast; it's called the tall poppy syndrome!"

On the other hand, says Penelope, "We say that we want to be the best program, that we get things in on time, that we work the hardest and are efficient. We are competitive, and I know that part of that is my influence. After all, I am the one who writes the grant proposals and coordinates the whole show."

Even in a sporting context, competitive success can somehow violate the sisterhood code; above all, we're supposed to be supportive. Even in a sporting context, girls and women tend to make decisions based on an "ethic of care" more frequently than do male athletes and coaches, who tend to employ an "ethic of self-interest," according to research by University of Pittsburgh sport sociologist Mary Duquin.[5]

Tennis pro Lindsay Davenport, after beating Mary Joe Fernandez in the 1996 Olympic semifinal, cried—not with joy but with sympathy for her opponent. Later she explained: "I was playing someone who's my best friend. I didn't want to go out there and see her lose."

France's Marie-José Pérec won the two hundred-meter run in the 1996 Olympics, sprinting past Merlene Ottey in the final ten meters. "When I passed through the finish line, I was quite happy," said Pérec, who, like Ottey, originally hails from the Caribbean. "But somewhere inside, I was also quite sad. I think you could see I was not overjoyed. [The fact that Ottey lost] bothered me."

"It's difficult to get really happy," said golfer Laura Davies after winning the 1996 Standard Register Ping title for the third year in a row and receiving her check for $105,000. Davies had been tied with Kristal Parker-Gregory as they began play on the last hole. Davies parred the hole; Parker-Gregory three-putted for a bogey. It was that bogey that muted Davies's celebration. She felt sorry for her opponent.

Harvard women's basketball coach Kathy Delaney-Smith says,

"It's hard for me to win. I never want the other person to lose." Delaney-Smith reports that after winning a basketball game, her first thought the next morning is "How bad does that coach feel? I feel really sorry for her because I know that when I lose, I feel deep misery."

Compassion for losers is not an exclusively female trait, thank goodness. When Greg Norman blew a six-shot lead in the 1996 Masters, winner Nick Faldo expressed similar ambivalence about his own victory.

Is it possible to have too much compassion? Madelyn Jennings, retired senior vice-president for Gannett, says, "If I would be accused of something, it's of having too much compassion. That's probably why I haven't won more. I never lost a golf game on purpose, but much as I wanted a competitive staff, I'd also take into account people's personal problems. To wake up in the morning and want to live with yourself, you have to have compassion."

But between and among women, compassion gets confusing. Sometimes women won't even allow themselves to compete. Sometimes, given a choice between being one up and being one down, women choose one down. It feels so much more familiar, so much less detrimental to others. Intimately acquainted with the pain of defeat, they don't want anyone else to lose.

Stephanie Grant writes eloquently and humorously of this paralyzing compassion in a short story called "Posting-Up."[6] The narrator is a high school basketball player at a Catholic school. She says of another player:

> Mary Jude . . . was shy, devout, not overly intellectual, extremely sweet, and oppressively pretty. She had been warming the bench for Perpetual Faith for three years, and had scored twice during brief cameos, once for the opposing team. Mary Jude touched my back lightly, just above my hip, with the tips of three fingers on her right hand. Her breathing was soft and even, and although

I couldn't see her face, I knew she was smiling: Mary Jude never didn't smile.

I sighed. Here I was again. How could I possibly compete against such goodness? How could I fake left, all the while knowing that I would be moving to my right, digging my shoulder into Mary Jude as I pivoted, and lightly pushing the ball into the basket? How could I leave her standing there, mouth agape, embarrassed, wondering what had just happened? How could I press my advantage knowing the punishment she would take from her teammates, punishment I knew only too well?

Later the narrator explains her profound ambivalence: "I knew the other centers wanted to win as much as I did, and I couldn't stand the thought of taking that away from them. It wasn't that I liked to lose; I hated to lose. But I guess I hated making other people lose worse. And besides, I was used to [losing]."[7]

Women are so good at caring. But we tend to forget about ourselves. We think, *Oh, those people would feel terrible if they lost.* Actually they might not feel terrible at all. That might be purely your own projection of *your* feelings about defeat. If your opponents are worthy—if they enjoy competition and are as skilled as you, or nearly so—the most loving thing for all might be to challenge them to compete with you. In fact a refusal to compete can be unkind. When practicing martial arts or self-defense, many women hesitate to attack their opponents because they are afraid of inflicting injury. Yet it's through direct attacks that the opponents will learn to defend themselves. Martial arts teachers must repeatedly goad female students into attacking with energy and commitment.

It's not wrong to enjoy a tie, to look for win-win solutions, to include and embrace your sister or brother competitors. It's not wrong to care how opponents might feel. We don't need any less compassion in the world. What's unhealthy is when women don't take their own needs and desires into consideration. Most women have a tendency not to feel too much for their opponents but to feel too little for themselves.

Stephen Covey, of *The 7 Habits of Highly Effective People* fame, has created a model for thinking about how courage and consideration affect outcomes. If you have a lot of courage but aren't very considerate, he says, you'll be inclined to strive for a win-lose solution. In other words, you'll be courageous enough to want to win yet won't much care what happens to other people or will want them to fail.

If, on the other hand, you're considerate but lack courage, you'll often end up in a lose-win situation. You'll lose because you'll be putting the needs of others ahead of yourself. People who lack both courage and consideration end up lose-lose, Covey says, while people who are highly considerate and courageous strive for win-win solutions.

Covey didn't specifically address women. But we're often more considerate than courageous, aren't we? We don't want the other person to lose, but we lack the courage to assert that we shouldn't lose either. So we don't let ourselves win, then resent the person who does.

Valarie Hannemann, a Los Angeles psychologist, has counseled female ice skaters, mountain bikers, skiers, and basketball players who resent how competitive their peers are. "If a woman's too aggressive, too 'out there,' other women won't like her," says Hannemann. "Women are socialized to be concerned about relationships, intimacy, what other people think. So they're conflicted about competition. They can do it, but they have to do it in socially acceptable ways. You have to be fair; you have to be nice."

Phoenix clinical psychologist Rosalyn Meadow calls herself "highly competitive." While playing tennis, however, "I'll feel bad if I win easily," she says. "I have a sense of, they're going to feel bad." Meadow, author of *Good Girls Don't Eat Dessert*, admits that such concerns "get in the way." She has also noticed that "sometimes it's a projection. Sometimes the other person doesn't feel bad at all."

Such reluctance to succeed extends well beyond sport, Meadow says. Women believe "if they're too successful, no one will love them. It all goes together: being nice, being accepted, being loved, not wanting to succeed. It's better to be a good girl and have people love you because then you don't risk abandonment. It's particularly problematic in heterosexual love relationships, but it's also problematic in women's friendships: If you succeed, your friends won't like you."

What about when women lose to their friends? That too can be problematic if one's identity is dependent on affiliation. A friend's success can be interpreted as a rupture of the intimate connection and thus disrupting to one's very sense of self. Especially when women have been holding themselves back, they can feel "driven to hold back another woman," write Luise Eichenbaum and Susie Orbach in *Between Women*.[8]

"I have never received the criticism for failure that I have for success, and it is clear to me that people in our society at least unconsciously hold the conviction that someone else's success limits their own, makes them lesser, and puts a permanent lid on their own chances," writes Marianne Williamson in *A Woman's Worth*. She says that we live in "a society deeply afraid of ecstatic women" and that in response, women don't "allow ourselves to shine fully" and "fail to let others shine."[9]

"The hardest part of success," Bette Midler has said, "is to find someone who is happy for you."

But are women really such ambivalent competitors? Are we really reluctant to win, reluctant to lose, unwilling to support our successful sisters? Do we really care too much what people think, care too much about the hurt feelings of the losers, care too much about the relationships and not enough about our own needs and desires?

When I asked the women in my survey to agree or disagree (on a five-point scale) with this statement: "Competition is a problem in many women's friendships," almost half (46 percent) agreed somewhat or strongly. About a third (34 percent) disagreed. White women were the most likely to agree (52 percent), followed by Asian-American women (46 percent) and Hispanic women (43 percent).

African-American women were by far the least likely to agree; only 28 percent did. They were the most likely to say that "friends should not compete with each other" (44 percent supported that statement, compared with 28 percent of Hispanics and 24 percent of both European Americans and Asian Americans).

Why would African-American women be less likely to find competition among friends problematic? Why would they be more likely to believe friends shouldn't compete with each other? The College of New Jersey psychology professor Ruth L. Hall says that African-American women are unlikely to compete with their friends because they've been raised with the "cultural values of cooperation and collectivism" rather than the individual, independent ethic that typifies many European-American cultures. These values are reflected in the phrase "I am because we are," a saying in the black community, notes Hall.

These values are also celebrated during Kwanzaa, the weeklong African-American celebration that begins the day after Christmas. Three of the seven guiding principles of Kwanzaa include unity (umoja), cooperative economics (ujamaa), and collective work and responsibility (ujima). None of the other principles (self-determination, purpose, creativity, and faith) includes competitiveness.

Athletes of all races seem to have an easier time competing with friends. In my survey 80 percent of the athletes said they had "enjoyed competing with friends or lovers," compared with only 50 percent of the nonathletes. Athletes were also less likely than nonathletes to believe that "Friends should not compete with each other" (25 percent of athletes agreed, compared with 37 percent of nonathletes).

Still, half the nonathletes seem to be indicating that they have enjoyed competing with friends or lovers in a nonathletic context. And overall, only 30 percent of my respondents agreed that friends should not compete with each other. So while many women, including athletes, indicate discomfort about competing with women, most are not opposed to friends' competing with each other, and many have actually enjoyed the experience.

Rumor has it that men can employ a "killer instinct" on a tennis court or in a court of law or in the boardroom, then pleasantly shake hands afterward. Champion sprinter Carl Lewis, for instance, in a speech at Peter Lowe's Success '96 seminar, said, "One of the people on the track training with me was my best friend. Every day at practice, I wanted to beat him, and I know he felt the same way about me. But we were able to separate the competition from the rest of life. When we left the track, we were able to leave the competition there."

The University of Tennessee's Pat Head Summitt, one of the most successful basketball coaches in the country, appeared on ABC's *Home Show* with me in 1991, after Tennessee had won the national championship. When I contended that competition can be a form of friendship, she responded, "I think you need to learn to separate. We develop some great friendships through competition, and that's very healthy and I wouldn't want us to change that, but also I'd like to see women be able to go onto the court and put their friendships behind them and compete to win. You can learn to step on the court and be very aggressive and competitive and step off the court and be a lady."

Soccer champion Carla Overbeck seems to have come up with a similar solution. When she first arrived at college, competing against her teammates and friends was difficult, she said. "Your friends are your friends, and you don't ever want to be mean or hurt them. But after a while, I realized that I could play hard and it didn't have to spill over into life off the field."[10]

"I see women getting frustrated by competition," reports University of Virginia psychology professor Linda Bunker. "I hear women say, 'I don't want to compete against my best friend; we won't be friends anymore.' They don't have the experience that men have, to know that what happens on the tennis court or in the pool has nothing to do with what happens in the locker room twenty-five minutes later. Men let it go a little bit better. I see that in the boardroom as well.

When I consult with Motorola or IBM or the Federal Executive Institute, we talk about how women will get into a heated debate around the conference table, then, when they walk down the hall, be worried about whether they hurt each other's feelings. So they're picking up the phone and apologizing, and sometimes that dilutes the message or the value of the competition. Whereas the guys go have a beer."

Is this true? Should women be more like men? Personally I don't think "learning to separate" the friendships from the playing fields is the answer. Nor do I think we need to drink more beer.

I see women looking for ways to integrate their desires to compete with their desires to be kind, and their desires to win with their desires to be friends, during the competition as well as after. I think there are ways to do this, to be kind competitors, ethical competitors, cooperative competitors. To engage in right competition.

Sometimes more competition is just what a friendship needs. If women hesitate to win, competition can help them become more assertive, more assured of their own right to fulfill their ambitions. If women are too merged or overidentified with each other's successes and failures, competition can help them differentiate. Once they separate sufficiently to compete with someone, they'll notice that paradoxically, the competition itself brings them closer. They don't have to give up compassion or empathy or intimacy in order to compete. The female propensity to care is not the problem. They also don't have to segregate their competitive selves from their caring selves. They just need to learn to care and compete at the same time.

Among my friends and colleagues the stereotypes about cattiness and pettiness do not hold true. I've never known women to stab each other in the back. Maybe I'm relentlessly positive, but it seems to me that most women I know compete honorably and rejoice in each other's victories. This is not to say that they never feel envious or threatened or miserably one down. But they don't let those feelings poison their friendships. They seem to find a way to stay connected as well as to differentiate, to celebrate each other's victories while striving for their own.

Is this because many of my friends and colleagues are athletes? Perhaps. According to my survey, female athletes are just as likely as nonathletes to perceive competition as a problem in women's friendships. But they're less likely to believe that friends shouldn't compete with each other (25 percent of athletes; 37 percent of nonathletes). They're less likely to be uncomfortable with competition (17 percent of athletes versus 52 percent of nonathletes). They're less likely to avoid competitive situations (12 percent of athletes versus 45 percent of nonathletes). They're much more likely to define themselves as competitive (93 percent of athletes versus 52 percent of nonathletes). So though they tend to see competition as a problem in women's friendships, they seem to choose to solve that problem without retreating from the competitive arena.

Maybe the problem is not that women care too much but that they compete too little. That they lack training and experience in competition. Robert Rotella, former director of the graduate program in sport psychology at the University of Virginia, says, "Gals who have had lots of experience competing know how to compete and aren't afraid to compete. Show me a guy who hasn't played sports, and he'll be afraid of competition too."

Maybe coaches who complain that their athletes aren't competitive enough need to teach them how to compete. Maybe they need to point out some things that other female athletes notice on their own: that you can care about another person and compete against her at the same time. That you don't have to hate your opponents in order to feel challenged by them. That you can appreciate your opponents in part because of those immense challenges they offer, both physical and psychological. That by competing with a friend, you offer her a gift, an inducement to do her best. That while two friends are competing together, they're still together.

Mia Hamm, the star of the Olympic gold medal–winning soccer team, credits her University of North Carolina coach, Anson Dorrance, with teaching her that "it's okay to compete against people you care about if done in a positive way, to help each other improve."[11]

Having produced more than three dozen all-Americans and having won thirteen national championships, Dorrance is generally regarded as one of the best coaches in the country. Originally a men's coach, Dorrance at first tended to treat his women's teams exactly how he treated his men's teams. His younger sister had been a better athlete than he was, and his mother was a better athlete than his father, "so I never had this illusion that women . . . were soft creatures. . . . I didn't come in with any social preconceptions about what these women could handle. My initial reaction was to run them just like the men."[12]

A turning point came in 1983, when he recruited April Heinrichs, one of the best female soccer players ever. "I was still a men's coach, basically," he says. "I had no understanding of women, and in all my recruiting calls Heinrichs kept saying the same thing: 'How does your team get along?' I was thinking, *Who cares?* I mean, the guys never ask me those questions. Well, after two weeks of practice it dawned on me why she kept asking that question. She beat the absolute hell out of everyone—in every situation, in every practice. And guess what? They hated her. Why? Because she wasn't afraid to be the best."[13]

"Women are uncomfortable competing," Dorrance has concluded. "It doesn't nurture them. They're afraid they'll lose their friends and that people will hate them if they come off as too aggressive."[14]

In practice, he notes, it's particularly difficult to motivate women to compete against their teammates. His players "have a very sensible hierarchy which says that my relationship with you is more important than . . . something as ridiculous as a soccer game and I credit them for that. They are not going to jeopardize their relationship by beating up their best friend in practice."[15]

With men, Dorrance says, "it's different. If you and I are best friends and play basketball, we will knock the crap out of each other during the game, doing whatever we have to do to win. Once it's over, it's over. We'll still be best friends.

"Women consider it all very personal. If there is a heated exchange in the middle of our practice, I sense a tremendous effort at reconciliation."[16]

Dorrance now tells his players to compete hard in practice *for the sake of the team*. Honoring women's desire to stay close, one of the most successful coaches in women's sports stresses "connectedness and relationships and playing for each other. Playing for each other is almost a theme song for my team."[17]

Playing for each other. Offering each other the gift of your excellence. Striving for personal success and hence strengthening the team. It's trickier this way; it's new; it's not the way competition is usually envisioned. But it's kinder and more congruent with the female propensity to care.

Chapter 20

But How Do Women
Compare with Men?

Americans tend to think in terms of dualities and gender stereo-types. So competition is the opposite of cooperation, and women are the opposite of men. Competition is masculine; cooperation is feminine. Men are from Mars; women are from Venus. Men are warriors; women are lovers. Men compete to avoid intimacy; women don't compete because it threatens intimacy. Men compete well; women don't.

What's true? Are women less competitive than men? Is this even the right question to ask? Many scholars have asked it. Their conclusion: Yes. These scholars were primarily psychologists and sociologists who studied competitiveness in the seventies and eighties, when gender-difference research was most fashionable.

Before offering a divergent perspective on male and female competitiveness, I'll review these purported differences.

Diane Gill, professor of exercise and sport sciences at the University of North Carolina at Greensboro, has been studying men, women, and competitive sports for many years. Along with a colleague, she developed a questionnaire that measures three "achievement orientations" in sports: competitiveness (a desire to "enter and strive for success in competitive sport"); win orientation ("a desire to win and avoid losing"); and goal orientation ("an emphasis on achieving personal goals").[1]

On average, male athletes scored higher than female athletes in competitiveness and win orientation. There were no differences in goal orientation. Gill concludes that women are as likely as men to desire success. Women are simply less oriented toward winning and comparing themselves with others.[2]

Other researchers have come to similar conclusions. In competitive situations, including games, academics, and work, men act more competitive, fare better in competitive situations, and are more likely than women to create hierarchies or pecking orders.[3]

Women assess the competitive trait less positively than do men[4] and feel more ambivalent about performing successfully in competitive situations, especially when competing against their romantic partners.[5] Faced with situations involving competitive achievement, women perceive danger, whereas men perceive excitement and challenge. (Men perceive danger in situations involving love.)[6]

According to business and education research, women and men have different styles of leadership. Women interact more with their subordinates and communicate decisions better. They are likely to eschew military metaphors in favor of language evocative of peace, family, dance, and music. Women tend to be democratic, flexible leaders who see it as their job to empower others. They meet, confer, cooperate, build consensus, emphasize equality, and, as Carol Gilligan has said, base decisions on an ethic of care for the good of all participants. Female subordinates expect leaders to collaborate, negotiate, and share information. They prefer cooperative over competitive styles and consensus over autocracy.[7]

Men are more likely to be visible, authoritative leaders. They're more likely to command, control, compete, establish hierarchies, and make decisions based on what Gilligan calls an ethic of justice and rules. Men respect and expect a more authoritative style.

Women and men also seem to think differently about their own successes and failures. Compared with men, women tend to evaluate their abilities as lower. They expect less of themselves.[8] Those women who consider their sex inferior—unfortunately many do—

are particularly likely to expect less of themselves. Relative to men, women see success as less important.[9] Whether successful or not, women generally attribute the outcomes of their performances to luck or the difficulties of the tasks, while men take personal credit for their success. Psychologists Mimi Murray and Hilary Matheson report that women "consider their tasks to be easier than men's, and consequently they have much greater shame for their failures."[10]

Scholars have also studied children in this regard. Girls at all grade levels report a consistent and strong preference for cooperative classroom structures. Boys are more enthusiastic about competition.[11]

Beyond the classroom, groups of girls also seem more interested in getting along than getting ahead. They establish elaborate social networks based on who is "best friends with" or "being mean to" whom,[12] writes University of California, Berkeley sociologist Barrie Thorne in Gender Play. They share secrets, divulge insecurities, and "engage in small-scale, turn-taking, cooperative kinds of play." By fifth and sixth grades, she says, "many of them spend recess standing around and talking."[13] Even when playing team sports, girls tend to choose teammates on the basis of friendships rather than use the typical boys' criteria: skill.[14]

Boys' social relations are more hierarchical. Boys are more overt in their desire to win. They're more physically aggressive, more active, and more likely to dominate or taunt competitors.[15] They like to make and argue about rules, and they break them more than girls do.[16] They rise quickly to competitive challenges, often in a spirit of fun and good sportsmanship.[17]

In other words, girls and boys in general inhabit different cultures, one based on intimacy, solidarity, and an "egalitarian ethos," the other based on status, hierarchy, and competition.[18]

Men and women inhabit different cultures too. In 1990 Georgetown University linguistics professor Deborah Tannen published the best-selling book You Just Don't Understand, in which she differentiates men's and women's speaking styles. Men use conversation "to preserve independence and negotiate and maintain status in a hier-archical social order," she says, whereas women talk as a way of "establishing connections and negotiating relationships." Men compete even in casual conversation, she notes, jockeying to impress others with their "report-talk," whereas women, hoping to avoid even "the appearance of superiority," refuse to compete, preferring the more inclusive "rapport-talk." When women do compete, Tannen adds, they're indirect about it, bragging about their children's or husbands' accomplishments rather than their own.[19] Tannen corroborates many people's observations and beliefs: that men and women are funda-mentally different in the ways they perceive and discuss the world.

The truth is more complex.
For one thing, many researchers assume that cooperation and competition are distinct and opposite, which is not necessarily how women perceive them. Female athletes often think of competition and cooperation as "interdependent rather than dichotomous con-cepts," according to University of California, Berkeley researcher Brenda Bredemeier and her colleagues, who have found that women "tend to value cooperation regardless of the degree of competitive-ness" of the activity.[20]

Also, statistically significant differences do not mean that all men are different from all women. "We tend to forget what philosophers call 'the law of the excluded middle,' which . . . is where most men and women fall in their qualities, beliefs, values, and abilities," notes social psychologist Carol Tavris in The Mismeasure of Woman.[21] Pi-oneering sex differences researchers Eleanor Maccoby and Carol Nagy Jacklin, describing one study in which 15 percent of the boys engaged in more rough-and-tumble play than any of the girls, pointed out that "therefore 85 percent of the boys were indistinguishable from the girls."[22]

When researchers stop comparing girls with boys and simply ob-serve how girls compete, they begin to see that they compete not "less" or "differently" but in diverse and complicated ways. Linda Hughes, writing in a journal called *Sex Roles*, notes that girls she observed playing foursquare "competed in a cooperative mode," aggressively trying to eliminate certain players so their friends could enter the game. They talked about "being friends" and "being nice" but also expressed more nuanced behaviors with phrases like "not really mean" and "nice-mean."[23] Similarly, Amy Sheldon notes in an article entitled "Conflict Talk" that preschool girls used a "double-voice style" that "masked self-assertion" while "maintaining group harmony."[24]

Barrie Thorne explains that such talk of "niceness" fulfills social expectations for girls "to display themselves as egalitarian and harmonious," while in fact "beneath all that rhetoric and overt concern with group harmony often lies considerable tension and conflict."[25]

A survey of sex differences literature found that "girls in middle childhood are equally strongly motivated to succeed as are their counterpart boys. However, girls appear more uncertain about ways to achieve their goals."[26]

Eleanor Maccoby discovered that competitive behavior in children depends primarily not on the gender of the child but on the gender of the playmate. Three-year-old girls are not passive when playing with each other, but when paired with boys, the girls "stand on sidelines and let the boys monopolize the toys," explains Tavris in her review of Maccoby's work. This behavior is unrelated to any individual personality characteristics. "Instead, it is related to the fact that between the ages of 3½ and 5½, boys stop responding to girls' requests, suggestions, and other attempts to influence them," says Tavris. Girls also tend to use indirect forms of verbal conflict (such as gossip) among themselves but more aggravated verbal forms, including insults, when arguing with boys. African-American girls and white working-class girls tend to be especially skilled in direct verbal conflict.[27]

Adults are also influenced by the gender of the person with whom they're interacting. Tannen reports that women speak more tentatively than men do, using more disclaimers such as "I may be wrong" and "I suppose." But psychologist Linda Carli, after observing pairs of people (male-male, male-female, and female-female) discuss topics on which they disagreed, concluded that women speak hesitantly only when speaking to men. Carli found that this was effective. "Women who spoke tentatively were more influential with men," she reports, though less influential with women.[28]

The biggest gender differences are social and economic: Men and women differ in their power, their status, their incomes, their family responsibilities for children and housework. Boys and girls differ in the toys they receive, the ways they're treated by parents and teachers, the images they see of themselves in the media.

All psychological differences, including competitiveness, can be attributed to sexist nurture, not innate nature, according to Carol Nagy Jacklin. In other words, if men are more competitive than women, it's because they've been placed in competitive situations from early childhood and rewarded for that behavior, while women have been praised for cooperating and sharing and stepping daintily aside to cheer for their brothers. Because of sexism, women can see competitiveness as "too male," too cutthroat and insensitive and cruel. Men can see cooperation as "too female," as a step down from the masculine imperative to win, to be dominant, to be on top.

The question of who's more competitive, men or women, is part of the problem. Dualistic thinking contends not only that men and women have different reproductive organs but that they are different, opposite sorts of people—and that one's better. As women compete and succeed in virtually all areas of society and it becomes increasingly clear that biologically based sex differences are few and largely irrelevant in most aspects of human behavior, researchers and journalists take an ever-increasing interest in the subject. They seem desperate to prove that men have bigger brains or better math ability or even a "natural" drive toward murder and mayhem because without proving difference, you can't justify hierarchy. If men and women are not so different, why pay men higher salaries? Why elect men to run the country? By harping on differences, real or imagined, men compete with women over who's better, who's superior, who "should" be the head of the household, the church, the state.

Tavris proposes: "Suppose . . . we move away from the narrow and limited question of Do men and women differ, and who's better? and ask instead: Why is everyone so interested in differences? Why are differences regarded as deficiencies?"[29]

Differences are regarded as deficiencies because men need them as weapons in what they jocularly call a battle of the sexes. Many men derive their very sense of masculinity from being not female and better than female. They create excuses for female subordination. These excuses are running thin over time, as women fly combat missions and serve as "superiors" to men in every conceivable workplace with the exception of professional football arenas, the Catholic Church, and the White House, but men cling to those few exclusions that remain: Women can't be football coaches because they didn't play football because they are physically inferior. Women can't be priests because God is a man and He would not approve. Women can't be President because, well, men wouldn't vote for them.

Answers to the "who's more competitive" question thus make winners out of men and losers out of women. If boys are understood to be "naturally" more competitive—and competition is understood to be either "naturally" good or at least socially and economically important—it would make sense to give girls extra training in competition. Yet illogically, the belief that boys are naturally more competitive is used to exclude girls from competitive opportunities, as in the case of college athletic directors who argue that women are inherently less interested than men in playing sports.

If girls are uncomfortable in competitive environments, it would make sense to teach them how to become comfortable or how to use their discomfort to their advantage. Yet, again illogically, the obser-vation that girls are uncomfortable with competition is sometimes used to justify the creation of specifically noncompetitive environ-ments for girls. No one would use this reasoning pertaining to math: Since girls are often uncomfortable with math, let's create a math-free environment. Yet that is increasingly being proposed in terms of competition. Teachers and administrators who try to create noncom-petitive environments for girls fail to ask themselves: What happens to girls who never learn to compete? What if girls were given alter-natives to the Conqueror's model? What if they were taught to com-pete like Champions?

When we say, "Women are not as competitive as men," we're using men as the standard against which women are measured, whether the result is to conclude that women should be more like men or that they should be accommodated because they're not like men. But why compare women to men? Regarding men's football games and corporate takeovers and military sieges, do we ever ask whether those men are more or less competitive than women might be? Male competitiveness—even when it leads to injuries and crimes and wars—is taken as a given. Rarely are men taught how to be com-petitive in a more complex, cooperative way: more like women.

The times it's most useful to compare female with male compet-itiveness are (1) when men act threatened by female victory, and (2) when men compete with women to deprive them of rights or oppor-tunities.

Unfortunately these things happen often. These dynamics are the subject of the next two chapters.

Chapter 21

"Many Men Feel Threatened by Female Victory"

In the novel *Taller Women*, two male physicians have this conversation:

> "Women are getting taller. They must be. It used to be rare when you saw a woman who was taller than a man, or, at least, as tall as a tall man."
>
> "Right."
>
> "But now, I see them all the time. I wonder about it. . . ."
>
> "The only change I see in women is that they're happier now, than they used to be. Or so it seems to me. . . . I just had this vision of a world full of happy women, and it depressed the hell out of me."
>
> "Why?"
>
> "There's something depressing about a happy woman."
>
> "Oh, I get it," the other doctor said, and laughed. "Taller, happier women, and where does that leave us?"[1]

Women *are* getting taller, physically and figuratively. They're getting stronger, gaining political and economic power. Maybe they're even getting happier. In any case, as more women flex their muscles, the issue of female success *relative to male success* takes on new symbolic importance. Now that women are mayors and governors and bankers and bosses and bodybuilders, some men (not all, but a vocal bunch) seem nervous. "And now you want to be high school wrestlers too?" they ask. "Where does that leave men?"

The most striking finding in my survey was the response to this statement: "Many men feel threatened by female victory." Seventy percent of all respondents agreed. Only 22 percent disagreed. (The other 8 percent had no opinion.)

This is not to say that the majority of men are indeed threatened by female victory, though there's plenty of evidence to support that. The federal 1995 Glass Ceiling Commission report reveals that only five percent of the Fortune 2000 industrial and service companies have female senior managers, though women constitute about 46 percent of the work force.[2] The authors conclude: "The glass ceiling exists because of the perception of many white males that as a group they are losing—losing the corporate game, losing control and losing opportunity. Many middle-and upper-level white male managers view the inclusion of minorities and women in management as a direct threat to their own chances for advancement." As women and minorities strive for top corporate positions, some white men "feel excluded and angry." When they competed only against each other, they "knew the rules." Their fear and anger now lead them to thwart the progress of others, the report says.[3]

Harvard sociology professor Orlando Patterson observes that one of the reasons for marital discord among African-Americans is the prevalence of the "male dominance ideology," especially among black middle-class men. He cites a Los Angeles study that found that 71 percent of black men believed that "husbands should have the final say in all matters" and 42 percent believed that "women in authority" are "against human nature." Black women strongly reject those sexist views, Patterson notes.[4]

Working-class men also seem threatened—if sexual harassment

can be interpreted as an attempt to intimidate and belittle women, as I think it can. Mitsubishi Motor Manufacturing of America made headlines in April 1996 when it was sued by the Equal Employment Opportunity Commission on behalf of about three hundred women at its Illinois plant. Female industrial workers at Chrysler, RJR Nabisco, Triad International Maintenance Corporation (an aviation repair company), and other plants are also complaining of sexual harassment and assault. At a time when record numbers of women are entering blue-collar jobs and record numbers of men are nervous about economic downsizing, disproportionate numbers of sexual harassment complaints are being filed by women in mining, construction, transportation, air traffic control, and manufacturing jobs—predominantly male industries. "The rate of filings was up to twice as high as service-sector jobs, where women have long held jobs," USA Today concluded after analyzing 15,691 complaints filed with the EEOC in 1995.[5]

"The idea that a woman is taking something that belongs to a man is increased when there are fewer good jobs to go around," explains Jane Lang, who represents fifteen women suing the Duluth, Minnesota–based mining company Taconite. "Our clients have been told they are taking bread out of the mouths of men."[6]

Another male-dominated institution, the military, also shows evidence that men feel threatened by female power. In the fall of 1996 the U.S. Army suspended more than twenty-five male supervisors at the Aberdeen, Maryland, Proving Ground for rape, sodomy, and sexual harassment of female trainees. Over the next few weeks young female recruits at seventeen other training facilities across the country identified themselves as victims of sexual misconduct and abuse, including rape. The scandal was compared with the Navy's 1991 Tailhook Convention, where drunken male aviators assaulted dozens of female officers, but subsequent interviews revealed that sexual crimes in the Army are routine. "It's just not that unusual. The Army has known of this problem," said Kerry Buckey, the Army's top defense attorney for the eastern United States until 1994.[7] Rape, adultery, assault, sodomy, and sexual harassment between male drill instructors and female recruits were "the single biggest problem we had in the scheme of serious offenses," said Richard Boller, a retired colonel who was the staff judge advocate at Fort Jackson between 1983 and 1987.[8]

Sexual harassment, more common in male-dominated professions than in traditionally female professions, tells women, "You don't belong here," or, "You're only good for one thing." It keeps them "in their place"—under male sexual control.

Sexual harassment is widespread in sports. The title of my second book, *The Stronger Women Get, the More Men Love Football*, points to the correlation between female strength and male retreat into the sports world.[9] The book bulges with evidence that many men are indeed threatened by female success in many forms. Seven national studies show that men who play basketball or football are more likely to rape, gang-rape, or engage in an array of other sexually aggressive behaviors. Male coaches frequently molest female athletes, justifying their behavior by calling it "dating."[10] Male athletes also harass female athletes. A recent study of 1,024 athletes at Canadian universities found that 57 percent of female athletes said male athletes had made sexist jokes or comments to them. An amazing 90 percent of the male athletes agreed that the university sports climate had become "almost intolerable" for women at times.[11]

The Texas Interscholastic Wrestling Association, protesting that high school wrestling should remain male only, argued that it must protect the boys against "blows to their egos." A wrestler at Harvard, one of two women who trained and competed with the otherwise male team in 1996, told me, "The men hate it. They don't want to do it. They say there's nothing in it for a man. They say, 'If we win, we were supposed to. If we lose, we've been totally disgraced and humiliated.' "[12]

The Colorado Silver Bullets, the pro women's baseball team, got up close and personal with male fears of female victory in 1994 when they started touring the country playing baseball against all-male teams. "It's incredible to us the things these men will do to win," President Bob Hope told me. "Cheat. Lie. Bring in ringers. Switch players in the middle of the game, as if we wouldn't notice. Anything not to lose."

Why do many men seem to fear female victory? Clinical psychologist Rosalyn Meadow traces men's fear to the perceived humiliation of the mother-son dynamic, in which mothers usually "won." In addition, "women can reject or accept a male sexually. They can leave and take a man's family with her. They're much more powerful than ever they have imagined."

One patient of Meadow's had gone back to graduate school and was living with a female executive. "He felt emasculated by being asked to pick up his dirty socks," recalls Meadow. "He said he was expected to be the woman, and he hated it. He wanted to be the breadwinner, in charge and in control. He ended the relationship, telling me, 'When I get married, it's not going to be to a woman like that.' "

Meadow also sees men for sex therapy. "They fear the power of women," she observes, and "their fears are reflected in their erections. When they meet up with a very beautiful woman or a very successful woman, they get anxious that this woman will leave them," and sometimes the men become impotent.

Michael Kimmel, associate professor of sociology at the State University of New York at Stony Brook, traces sexual dysfunction to competitiveness in a different way. Since women have more sexual freedom than they used to, men now compare their sexual prowess with that of other men. "When women become sexually adventurous, a large number of men get insecure," says Kimmel. "They ask, 'How will I know I'm the best? How will I know I'm the biggest?' "

Linguist and author Deborah Tannen has noted that men tend to perceive relationships in terms of hierarchies, so if they're not on top, they must be on the bottom. Powerful women can thus threaten men's sense of dominance.

Some men perceive opportunities for women to succeed as discrimination against men. Female gain feels like male loss. Laurie Priest noticed this when she was the athletic director at Marymount University as it made the transition from a women's college to a coed one. Priest was careful to be fair: She split the budget down the middle, arranged to have the men and women share the gym and the playing fields, hired the same number of coaches for men and women, and scheduled games and practices so that neither men nor women were favored. "You know what happened?" she confided later. "The male coaches and athletes felt like I was discriminating against them. I said, 'What do you mean? I've been so careful to give you exactly half of all the resources!' Then I realized what they meant. They were so used to having privilege they felt like fifty-fifty was unfair."

Powerful women can also be perceived as "emasculating." When a man loses to a woman, he says (or other men say) that she busted his balls; she's a ball breaker, a castrator. Have you ever heard a woman say, "I broke his balls"? Women don't seem to think like that. Yet even a woman who is simply loud or aggressive, without defeating any particular man in any particular arena, can be called castrating.

Why do men equate female advancement or victory with the "breaking" of testicles? Why are women, but almost never men, said to be ball breakers? Why do women have this unique power to rob men of their manhood, albeit only metaphorically? And why the testicles and not the penis? Even Lorena Bobbitt left her husband's testicles alone.

Boys learn early that getting kicked or hit in the testicles causes extreme pain. Is this what men are referring to: that female achievement is excruciating to them? Or is it about manhood? Without testicles, the penis will not become erect; without erections, men cannot have sexual intercourse. Does female achievement make men impotent, as Roz Meadow suggests?

The dictionary defines "emasculate" as "to deprive of virility or procreative power." This explains it: Male power, masculinity, and sexuality are inextricably linked, as evidenced by the word "impotent," connoting sexual dysfunction but actually meaning "without power."

For a man to be defeated by a woman is for that man to lose sexual power, his very sense of himself as a man. The stakes are enormous.

So men do everything in their power to save testicles. They make sure they never lose to women, even in an argument. They ridicule or sexually harass women who achieve, especially in arenas that men have used to define masculinity. If necessary, they physically beat women.

Male domination starts early. In elementary school boys mock girls, invade their play, and taunt weaker, more submissive boys as "sissies," "fags," and "girls."[13] The message: To be tough is male; those who are not tough are not male and are inferior. Why do boys behave this way? "It may be that children are mimicking the adult patterns of male dominance that they observe," speculates Carol Tavris in *The Mismeasure of Woman.*[14]

Boys also dominate because adults let them. "Adults may even feel quietly reassured that a boy who behaves in aggressively sexist ways is affirming "normal" masculinity; after all, dominance and control, in less harassing and more modified forms, are valued in adult men," notes Barrie Thorne in *Gender Play.*[15]

Sports often become a way for boys to assert their difference from girls and their superiority over them. Phrases such as "You're acting like a girl" establish female behavior as worthy of scorn. Much male competition is motivated by a desire not to be debased as womanlike.

For boys, not losing may be even more motivating than winning. Researcher Carol Ames has concluded that "the consequences of failing in competitive situations appear to have been more ego threatening for males than females."[16]

"Show me a good loser, and I'll show you a loser," some football coach said. Fans nodded at how wise that was. But in fact knowing how and when to lose is one of life's great arts. Show me a bad loser, and I'll show you a potential wife beater or rapist—or at least a man who is no fun for women to be around.

Nevertheless I'm more concerned with female perception than with male paranoia. What does it mean that researchers, therapists, and the majority of women in my survey *believe* men to be threatened by female victory? How does that affect women's behavior? How does that affect women's desire to win and their willingness to defeat men?

In her doctoral dissertation at the University of Michigan in the 1960s, Matina Horner coined the term "fear of success" to explain women's apparent reluctance to compete with men for traditional masculine goals.[17] Rather than fear the shame or disappointment of failure, women fear the perceived repercussions of success, Horner postulated. She tested her hypotheses by asking undergraduates to complete a story about a student (the same gender as the subject) who had graduated at the top of her (or his) medical school class. About two thirds of the women, but only 9 percent of the men, wrote stories in which the medical student suffered horrible consequences: loneliness, social isolation, even suicide. Such tests are said to reflect the storyteller's psychological state. Horner concluded, after further research, that (1) for many women, to succeed is to lose femininity, since success requires competitive, achievement-oriented behaviors that conflict with the traditional feminine role; (2) women show more evidence of fear of success than do men; and (3) women who fear success perform better in noncompetitive environments.

Horner's work birthed a rash of interest, speculation, and research. Her conclusions were confirmed by some researchers and refuted by others. One study found that in competitive situations, women who do not fear success outperform those who do.[18] Another found that female athletes do not fear success.[19] One summary of twenty-two studies found no significant gender differences.[20]

In *No Contest: The Case Against Competition*[21] Alfie Kohn suggests that Horner and others have confounded fear of success with "aversion to competition." One researcher, he says, "assumed that anyone disagreeing with such statements as 'I am happy only when I am doing better than others' . . . was exhibiting fear of success. This raises the possibility that women are backing away from the prospect of having to beat other people, not from success itself."

Kohn approvingly notes the master's thesis of psychologist Georgia Sassen, who found that men (more than women) tend to define success in terms of competition. Sassen speculated that Horner's subjects were indicating "a heightened perception of the 'other side' of competitive success, that is, the great emotional costs at which success achieved through competition is often gained—an understanding that, while confused, indicates some underlying sense that something is rotten in the state in which success is defined as having better grades than everyone else."[22]

Kohn might be right that female fear of success reflects a reluctance to compete and especially to defeat others. I disagree with his conclusion: that competition itself is the problem. I don't think women are the problem either. I think Horner's subjects were indicating that female winners are often punished by men. There are negative consequences to competition for women, which leads me to conclude not that women suffer from any particular "fear" but that something is rotten in the state in which women who win are castigated, ignored, ostracized, or framed as castrating bitches.

In 1996 a New York-based research organization called Catalyst surveyed 461 Fortune 1000 senior women executives. These women, who earn an average of $248,000 a year, were asked to explain the keys to their success. The second most common answer, after "superior performance," was "developing a style with which male managers are comfortable."[23]

So even the richest women in the country cater to male egos, gearing their behaviors toward a style that will make their male managers comfortable. It's not easy, though; often it's impossible. In follow-up interviews many of the women reported that men are not at ease with a female presence, even after years of working together. "They are never fully comfortable because it's not a hundred percent men," said one. "They treat you differently," said another. It's "hard to create trust and comfort with male colleagues," said yet another. One offered this advice: "Don't be attractive. Don't be too smart. Don't be assertive. Pretend you're not a woman. Don't be single. Don't be a mom. Don't be a divorcée." Asked, "What prevents women from advancing to corporate leadership?" a majority of the women answered: "Male stereotyping and preconceptions."

Ann Landers was recently presented with a question from a concerned mother. She and her husband had given a set of weights to their seventeen-year-old son, Michael, but their fifteen-year-old daughter, Diane, had been lifting them, then challenging Michael to arm wrestling matches. "Of course, she always wins," the mother wrote. "My husband and I find the competitive aspects of this unhealthy, and we are at a loss in dealing with it."

Ann's reply: "Diane sounds like a female bully and Michael is a wimp to allow her to humiliate him this way. Order those two to cut out the nonsense."

Apparently Landers (and others) believe it is inappropriate for girls to beat their brothers, at least in tests of strength. Landers goes on to recommend that the siblings play golf or swim together. Presumably a female victory in those realms would not so humiliate Michael. Or maybe Landers believed Michael would be more likely to win there. In any case, Landers implies that girls and boys should not even engage in activities in which male loss might be perceived as humiliating.

Margaret Mead explains, maleness "is not absolutely defined; it has to be kept and re-earned every day, and one essential element in the definition is beating women in every game that both sexes play, in every activity in which both sexes engage."[24]

During Bill Clinton's first presidential campaign, former President Nixon offered this unsolicited advice to Clinton via *The New York Times*: "If the wife comes through as being too strong and too intelligent, it makes the husband look like a wimp." That could seem like outdated advice, but it proved prophetic; Clinton was subjected to much ridicule based on the public perception that Hillary Rodham

Clinton was too strong and too intelligent. This included jokes about "the President and her husband."

The question "Should You Pamper the Fragile Male Ski Ego?" was seriously considered in a pair of articles in a recent issue of *Powder* magazine. In "Treat It like the Eggshell That It Is," Jill Adler explained that she'll let a slow male skier "believe he's as good as he thinks he is" because if you're "straightforward with a guy," he'll either "turn the entire ski day into a competition or retaliate with moodiness or indignation." In an opposing article entitled "Crush It like a Bug," Kristen Ulmer argued that "it's not good to leave the male ego unsupervised; we could all wind up back in caves."[25]

Even athletic, outspoken high school girls struggle with this issue: whether to confront or placate the male ego. In the fall of 1996 I gave a speech at Marymount College in Tarrytown, New York, in honor of National Girls and Women in Sports Day. More than 450 female high school athletes from area schools were selected to attend. After the speech they gathered in groups of thirty, then each group asked me one collective question. One group's question was "How can we stand up for equal rights in sport without making boys mad at us?" Another group asked, "When we play against boys and they lose, how can we convince them that we know they really *were* trying, even though they claim, afterward, that they really *weren't* trying?"

A story about the Greek goddess Artemis offers a chilling parable about female competition with men. A hunter, Artemis used her skills to protect other women (including her own mother) from male rape and assault. She also liked to hunt for fun, for the sheer joy of competing. So when her twin brother, Apollo, challenged her to shoot an arrow at a round target bobbing in the dark ocean, she welcomed the chance. She didn't realize the target was the head of her dear friend Orion, who had waded into the water for a swim. Jealous of his sister's affection for Orion, Apollo had tricked her into killing her friend. Interpreting this myth in *Goddesses in Everywoman*, Jean Shinoda Bolen concludes, "Thus, the one man she loved became a casualty of her competitive nature."[26]

How come the woman gets blamed? Why *shouldn't* she have accepted the archery challenge from her twin brother? Was she too trusting? Too competitive? Why is this her fault, instead of the fault of her jealous, hateful brother?

Women's reluctance to compete with men can often be traced to this: If we win, we will inadvertently kill men or kill our own chances of being loved by men. How dare we best our brothers? To be fearlessly, deliberately competitive with a man is, for a woman, risky. How could any red-blooded American man tolerate a victorious, sharp-shooting warrior woman? Her very competence would slay him.

"Women's direct use of their own powers in their own interests frequently brings a severely negative reaction from the man," notes Jean Baker Miller in *Toward a New Psychology of Women.* "Because of experiences of this sort, many women have developed an exaggerated inner equation: the effective use of their own power means that they are wrong, even destructive."[27]

So women work at home or start their own companies or refuse to apply for jobs or grants for which they'll have to compete with men. They date only taller, stronger, richer men. I don't blame them. All of us want to be loved. Besides, some men are dangerous to compete against. So desperate are they to defend their sense of masculine superiority that they'd rather die—or injure their female opponents—than "let" a woman win.

The truth is, female victory doesn't kill men; it only kills their ideas of who men are and how they should dominate. Yet women often fear something drastic will happen if they win, so they hold back. "I tend to put myself number two with men," a business owner told me. "It makes dating hard. It's not necessarily his fault. I put myself down, but at the same time, I resist doing that. It becomes a power struggle."

I ask Roz Meadow what she tells women who fear that their competitiveness will threaten men.

"You can't live your life because you're afraid nobody will love you," she says. "This is the way women have lived. They have to put silicone in their boobs, they have to conform, they have to be skinny, or no one will love them. What kind of life is this? They have a fantasy that they won't be loved for themselves."

"On the other hand, maybe they won't be," I say.

"So then recognize you're not going to be loved by everyone," counters Meadow. "That doesn't mean you have to give up your identity. Many women's fears are imagined. I know women who are fearful of getting a graduate degree; that's unrealistic. Maybe you won't be liked if you're president of Dial corporation, but for the majority of women, that's not their goal. They just want to get an M.D. or get into another profession. Women's fear of being threatening to men even extends into fields that aren't so threatening."

I n my survey, competitive and athletic women were especially likely to agree that "many men feel threatened by female victory." Of the competitive women, 72 percent agreed; only 60 percent of non-competitive women did. In addition, 75 percent of self-defined athletes (88 percent of pros, and 81 percent of college varsity athletes) agreed; only 53 percent of nonathletes did.

Why would competitive and athletic women be more likely to believe that many men are threatened by female victory? Is it because women who compete (whether in sports or elsewhere) are the most likely to have direct experience competing with men and thus have seen for themselves that men are threatened? Or is it because competitive, athletic women are more likely than their sisters to be more successful in traditionally male arenas (including sports) and thus more likely to threaten men? Both might be true. Competitive, athletic women might meet more insecure men, and these same women might instigate more fear in men.

Not much seems to have changed since 1958, when a similar survey question asked Ohio sportswomen if men were critical of women who were "too good" or highly proficient athletes. Two thirds said yes. "It depends on his ego," said one. "The feminine charming girl might carry it off."[28]

But even the majority of nonathletic and noncompetitive women I surveyed agreed that many men feel threatened by female victory. So it's not just outspoken, aggressive, or athletic women who perceive men to be threatened. The majority of all women did.

In answer to another of my survey questions about whether they generally compete with women, men, or both, a majority (68 percent) said they "generally compete with women or men." Only 3 percent said they generally compete with men. About one fourth (23 percent) said they generally compete with women.[29]

It seems significant that almost one fourth (23 percent) of the women I surveyed tend to limit their rivals to women. I saw evidence of this during interviews. When I'd raise the subject of competition, women usually assumed that I only meant competition between and among women. These women seem to have learned their childhood lessons well: Girls should not compete with boys. It's absolutely out of the question.

Yet the majority of my respondents (68 percent) do not seem to be refraining from competing with men despite their belief that many men are threatened by female victory. So they must be finding ways to compete despite their perception that men are threatened. They must be finding ways to integrate their own competitiveness with their belief that men don't like to lose to women.

Sometimes they play the Cheerleader game, assuaging male egos by looking pretty and acting deferential. Other times they ignore or laugh at male defensiveness. One optimist wrote on my survey: "Men are praised for their competitiveness, and finally women are being acknowledged as well. It's still threatening for some men, but they'll get over it."

Chapter 22

Desperate Tactics
to Watch Out For

When I was sixteen, my family moved from Philadelphia to Phoenix. My new high school offered no girls' basketball team, so I asked the boys' coach, an astronomy teacher, if I could try out for the boys' team.

We were standing outside his classroom next to the celestial map. He was tall, one of the few teachers taller than I. He looked at me quizzically. "Your breasts would get in the way," he said. He stood close to me; he riveted me to him with the shock of his words. "Your breasts could get hit with an elbow," he continued, and his elbow was close enough to my body to demonstrate the maneuver.

"I want to try out anyway," I insisted, stepping back. "I played basketball at my old school. I'm good."

"Only if I can personally bind your breasts," he said, eyes twinkling.

Girls didn't sue teachers in those days. The term "sexual harassment" had not been invented. But I did notice that my astronomy teacher's response was different from anything a female teacher might have said. The encounter started me thinking about the ways men compete with women, especially when those women want to compete in arenas men have reserved for themselves. It taught me that if I intended to compete with men, whether in basketball or other endeavors, I was going to have to learn how men compete.

Years later, during hundreds of radio and television interviews related to *The Stronger Women Get, the More Men Love Football*, I received a crash course on male styles of competition. Over and over, I was challenged, attacked, blamed, screamed at. Angry men called me the worst names they could think of: feminist, radical feminist, femi-Nazi, man hater, male basher, castrator, and lesbian. They said, "If a woman played football, she'd be crushed in the first play. Crushed! Demolished! Killed!" They said, "You're trying to make men into wimps. Who's gonna fight the wars if men get soft and sensitive?" They said, "Are you trying to say there's no natural, inherent differences between men and women? What about genital differences? Don't you think there are any genital differences? What about genitals? Huh? What about genitals?" (Translation: I have a penis, and you don't.) They said, "This woman's a lesbian! I heard her admit it on another radio show!" And they said, "Tell me, in bed, are you on top or on bottom?"

It was quite an experience.

My intention was only to discuss my book. But partly because of the subject matter (a feminist critique of sports), partly because of the male culture of which football is a part, and partly because of my timing (O. J. Simpson was arrested the day the book was released, and I mention in the book his history of violence against Nicole, as well as a widespread pattern of sexist abuse by male athletes), about half of my male hosts, guests, and callers reacted with fury and tried their best to discredit me.

These interviews were not conversations. They were debates, verbal competitions. The men did not listen; they rarely asked good questions. Often they asked no questions at all. Instead they ridiculed my ideas, challenged my authority, did their best to dominate the conversation, and, when all else failed, resorted to sexual harassment. All of which only proved my point: For many men, football is an emotional issue and symbolic of male power.

Some men (about half) "got it." Author Naomi Wolf calls them the egalitarians, as opposed to the patriarchalists. They want their daughters to have equal rights. Or they simply respect women. Two former pro football players who appeared on television shows with me admitted that they had beaten their wives in the past and acknowledged a connection between male dominance and football. One, John Niland, joined me on the *Maury Povich Show* with his former wife, whom he had beaten, and his present wife, whom he does not beat. "Amazing what passes for a hero these days," my father noted dryly.

I also encountered another type of man, the one who fervently believes in equality—for men. These men are concerned about fathers' rights, discrimination against men in the draft, and why boys aren't allowed to play high school field hockey.

During this media tour and during speaking engagements at conferences and on college campuses afterward, I learned some things about male forms of competition. My observations were garnered from an extreme situation: I was in public forums in the United States, criticizing the football culture, which is akin to criticizing the pope in Italy. What I learned was not how all men compete with women but how some angry men compete when they perceive a woman to be "attacking" something they hold dear.

The men who tried to defeat me might represent only a small group of very threatened, very angry, very conservative men. They surprised me; my own male friends and family members don't act this way. Hundreds of men have written me letters of support. On the other hand, my experience was not unique. Many of my observations have been corroborated in books about male behavior, from Deborah Tannen's work on male and female communication styles to books by men about conflict, war, and how to "win" conversations. Here are the six major competitive strategies I observed, usually in order of presentation:

1. Disqualification

First they say, "You can't play with us because you're not good enough." ("Although rivals may resort to literal destruction of their opponents, they usually seek to disqualify them from the field of contest," James P. Gustafson and Lowell W. Cooper write in *The Modern Contest*.[1]) Hence women can't achieve the way men do because women are "naturally" inferior. Women are too weak, too emotional, too short, too involved with their children, too unattractive, too attractive, too likely to get pregnant and leave the job. Their breasts would get in the way. Or women are unqualified because men don't trust them or because ancient religious and philosophical texts deem them unfit to compete on an equal basis.

The Old Testament tells women, "Your desire shall be for your husband, and he shall rule over you."

Muhammad says in the Koran: "Men are superior to women on account of the qualities in which God has given them pre-eminence, and because they spend of their property [for the support of women].[2]

Confucius said, "It is the law of nature that woman should be held under dominance of man."[3]

Plato said woman's "native disposition is inferior to man's."[4]

Aristotle said, "The male is by nature superior, and the female inferior; and the one rules, and the other is ruled. The lower sort are by nature slaves, and it is better for them as for all inferiors that they should be under the rule of a master."[5]

Of course, women have proved themselves perfectly capable of voting, holding public office, playing Little League, being astronauts, announcing the evening news, serving on the Supreme Court, fighting in wars, laying bricks, putting out fires, and running businesses. (They manage to do all these things without having wives at home to do the dirty, behind-the-scenes work, which helps "qualify" so many men.) Nevertheless the "you're not qualified" refrain remains common, and the rationales remain irrational. House Speaker Newt Gingrich, while teaching a college course, claimed that women shouldn't participate in combat because they get "infections."

It's too late to say with any credibility that women can't play sports, so now the arguments in the athletic domain have shifted: Women are unqualified to *coach* or *broadcast* sports. "How could a woman coach football if she's never *played* football!" men on radio shows shouted at me. Never mind that Bela Karolyi has never done a cartwheel on a balance beam. "How absurd! Ha-ha! How hilarious, how ridiculous!" Men who compete like this laugh a lot and use the word "ridiculous" a lot.

On the three television networks only one woman is regularly employed to comment on men's golf. ABC commentator Judy Rankin, a former professional player, has repeatedly been told she's not qualified. "I hear all the time that a woman can't hit it 270 yards, so how could she talk about the men's game?" says Rankin. "But that doesn't mean I don't understand how it works. I have played the game. I think I know what I'm talking about."[6] Rankin is too diplomatic to say it, but most male commentators can't hit the ball 270 yards either. Some don't even play golf.

In the case of my critique of sports sexism, men (such as Robert Novak on CNN's *Crossfire*) challenge my qualifications with this opener: "Have you ever gone into a pro football locker room?" When I say yes, they ask how many times I'd been there, or if I've been there lately, or if I've also been in a college football locker room, or if I've ever played football. The hope is that if they continue to refine the qualifications, I will eventually be disqualified.

A variation on the disqualification is "I'm *more* qualified." "I'm sixty-four, and I've been going to football games since I was ten," Novak told me on *Crossfire*.

"I've been a sportswriter for twenty-seven years," *New York Times* columnist Ira Berkow told me during an argument on *Good Morning America*. Since Novak and Berkow are older than I, they "won" these points, at least in their minds.

2. DENIAL

Several male sportswriters have told me that in all their years in locker rooms, they have never heard men joke about rape or wife beating, or they have never heard any sexist comments at all. Such denials can seem absurd to women (where would we be if we had waited for men to notice sexism?) but are uttered in all seriousness, as if the fact that they don't see sexism means it isn't happening. It's an attempt to invalidate female reality and establish male reality as the singular truth.

3. INTERRUPTIONS

Another way men compete is by dominating conversations with long stories and interruptions. Taught to be polite, many women (especially European-American women) allow men to interrupt. I did too until I figured out that they weren't letting me participate. This technique serves as a way to push women off course, to take up all the space, so women have no room to maneuver. In this game the person who talks the most wins.

4. SPECIAL AND SECRET RULES

Women in male-dominated arenas are expected to play by different rules from those men play by. Women are supposed to be charming, attractive, smiley. They're supposed to dress in a way that's not too feminine and not too masculine—a challenge. They're supposed to "keep a sense of humor," meaning they're supposed to put up with relatively small slights: being called by their first names, being called dear or miss, being touched "all in good fun." Finding a competitive style that is suitable—*for a woman*—is not easy.

When a *USA Today* reporter asked actress Ellen Barkin if she was "tough," Barkin responded, "Why are only women asked if they're tough? People are much less resentful of male stars. Why do you have a different set of rules for me than you do for that man over there? Basically, to the men who make movies, women actors are Barbie dolls. . . . Women are frivolous creatures and men have substance."[7]

Washington lawyer Celinda Lake explains the rules this way: "It's okay for a woman to be tough, but only if she has come through personal tragedy or if she's tough not overall but on a certain issue. That's passion. That's feisty. They like feisty, they don't like tough."[8]

Even the rules of arguing are different for men and women. Men really do argue heatedly, then go drink beer together. But they rarely extend that chummy "Let's go have a beer" offer to women. At least in my experience, men who disagree with me politically virtually never conclude the encounter with a gracious invitation to socialize. Some won't even look at me. If you're a woman, it's hard to be buddy-buddy. You're not a buddy, and men don't seem to forget that. After the filming of television shows there have been some chilly silences as my hosts have fumed. My impression is that after these public verbal competitions—perhaps because they thought I had "won"?—some of my male opponents seemed to hate me.

Men also play by unwritten rules and break rules that women take seriously. In other words, they play dirty. When I told a friend that I encourage women to compete with men, he responded, only half-jokingly, "How can women compete with men? Men cheat."

One woman wrote in my survey: "I think one interesting aspect of competition is when morals, rules, and sportsmanship are jettisoned. Men do this either immediately (just because their competitor is female) or the instant they feel threatened."

Howard University women's basketball coach Sanya Tyler knew for many years that the men's coach was being paid four times as much as she was, and it was obvious that her office was much smaller than his. Still, she coached for thirteen years before taking action to rectify the situation because she mistakenly believed in playing by the rules. "I was loyal," she says. "I was a team player. I believed them when they said that the discrimination was not intentional, that there just wasn't any money. I thought I was on the whole team. Then I realized there were two teams, and I was just on the women's team."

In 1993 she sued her university for sex discrimination—for being paid less and treated worse than the men's coach—and was awarded

$2.3 million by a Washington, D.C., Superior Court jury. Later the award was reduced to $250,000. Tyler received a new locker room, a new office, and a higher salary—though still lower than that of the men's coach. More than four years later she is still angry about not being considered a teammate by the male administrators at Howard. "Some African-American men have difficulty with strong, competent women," she says. "It's so hard for them to let their egos go. Winning even in a bad situation is better for them than losing to a woman."

5. NAME-CALLING

The playground technique of name-calling remains popular among adult men. Such words as "weird," "outrageous," "ludicrous," "cuckoo," "nuts," and "silly" all fall into the "you're insane" genre. Then there are political labels: "feminist," "radical feminist," "femi-Nazi," "liberal," "far left," and "out of the mainstream." When these terms fail to silence women, men attack women as women: for being female ("bitch"), for being too sexual ("ho"), for being not sexual enough ("frigid, prude"), for being sexual with the wrong sort of person ("dyke"). After the all-female crew won an early race in the previously all-male America's Cup trials in 1995, former champion Dennis Conner told *The New York Times* that the women were racing in a "lesbo boat."

In 1995 the *Wilmington News Journal* quoted CBS commentator Ben Wright as saying that women's "boobs" inhibit their golf swings, that "lesbians hurt women's golf," and that "parading" lesbians are becoming increasingly "defiant." Wright was criticizing the women for being female, for having breasts. He was also criticizing women for being the wrong kind of female: not heterosexual and not submissive.

University of Pennsylvania law professor Lani Guinier and her colleagues described male name-calling in an article entitled "Becoming Gentlemen: Women's Experiences at One Ivy League Law School." When female students speak up in class, the authors note, male law students subject them to a kind of hazing, ridiculing the women's comments or attempting to bait them with terms like "feminist" and "lesbian." Though the female and male students entered law school with the same qualifications, the women were less likely to succeed academically and were less likely to be chosen for the law review, prizes, and prestigious clerkships.

I'm convinced that all outspoken women, if they live long enough, will be called lesbians. Sometimes "feminist" itself is a code word for lesbian, but when men are sufficiently threatened, the accusation is direct. "Lesbian" is their big gun, so to speak. When discussing football in public forums, I've been told repeatedly, "You're probably a lesbian," and "I bet you're a lesbian." The implication is that only a lesbian would criticize men or male violence, which is ironic, given the fact that straight women are more likely than lesbians to be victimized by male violence in their own homes.

In my case, since I *am* a lesbian, it gets tricky. If my opponent knows this, he invariably tries to use it against me directly. If he doesn't know it but baits me—"You're probably a lesbian, aren't you?"—he is usually so shocked at my affirmative response that he stutters, stupefied. "Yes, I am a lesbian" is a wonderful conversation stopper, and I highly recommend it, whether you are a lesbian or not. If you're not, it's a valuable way to confront someone on his homophobia, plus it's safe because you can always recant later. If you *are* a lesbian, it's a valuable way to maintain integrity and self-esteem. There's a tremendous amount of personal freedom in telling the truth, and a lot of political power. Ever notice how no one *accuses* Martina Navratilova of being a lesbian anymore?

Joking is also useful. I tell women: "I think we ought to get used to saying the word 'lesbian' out loud, so it doesn't have so much power over us. If you want, you can warm up to it by saying the word 'thespian.'" I say, "Don't worry if you don't know much about homophobia; I used to think it meant fear of going home." At a bookstore one time, when a man baited me with "You're a lesbian, aren't you!" I pointed to two male colleagues in the audience. "Yes," I said, "I am, but several of the people I quote in the book are not. Right here in the audience, for example, are two scholars, Jackson Katz and Todd

Crosset; both of them have done extensive work on male violence in sport. And you guys aren't lesbians, are you?" They blushed.

6. ASSAULT

If verbal competition fails, the final strategy of male domination is physical or sexual assault or the threat of such assault. The first woman officially to enter the Boston Marathon (Kathrine Switzer) was physically dragged from the race. The first woman to assert her right to attend the state-funded South Carolina college called The Citadel received death threats. Two of the next four women to enroll dropped out after being sexually and physically harassed. Sexual harassment, domestic violence, rape, gang rape, and murder all can represent men's last-ditch efforts to gain dominance. Other feminists have described these as acts of aggression and hostility, and I don't disagree with that, but I also see them as competitive strategies in contests men refuse to lose. In the minds of some men, masculine supremacy itself (often referred to with code words like "tradition" and "family values") requires women to stay "in their place." The ways men attempt to keep women in that subordinate place are sundry and seasoned and to some extent effective. They're effective enough to persuade some women not to compete at all.

Chapter 23

Too Competitive

When I look back on my life, I see a tall, lanky girl who discovered her own beauty and grace by immersing herself in sports. Sports gave me an identity, a place in my family, a social support system, a profound confidence in my ability to achieve, and an appreciation for a long, lean body that might otherwise have seemed merely geeky. Everything I know about courage and effort and achievement and persistence and teamwork and competition, I've learned on the playing fields, on the courts, in pools and rivers and oceans.

But I won't compete in today's swimming meet at Hains Point, an outdoor fifty-meter pool in Washington, D.C. The starter, a serious man dressed in white shirt and shorts, will command in a low, clear voice, "Take your marks . . ." and eight swimmers on the starting blocks will bend over, eyes fixed on the still water below, hands near their toes, motionless. At the sound of the gun they'll spring forward and fly above the cool blueness. The Washington Monument, just a mile away, will peer over the fence with its pointy head, as if watching.

I'll be watching too, cheering for my friends. Like the starter, I'll be wearing shorts. I won't even have my swimsuit or goggles with me.

I won't step up onto those blocks. During the course of writing this book I gave up competition.

Not all competition, just the competition I love best: sports.

How can I encourage women to compete when I have relinquished that particular quest for perfection? I didn't want to, believe me. I went down kicking and screaming. I gave up competitive sports the way an alcoholic gives up alcohol. "Reluctantly" is too mild a word.

I had wanted to impress you. I had planned to enter the U.S. Masters Swimming Long Course Championships in August 1996. I turned forty that spring and meticulously compared my times with those of women in my age-group (forty to forty-four), excited by what I saw. I planned to write the story of these national championships: my anticipation; my discussions with other competitors; my feelings about winning or losing or achieving personal bests. I had hoped to say, "I'm one of the nation's top five women in my age group." Would you have been impressed?

Who cares? Now that I've retired, my swimming speed relative to other women my age seems trivial, even to me. Goals are like that: They seem terribly important when you want them, but when you stop wanting them, either because you've already achieved them or because you've changed your mind, their power drains away.

When I was eleven, my big brother sold me his used basketball (half price), and I fell in love. I'd caress the ball as it rolled under my palm, guiding it around the cars and potholes in our driveway. I taught myself to shoot, aiming high so the sunset would sink through the hoop quietly, with no ambivalence. After hours of reverent, solitary play, I'd wash the ball in our basement sink, carefully rinsing away the driveway's gravel or snow. Later, lying in bed, I'd spin it straight overhead, trying to make it kiss the ceiling before settling in my happy hands. In the morning before school I'd bounce my beloved off my bedroom wall, one hundred little taps with my right hand, one hundred with my left.

As I devoted myself to this basketball, learning to shoot it, catch it, pass it, and care for it, the basketball in return seemed to caress, care for, and even shape me, stretching my fingers, strengthening my willowy arms and legs, widening and lengthening my feet so they'd offer a good place from which I could jump and to which I could land. Basketball became a gift I could share with friends and strangers: "Here! I'll pass you the ball!" As I grew ever upward, toward the basket, my body began to speak of the sport, so that my very presence in a room—head near the ceiling—would prompt people to ask, "Do you play basketball?"

(Later, as my hair began to turn gray, the question became "*Did* you play basketball?")

I sprained my first ankle when my foot slipped off my bike's pedal and got caught between the frame and the wheel. Swelled like a pregnant belly. Required crutches. Fascinated me.

I remember the squishy swelling, the Ace bandage that left its imprint in my skin. The pain was not so much agonizing as interesting. Negotiating stairs on crutches was simply another athletic feat. The wooden crutches themselves intrigued me, with their rubber padding for hands and armpits. The crutches could be adjusted if I turned their tiny silver wing nuts, so I could lower them and lend them to shorter girlfriends. Or I could leave them adjusted for me and let friends pole-vault down the school halls while I sat, leg propped up, laughing. The crutches became a status symbol, a tomboy's trophy, proof: I'm an athlete.

I sprained each ankle several times in high school. I also damaged my right shoulder by spiking volleyballs. After high school graduation I had surgery for chronic subluxation (repeated partial dislocation). Recovery was slow and shocking; I hadn't expected so much pain. Still, physical therapy felt like another game, another corporal task at which I could excel.

In my sophomore year of college, as I intensified my basketball training in an unsuccessful effort to make the 1976 Olympic team, both knees developed tendinitis. I began what became a many-year regimen of weight lifting, ultrasound, tape, ice, and heat. And kept playing.

One Halloween my housemate dressed up as me. I was amused by the sight of Sheila in my Stanford basketball uniform, but when I saw the two bags filled with cotton balls, representing ice, I realized that injuries had become part of my identity, an integral part of my athleticism.

After college I had another shoulder operation to repair a screw that had come loose from the first surgery. I played basketball for a year in France, then briefly for the New Jersey Gems of the Women's Professional Basketball League. The more I jumped for joy, the more my knees hurt upon impact. "Something's wrong here!" they seemed to be shouting. "Pay attention to us!"

But knees are so small and so far from the willful brain. So insignificant when the gym is overflowing with adoring fans. So trivial when an athlete is hooking a ball up and over an opponent in a perfect arch. So irrelevant compared with the ineffable joy of teamwork. By the time I quit playing basketball at age twenty-three, the cartilage under both kneecaps had been permanently shredded by a condition called chondromalacia. I could no longer run.

Ever the optimist, I decided that my injuries were a blessing. "Sit down," my body seemed to tell me, and after bilateral knee surgery I had no choice but to listen. I sat in front of my first computer and at twenty-four began to commit myself to the one thing I love as much as sports: writing.

Two years later I rediscovered my first sport, which is gentler on the knees: swimming. Brooke Dick, the coach who introduced me to masters swimming, told me that swimming is "forgiving." I've been a masters swimmer ever since.

Masters swimming provides a nearly perfect model for Championship competition. Swimmers practice in lanes that are determined by speed, not age or gender. They tend to compete primarily against their personal bests, but they also race with each other, inspiring each other to excel and offering mutual support. They're dedicated, hard-working people who take themselves lightly. (One favorite T-shirt says, "The older I get, the faster I was.")

On my D.C. Masters team, the fastest women and men, including some college students and some champion ultra-distance (twenty-five mile) swimmers, zip along in Lane 8. Older swimmers plus novice young folks poke along in Lanes 1 and 2. Some of the old folks used to swim in faster lanes years ago. That's how it works: If you swim long enough, you get slower, ineluctably demoted from the zippy lanes to the poky lanes. It could be depressing but isn't, in part because there's a lot of intergenerational camaraderie. Before and after practice people with sagging stomachs and crinkly skin chat with Olympic types whose bodies are as hard and lean as the lifeguard stands.

One recent morning I arrived to see a bucket of red carnations at the end of Lane 2 and immediately knew someone had died. (This is a masters tradition, or should be.) It was Frank Murphy, a popular seventy-eight-year-old Pearl Harbor survivor who had been a team member for seventeen years. He had died of a heart attack, right there in Lane 2, the previous morning. Frank and his wife, Lorraine, a Lane 1 swimmer, had been married for fifty-five years. Fifty swimmers of all ages showed up at the funeral.

I'm in Lane 5. Before I quit competing, I used to lead the lane, and I took that job seriously, listening to Coach Flanagan's instructions, then trying not to mess up the intervals (the amount of time between laps). Behind me were Sue and Ruth and Julie and Patrick and George (age range: twenty-eight to fifty-one). I fancied myself a team leader, offering encouragement to my lanemates as they finished. "Nice job," I'd say, "just one more set to go." Then I'd disappear underwater, align my feet against the wall, and push, my body streamlined as a surfboard.

After each set Ruth would ask me, "How'd you do?" She meant, "How fast?" "One twenty-three," I might say; one minute, twenty-

three seconds for a hundred meters freestyle. I liked it that she cared.
I liked chatting with her afterward, while showering and dressing, our
bodies exhausted and exhilarated. It's hard to explain this to noncompetitive people: why it's fun to strain and push and sweat (even in the
pool you sweat) until your muscles ache and you can hardly breathe.
I find it thrilling. I like the speed, the effort, the success, the teamwork. I love the moment when the morning sun oozes over the cot-
tonwood trees and spills pink paint into the pool so I can feel my
back burning hot while underwater my belly and thighs and face stay
shivery cool. Sometimes that's enough: the rapture of cold water and
hot sun and good company and a lean body stroking. But then, after
a while, I want to compete.

Between the ages of twenty-six and thirty-eight I competed in a
few local meets each year, first in the San Francisco Bay Area, then,
when I moved back East, in Washington, D.C. I joined two men's
water polo teams for a while and found in water polo a wonderful
combination of my two favorite sports: swimming and basketball. I
joined a rowing team and competed in regattas in singles and doubles.
But even these "sitting and floating" sports—at least the way I played
them, always giving the proverbial 110 percent—became too stressful
on my knees and shoulders, so I ultimately limited myself to swimming.

In early 1994 I signed up for four swimming events in the upcoming Gay Games. My only previous international swimming experience had been the original 1982 Gay Games, and I'd relished
sharing the joy of sports with athletes who did not hide their love. I
also appreciated the philosophy of the games: Anyone—even straight
people—can enter. Though the games are competitive, the emphasis
is on personal bests, not gold medals. Still, gold medals are fun; I
won two in those first games, plus two silvers. Between 1982 and 1994
the games had grown from three thousand participants to an expected
eleven thousand. I was eager for the fun and camaraderie. And curious: How would I fare this time?

As I trained, I began to experience an ache in my left shoulder, which until that time I had thought of as my one remaining "good" joint. Nevertheless I entered a local meet as a warm-up. I drove to the event with a friend and remember saying to her, "My shoulder is unbelievably sore." Yet it did not occur to me to scratch myself from the meet. In my mind I "needed" that experience in order to swim well at the Gay Games.

In that local meet I swam in three events. That night the tendons in my shoulder became so inflamed I couldn't sleep. In the following days I was unable to yank on a T-shirt or wash my hair without severe pain. I was unable to swim in the Gay Games, and it took a full year (and one cortisone shot and lots of physical therapy) before I could slip into the pool again.

That was extreme: a year out of the water. But the pattern is one I've repeated throughout my life: physical exertion followed by pain, followed by more exertion despite the pain, leading to overuse injuries and, often, permanent damage.

Sounds silly, doesn't it?

Athletes do it all the time. Mary Decker Slaney, who set thirty-six American and seventeen world records, incurred her first stress fractures as a teenager and has endured more than twenty surgeries for various muscle, tendon, and bone injuries. The injuries kept her off the 1976 Olympic team and kept her from racing well in the 1988 Olympics. Just before the 1996 Olympics she said, "I dream about being healthy. That's all I need to be." Slaney was healthy enough to make the team but, at age thirty-nine, not fast enough to qualify for the final race. How healthy might she have been and how many more races might she have won if she had learned to slow down before injury or at least rest afterward? Is permanent damage always the price of greatness?

No. In fact "really great athletes baby their bodies," says Olympic swimming champion Nancy Hogshead. "You grow up with the axiom 'No pain, no gain,' but it does not apply. You push yourself right up to the point where your body wears out, but you never cross over that point. Rather than see your soul and your body as two separate things, you have to be teammates. The body is full of wisdom, and so is the mind. You have to get over the finish line together."

Yet our culture rewards short-term victory over long-term wellness. Boxer Muhammad Ali, suffering from Parkinson's syndrome as a result of repeated blows to the head, lit the torch at the opening ceremonies for the 1996 Summer Olympics, his hands shaking. Yet the tragic consequences of his career didn't seem to bother the fans who cheered with admiration for "The Greatest."

Nor did many fans express concern about the health of Kerri Strug, the 1996 Olympic gymnast who valiantly completed a second vault after injuring her ankle on the first. With the second vault she helped secure a gold medal for the American team and tore two ligaments in an already weakened ankle. Crying and unable to walk, she was declared a national hero. That's what great athletes do, right? Like soldiers, they're supposed to sacrifice their bodies while pursuing a greater good: victory. Right? Is this what feminism means: Women now receive equal encouragement to injure their bodies in the name of winning?

I n 1995 my shoulder was still too sore for competition, a huge disappointment for me when I accompanied my mother to her first Masters Nationals. But by 1996 my shoulder had healed sufficiently that I was sprinting again in practice. I decided to go to Nationals that year in Ann Arbor, Michigan. I had never competed in Nationals, and the prospect intrigued me. I reserved a hotel room and exchanged some frequent flier miles for an airline ticket. I worked on my technique, reminding myself to finish each stroke the way Nancy Hogshead had once shown me. I concentrated on rolling from side to side the way distance champion Diana Nyad had shown me. One of my teammates critiqued my flip turn, saying, "Chin to chest, chin to chest," a mantra that helped me flip faster. I started feeling sleek and swift and downright Olympian as I "nailed" my flip turns the way gymnasts nail landings, two feet firmly on the wall.

Almost immediately my body started aching. My left knee hurt, my left shoulder hurt, and I developed new pains: a sore elbow one day, a tight, annoying muscle in my back the next. Nevertheless every day I thought about the upcoming Nationals. Every day, as I tried to improve my stroke, I imagined swimming the fifteen hundred meters or the eight hundred or the four hundred, rolling, finishing the stroke, flipping fast, chin to chest. It gave me a goal, a purpose.

One day I even thought about winning. That was unrealistic. My best times are far slower than those of, for instance, Sandy Neilson-Bell, a 1972 Olympic triple gold medalist who happens to be my age and now competes in Masters swimming. But I felt so fast and happy I had delusions of grandeur, and these delusions gave me something to focus on besides the pain.

Another day I learned how to dive in with my goggles on. Millions of kids take this for granted, but it was an accomplishment for someone whose primary swimming career took place between 1962 and 1972, before goggles were invented. The day I finally *got it* I was so happy I did at least twenty racing dives, over and over again, celebrating my new skill.

The following day my shoulder screamed at me. When severely inflamed, rotator cuff tendinitis feels as if a woodpecker were drilling its beak deep into your sensitive tissue. The pain is impossible to ignore. I stayed out of the pool for a week.

The decision to quit came gradually, after long, voluble quarrels between my mind, which always argued for competition, and my joints, which were sick and tired. Should I compete at Nationals, because I'd love to do it, or not, because my body doesn't want to? As if "I" and "my body" were two warring factions. Like any addict, I tried bargaining with myself: I'll compete only in this one meet, in one event. I'll compete only if I'm pain-free that day. I argued with myself while swimming, while cycling, while walking my dog, while lying in bed before sleep, even while sleeping. I dreamed I was on the sidelines of a basketball court and a coach said, "It's okay, Mariah. We don't need you to play anymore."

I started meeting people who hobble on artificial joints. "I've had both knees replaced," they explained, limping past. My aunt Carol, my mother's sister, told me that she had had both shoulders replaced, reminding me that weak joints can be inherited.

Still, I thought: *If I never get to stand on those starting blocks again, feeling proud and excited and eager to show off my new dive, I'm going to miss it terribly.*

Then I'd think: *If I have to get my shoulders or knees replaced by plastic ones, I'll miss them even more.*

I talked to my friend Gloria Joseph, a former semipro softball player with knee problems. I told her I was trying to accept my physical limitations. "What other choice do you have?" she said directly.

I asked my friend Sue Schaffer why she didn't compete anymore. Sue won three gold medals at Nationals when she was forty; that was about ten years ago. "There comes a time in your life when it's not worth it to hurt anymore," she said.

"Don't you miss having the goals?" I asked.

"My goals have changed," she said. "Now my goal is to stay in good shape."

I talked with Carol Galbraith, another swimmer friend. "I might not go to Nationals," I told her. "I don't want to win a bunch of medals but destroy my joints in the process."

"No, definitely not," said Carol, reminding me: "You already did that in basketball."

I talked to my partner one day over breakfast. "My shoulder's sore. I shouldn't have pushed myself so hard in practice this morning. But that fast triathlete Rose was there, and I was trying to keep up."

"Eventually you're just going to have to let that go," she said gently.

I consulted sport psychologists. (One advantage of being an author is that you get to interview therapists, then, at the end of the interview, sneak in some questions about your own personal quandaries.)

They responded with their own good questions: "Why are you competing?" (Sharon Drake Petro, sport psychology consultant, Charlottesville, Virginia). "What would it say about you if you quit?" (Jane Miner, sport psychology consultant and president of Personal Solutions, Bountiful, Utah).

Dave Provorse, an assistant professor of psychology at Washburn University in Topeka, Kansas, told me that when he competes in triathlons, he puts forth only about 85 percent of his maximum effort in order not to injure his body. I wondered, could I do that? If someone challenged me in the next lane, could I hold back?

Finally, about two months after my fortieth birthday, I retired from competitive swimming. I decided to call it retiring instead of quitting; it sounded more mature. An earned privilege, a wise thing to do in one's older years. I dropped out of Nationals and canceled my plans to compete in local meets that summer.

I had expected to grieve. Instead I felt a tremendous weight lift from my shoulders—and my knees. Ahhh. I don't have to do that anymore.

The chatter in my head stopped. I stopped arguing with myself, stopped replaying the obsessive "should I or shouldn't I?" tape.

Was my body miraculously healed? I thought this might happen. It didn't. In fact I became more aware of how much my joints hurt. At least one knee hurts every day. At least one shoulder hurts most days. The degrees of pain vary, but I am rarely pain-free.

I had thought I was paying attention before, stretching, eating well, sleeping when tired. Now I see that my intense desire to compete and my obsession about whether or not to compete were preventing me from perceiving clearly. I was like the alcoholic who can't acquire self-awareness until she stops drinking because the alcohol itself clouds her perceptions. I needed to quit competing before I could attend to my body.

But over time, as I'm learning to respond to my body's pain with rest and tenderness, my joints are beginning to heal. It's a gradual, subtle healing, but I'm hopeful; as with the ex-smoker whose lungs can eventually regenerate healthy tissue, it may take years. It may also take weight lifting, physical therapy, and possibly even more surgery. Not so that I can swim faster but so that I can swim forever.

The grieving, when it came, wasn't for lost athletic opportunities after all. It was for lost abilities, for the healthy body I once had. As I emerged from my denial, I thought, *I am permanently disabled!* And: *Wow! What have I done to myself?*

I've long subscribed to the theory that when a person represses one emotion (anger, for instance) or one piece of information (a painful childhood memory, for instance), she inevitably represses other emotions and insights as well. Now I see that the reverse is also true. When I stopped repressing the fact of my own physical fragility, other repressed facts surfaced.

When I let go of competitive sports, I acknowledged that I have physical limitations, weaknesses that matter. By acknowledging those weaknesses, I began to give myself permission to have other weaknesses: not to be a perfect friend, a perfect daughter, a perfect writer, a perfect public speaker. As an athlete I'd been competing with an impossible standard: perfection. Once I let go of that, I began to see the other ways I'd been competing with impossible dreams. My ambition to excel didn't subside, but I started saying no more often and more easily. I began to give myself permission to fail, to be frail, to be vulnerable, to have wounds and scars that still hurt. To have a brain that makes mistakes, a heart that aches, a tongue that can say the wrong thing. Not to be the best. Not to prove myself, over and over again. What a relief.

The most popular magazine article I ever wrote was "I'm Dancing as Slow as I Can," for *Women's Sports + Fitness.* (The cover line of the magazine read, "When the Spirit Is Willing but the Knees Are Weak.") In the article I shared my mourning process when, after double knee surgery, I realized I would never run again. The essay struck a chord with hordes of injured athletes who wrote to tell me their impassioned stories. That was in 1985. Now I no longer feel a conflict between my willing spirit and injured body. My spirit has become willing to do what the body needs.

So swimming was my last competitive sport, as well as my first. Swimming may be "forgiving," but ultimately this swimmer had to forgive herself for getting confused about how to integrate her fierce desire with her frail joints.

Those of us who are too competitive—whether we express our obsessions in athletic arenas or business meetings or around the family dinner table—hurt ourselves: our bodies, our integrity, our chances for future happiness and success. We also hurt others: the loved ones we ignore because we're too fixated on victory, the rivals we cheat because winning becomes the only thing, the potential teammates we alienate when we compete inappropriately, in the wrong times and places. While writing this book, I stumbled upon this truth: Choosing not to compete can be a victory in itself.

W hy are some athletes repeatedly injured? Endorphins play a role. These natural opiates in the brain can mask pain and even create euphoria during physical exertion. High pain tolerance is also part of the problem. Our culture itself has a high tolerance for ath- letes' pain. The sports physicians I consulted always recommended tape and treatment, not rest or retirement. The coaches didn't explain that giving 110 percent is impossible—that it is, by definition, strain- ing oneself beyond one's capabilities. Only once during my four years at Stanford did I miss a game. Though I was undergoing an elaborate daily ritual of ice, heat, tape, and ultrasound for my knees, no one asked the question, Should this person keep playing basketball?

Lack of proper training and equipment also plays a role. Women in my generation (and many girls today, unfortunately) played on in- ferior surfaces, in small gyms, wearing shoddy sneakers. Knee injuries are much more prevalent among female than male basketball players, according to several studies. During the 1988 Olympic trials, for instance, 13 percent of the men and 54 percent of the women sustained knee injuries. Between 1989 and 1991 women accounted for 78 percent of the anterior cruciate ligament injuries suffered by NCAA basketball and soccer players, though they constituted only 34 percent of the athletes. Though no conclusive reason for the disparity has been found, many studies have pointed to women's inferior training and conditioning. Researchers at the U.S. Naval Academy, for instance, found that women entering the academy were injured more often than men, but as women grew acclimatized to the rigors of training, their injury rates equaled the men's.[1]

During my first two years at Stanford, the only training room was in the men's locker room. No one taped my ankles until my junior year of college; after that I had no more sprains.

In *Women Who Hurt Themselves*, a psychologist named Dusty Miller describes what she calls Trauma Reenactment Syndrome, in which women reenact in symbolic ways their traumas from childhood. Through eating disorders, alcohol abuse, drug abuse, and self-inflicted wounds, these women demonstrate "self-hatred or self-punishment or a need to control."[2]

Self-hatred and self-punishment and a need to control can be factors in exercise addiction too, especially when combined with eating disorders. Even many recreational athletes, in their desperate quest for ever-thinner bodies, exercise in compulsive, self-destructive ways, perhaps enacting childhood traumas—or at very least deeply ingrained beliefs that women must be small. Barbara Drinkwater and other leading sport physiologists have described a common phenomenon in elite athletes called the female athlete triad: eating disorders, osteoporosis, and amenorrhea. Seems to me it's actually a tetrad, including this fourth factor, sports addiction.

In my case my self-inflicted wounds seem to reflect an out-of-control need to feel like a winner, perhaps to prove that I am what British psychologist D. W. Winnicott calls "good enough." I played sports primarily because I loved playing sports; they were the first way I learned to feel powerful and graceful. But sports were also my first niche, my first "occupied zone" in an unspoken competition with my older lawyer siblings and physician parents. "There are only two professions: law and medicine," someone once told me. "Everything else is just a job." Eventually I became a professional writer and speaker, but long before that I had become a professional athlete. I remember saying to myself at that time, "I *did* become a professional after all."

So my efforts to remain a "star" in the sports arena despite myriad injuries might be rooted in a youngest child complex, in an ongoing need to prove myself "in the same league with" my family members. Yet in masters swimming I also discovered a level playing field because swimmers only compete against others their age and gender.

When sport psychology consultant Jane Miner asked me, "If you gave up competitive sports, what would you be giving up?" my answer was: "My identity." Because I started competing at a very early age, my identity as "athlete"—and winner—is right up there with "female" and "writer," integral to how I define myself.

When I speak to groups of women, I encourage those who participate in sports to think of themselves as athletes, whether they're competing or not. I encourage them to make intelligent decisions about when to compete and when not to. So by my own definition, I'm still an athlete. The truth is, I retired from competitive sports in order to remain an athlete—a swimmer and cyclist and hiker and golfer—throughout my life. An endurance athlete. An athlete with longevity.

Jane Miner also asked: "What would it say about you if you quit?"

"That I'm wise enough to respect my body," I responded.

So I've found a way to frame retirement in a way that focuses not on loss and disability but on endurance and wisdom.

It also helps to frame it in terms of addiction. Sport psychologists don't talk much about sports addiction. When they do, they don't differentiate between exercise addiction—a compulsion to exercise despite the costs—and sports addiction (my own self-diagnosis), a compulsion to compete despite the costs. Psychologists do differentiate between positive addiction, the kind that motivates you to work out, and negative addiction. Negative addicts "insist on exercising in the face of physical pain or injury,"[3] allow sports to dominate their lives, compete often, fail to use good judgment about when to compete, and get injured a lot.[4] In one study 60 percent of injured runners considered themselves addicted to exercise.[5]

Like the alcoholic, the sports addict indulges in a pleasurable experience even when the painful side effects become debilitating. Like the alcoholic, the sports addict derives social benefits from the addiction, as she jokes and talks with other athletes before and after competitions. To the sports addict, the prospect of giving up competitive sports is as unfathomable and unappealing as an alcoholic's prospect of giving up the bottle.

Like the alcoholic, the sports addict feels unable to control her behavior. When challenged to compete, she feels unable to say no, and once competing, she feels unable to limit her effort. "Once I'm in a competitive situation, I don't seem to be able to stop myself from pushing past the point of injury," I explained to my D.C. Masters coach, John Flanagan.

John, who also competes in (and wins) masters meets, looked at me blankly. "Oh, I'd never swim fast enough to injure myself," he said matter-of-factly.

I asked Anne Audain, a New Zealand track star whose career spanned twenty-two years, how she had managed to remain injury-free all that time. Audain was born with deformed feet and underwent extensive surgeries as a young teenager, but she set a 1982 world record, won 75 of the 122 races she entered, and earned a place on six Olympic teams. "Maybe because of what I went through with my feet—all that rehabilitation and physical therapy—I learned to listen to my body, and never pushed past stress and into injury," she said simply.

I began to get a sense of how nonaddicted athletes compete. Like nonaddicted drinkers, they stay within their limits.

In *Drinking: A Love Story*, Caroline Knapp describes what alcohol addiction is like for her. After she gets sober, she lies awake at night wondering whether she's *really* an alcoholic. She bargains with herself, trying to find a way to start drinking again without destroying her life. Finally she asks herself: "Do nonalcoholics sit up at night wondering if they're alcoholics?"[6]

Of course not. And people who aren't sports addicts don't lie awake engaged in the kind of obsessive thinking that I tortured myself with for months. The obsession itself was an indication of a problem. I suspect this is true of all obsessions.

When I made the decision to stop competing in meets, it took me a while to stop competing in practice—or, rather, to change the way I compete. I felt pressure to report fast times to Ruth, afraid I'd disappoint her. I found it hard to say, "You lead. My shoulder's sore. I need to take it easy."

But eventually I noticed that no one really cares how fast I swim. The pressure I felt had been a projection of internal pressure to live up to my own standards, standards of performance that go back at least twenty years.

Many women need to learn that they can do more than they think they can. I needed to learn that I can do less than I think I can.

Ruth and I have had to redefine our competitions, finding new ways we both can win. She still works on lowering her times, with encouragement from me, but now she and I also compare strokes per lap (the fewer the better, generally). I take pride in holding steady at forty. This is a good goal for me because sprinting generally increases stroke count, so in order to "win," I can't sprint. Other times I try to swim each set of laps at exactly the same pace—finishing in exactly 1:32, for instance, for each of six one hundreds freestyle.

These days I try to swim *well*, to feel smooth and efficient, to enjoy the physical poetry of swimming. Sometimes when everyone else is sprinting, I'll drift to the back of the lane and swim elementary backstroke, an old-fashioned stroke that serious competitive swimmers never do. It feels frivolous and luxurious. I watch the clouds, grinning. My resting pulse is still forty-eight, so if I feel a need to brag, I can brag about that. But I have a new goal: lifetime fitness.

So when the swimmers take their marks and go off the starting blocks today, I won't go with them. Meets are mostly for people who want to swim fast, and at this point in my life I'm more interested in swimming slowly. But a few months ago I did compete in one final meet (which happened to be a world championship, the International Gay and Lesbian Aquatic Championships). After months of not competing in practice, I grew curious: Could I not compete in a meet? Could I hold back, swimming at only about 85 percent of my best performances? Could I prove to myself that I was not, after all, hopelessly and masochistically addicted to sports?

So I competed, so to speak, in two events (the four hundred and eight hundred meters) plus three relays. During the races I enjoyed the simple, sensuous pleasures of efficient freestyle. I successfully swam my slowest times ever (about 95 percent of my personal bests, as it turned out) and, because few other women my age entered the meet, won five gold medals anyway, helping my team, DCAC, win its second world title. Afterward nothing ached, nothing was injured, and I had no regrets.

My teammates, hearing that I was satisfied with slow times, were perplexed. I tried to explain: I'm learning to value the process of competition as well as its outcome. I'm gaining the freedom to compete or not compete, as I choose. I'm teaching my soul and body to be teammates. All essential qualities, I now realize, of a Champion.

Part Five

Embracing Victory, Embracing Defeat: Guidelines for Champions

Chapter 24

Give Yourself Permission
to Compete

While addressing a group of high school girls in Wisconsin, I told them, "You have a right to compete for what you want, as do your competitors. But first you have to remind yourself that it's okay. Give yourself permission to compete."

During the question and answer period one of the girls stood up and put her hands on her hips. "Why do we need *permission?*" she said. "Shouldn't we just go ahead and compete?"

I smiled. *This is progress*, I thought. But many women, perhaps especially older women, still feel pressure to be dainty, delicate, and deferential to men. We need to give ourselves permission to pursue our own passions, to be successful, to sprint across the finish line first.

When Grantland Rice wrote, "For when the One Great Scorer comes to write against your name—He marks not that you won or lost—but how you played the game," he was assuming that you're playing the game. If you avoid competitive environments, you'll never find out how successful you might be. Howard University basketball coach Sanya Tyler says it this way: "If you want to win, you have to get in." It's a lesson swimmers know well. Most of us hate the cold water, but when you force yourself to get in, the immense, ineffable joy of swimming soon outweighs the misery of those first few breath-catching moments. If you want to win, you have to get into the swimming pool or the graduate school or the entry-level job or the job you've always wanted but dared not apply for or create. Often the water is very cold. Often the climate for women is very chilly, especially if few women have immersed themselves in that environment before. But if you want to win, you have to get past that initial discomfort and participate. Even if you're not sure if you want to win, it's still a good idea to test the water, to find out how others play the game, how you can play it yourself.

How can you find the courage to participate, especially when it seems that women shouldn't or can't? Through practice. Practice competitive behaviors (card games, bowling, whatever seems trivial to you) in a safe setting (with friends). Familiarize yourself with the competitive basics: goal setting, teamwork, performing under pressure, keeping score, devising rules to keep the contest fair and fun, acting gracious in victory and defeat. Even seemingly meaningless contests offer a chance to get comfortable with competition.

The poet Audre Lorde writes, "We have been raised to fear the 'yes' within ourselves, our deepest cravings."[1] Just say yes. Go ahead and compete. Decide where you want to be; then go there. Get in the water. Immerse yourself. Begin.

Chapter 25

Seek Victory Unapologetically

In an amusing television commercial by Nike, sprinters Gail Devers and Michael Johnson sit in a circle with race car driver Al Unser, Jr., a FedEx delivery man, and a Benihana chef. It's a support group for fast people. Gail reads a story: "Once upon a time there was a faraway land where people fast and slow could join hands and sing in harmony, where you were judged by the size of your heart, not the size of your lead." The group leader, who holds a coffee cup with the slogan "Fast & Fine with It," nods appreciatively. Nike's tag line: "It's okay to be fast."

While I don't want to overanalyze Nike's joke, it might not be a coincidence that Devers, the only woman besides the leader, is the one who verbalizes the group's longing for that place where it's okay to be fast. It does seem more difficult for women—especially women surrounded by men, as Gail is in the group—to seek success unapologetically.

So take it from me or from Nike: It's okay to be fast. It's okay to be the fastest of all. You can learn a lot by losing, people say, but you can learn a lot by winning too. It's okay—important, even—to win. Not just to tie, not just to get your fair share, not just to have half, but to be victorious. It's okay to seek victory for yourself and for other people you support. Let go of those old scripts that told you winning isn't feminine, isn't feminist, isn't wise because some guy's going to get his feelings hurt and take it out on you. Stop letting that sort of thinking defeat you. Competition is not domination. Winning is not cruel to others. Those others can learn from you, they can learn from their own effort, and if they try hard enough, maybe they will win next time.

Honora Dent, a Washington, D.C., registered nurse, says, "I want to be the best nurse. I don't think there's anything wrong with that, because I want to take care of my patients the best possible way. I learn from the other nurses, ask them how they do things well. I take into account my limitations, but I'm always striving to be the best that I can be. It comes with maturity. I will not feel like a loser if I'm not the best, but I think it's good to want that, to try for that. I find it energizing."

University of Minnesota professor Mary Jo Kane says, "I always keep score. If I go shoot some baskets, and the other person doesn't want to, I keep score anyway, silently. It matters to me whether my abilities are equal to or better than another person's abilities. Many feminists tell me I'm too male-identified. Softball players say, 'Mary Jo, cool it, we're out here to have fun.' I say, 'It's not fun for me unless we're keeping score.'"

Kane, who holds the nation's only endowed professorship related to women in sport, says "I like being the best. It gives me a sense of self-worth and pride. That was my training at the University of Illinois: You've got to be the best. I don't know of any professional situation where something really mattered to me where I didn't succeed.

"But I don't go after things that are not sure bets. When you go up for tenure, the rule of thumb is you need ten to thirteen published articles. There was no way I was going to go up without fifteen to eighteen. To lose tenure would be professional humiliation. Losing anything hurts. But I do remember lessons from sports: It happens. Also, I believe there can be more than one winner. I'm happy for people when they do well. I'm very gracious. It's not a zero-sum game."

Get comfortable with winning. Give yourself opportunities to win. Practice feeling like a winner—like one of many female winners, a member of a large team, a sorority perhaps, of Champions. Learn to win without apologizing afterward. Tell others that you won. Act like a winner. Walk the way a winner walks. Approach competitive situations as if you expect to succeed. Watch Olympians and other women who openly, unapologetically seek victory and say to yourself: "Me too. If they can win, I can too." Train yourself to succeed. Get used to success. Rise to the occasion. Don't hold back. Don't back down. Winning is fun and female. It's a pleasure. Enjoy.

Chapter 26

Don't Settle for Second

Women so often settle for less than we're worth, less than we could hope for if we thought of ourselves as Champions, if we believed we deserve to win. We get accustomed to being subordinate, to being second-class citizens, to being the second sex. It comes to feel natural to us; it's the water we swim in. "When women say that all is well, what they're often really saying that they accept what they get and have learned not to ask for more," notes Judith Kriss, director of the women's center at the University of Nebraska at Lincoln.

A few years ago I served as the assistant varsity girls' coach at a high school that had two gymnasiums. One gym was old and small. The other was newer and bigger. The old, small one was called the girls' gym. The new, big one was called the boys' gym. The varsity girls played games in the big gym, but all the girls practiced in the small gym. All the boys practiced and played in the big gym.

When they hired me in 1993, I said, "Gee, there's this law called Title IX. Anyone heard of it? It says you can't discriminate on the basis of sex in schools or colleges." I proposed that we comply with Title IX by having the varsity boys and girls share the big gym and the other kids share the small gym.

What amazed me was this: None of the other girls' coaches

wanted to go along with my plan. All three were women, young women, even. But they had grown comfortable with the small gym. They thought it was sufficient.

I said, "What kind of statement is this making to our girls?"

They said, "Our offices are here, near the small gym. If we practice in the big gym, we'll have to carry the balls all the way down the hall."

I said, "Since when is basketball transportation a major hardship for a coach? Besides, why are your offices near the small gym and the men's near the big gym?"

Finally we asked the boys' head coach if we could share the big gym. He said okay. He had been at the school for more than twenty years, ever since Title IX was passed in 1972, so he'd been expecting this for more than twenty years. He didn't fight against us.

Nor had he fought *for* us. All those years, and he hadn't seen it as his responsibility to give the girls equal access to the big gym. Like many other men in positions of authority, he had not spoken up for women.

No group in power has ever handed equal status to the underprivileged group. It's up to the underprivileged group to demand it. To compete for it. To assert its right to its fair share. To refuse to remain second-class citizens.

If you can't do it for yourself, do it for all the high school girls or grade-school girls or daughters or nieces or neighbors who are looking up to you, who are watching to see if you'll stand up for them, for women's rights. They're wondering if they're as valued as the boys, as worthy. They're wondering if they too should settle for second best. They need you to show them the way.

Chapter 27

Forgive Yourself Immediately
for All Mistakes

"To raise a child well one ought not try to be a perfect parent, much as one should not expect one's child to be, or to become, a perfect individual," writes psychiatrist Bruno Bettelheim in *A Good Enough Parent*. "Perfection is not within the grasp of ordinary human beings." Instead, Bettelheim says, parents should strive to be "good enough."[1]

I find this "good enough" principle helpful in competitive situations. When you risk competing, you're going to fail sometimes, so give yourself a break. Decide that you were, given your effort and your talent and the other circumstances that kept you from being perfect, good enough.

In other words, forgive yourself immediately for all mistakes. This is something I learned on the basketball court. During a basketball game everyone makes mistakes. Turnovers, missed shots, and fouls are part of the game. Remember that kid in junior high who scored in the wrong basket? Some errors are worse than others, but basketball teaches you to forgive yourself. Maybe you steal a ball and dribble furiously, the basket just ahead, like a promise. But something goes wrong, and you bounce the ball too hard off the glass. It ricochets into the eager hands of an opponent. The crowd groans. You might want to hang your head in shame, but you can't. There's no time. Nor can you chase after the rebounder and foul her. You have to sprint back downcourt and play good defense. That's all. If you don't do that, you're making two mistakes. Basketball is like that, very swift.

Life is like that too. It flies by quickly, and for every moment you spend regretting what happened or punishing yourself for your mistakes, you're missing the next present moment. You can *learn* from mistakes, but there's no time to get mad at yourself about them. You have to sprint back downcourt, ready for life's next adventure, whatever that may be.

Perfection is not within the grasp of ordinary human beings. Strive for excellence, but when you inevitably fall short, forgive yourself immediately. Think of basketball. Tell yourself, "Hustle back downcourt!" I say this to myself all the time, especially when I start to feel foolish about some stupid thing I've said or done. It's amazing how well it works. It's amazing what can happen when you offer yourself a little tenderness. When you remind yourself that, win or lose, you're good enough.

Chapter 28

Be Willing to Lose

E leanor Smeal, political organizer and the president of the Feminist Majority Foundation, traveled around the country recently to recruit record numbers of women to run for public office. She gave hundreds of speeches as part of a Feminization of Power Campaign. "Invariably a question would be asked about losing," she recalls. "What would happen if you lose? Would it ruin you?

"You have to risk loss," she told her audiences. "If you say, 'I must win every time I run,' then surely you will not run."

Sometimes politicians actually plan a defeat, knowing that this campaign will put them in the pipeline for the next race. "There are very few politicians who didn't lose," Smeal notes. "George Bush ran three times and lost before he won. Clinton had a major loss in 1982, then came back to win. So losing isn't a big deal. It's part of the process of competing. It's no disgrace."

You can also win with a loss, Smeal explains. "If you run and lose, you're no longer a volunteer. You're a leader, a person with a constituency. Jesse Jackson won only nineteen percent of the vote when he ran for President, but the election increased his stature. It shows you have a following. People begin to look at you differently. It gives you name recognition."

Smeal puts it to her audiences this way: "Playing the game makes you a player. Being on the sidelines cheering for others makes you a cheerleader. Which would you rather do, play or cheer?" Once women think about it that way, "the fear of losing decreases," says Smeal.

She quotes Eleanor Roosevelt: "You must do the thing you think you cannot do." She also reminds women to "analyze victories and defeats. Not to lay blame or heap praise, but to see what actually happened so you can improve your performance and find model steps for the future."

When the *America³* set sail in the 1995 America's Cup with the first-ever all-female crew, billionaire boat owner Bill Koch's goals were to draw attention to yachting, to show the world that women could compete on an equal basis with men, and, of course, to win. "The point, always, is to win, and he thought an all-female team could do it," said crew member Dawn Riley.[1] The fact that the crew was female was essential to the initial concept of success.

But when the crew lost most of its preliminary races, Koch replaced starting helmsman J. J. Isler with a man, David Dellenbaugh. It was a controversial decision that many observers believed undermined the unique all-female concept. The crew members themselves grappled with which was more important: Maintaining the integrity of the all-female team or improving their chance of winning the championship, which was, after all, the stated goal of the competition. One crew member told the San Diego *Union*, "If we were going to lose, let us lose with the dignity of what we had accomplished. We knew what we were trying to do, and that's pretty much been trashed."[2]

They lost anyway, as it turned out, but many people were impressed with how well they had done and how close they had come to winning. They still seemed like Champions.

Paradoxically, some of this nation's most beloved women are losers in the traditional sense, women who have been defeated. They're loved or admired because they risked defeat, because they edged all of us closer to success, or because they pursued victory with style and courage.

Anita Hill, for instance, inspired thousands of women to come forward with sexual harassment complaints despite the fact that the Senate Judiciary Committee treated her disgracefully and voted to confirm her alleged harasser, Supreme Court Justice Clarence Thomas.

Joycelyn Elders, fired from her job as the surgeon general after she acknowledged that children masturbate, has become a popular speaker on the lecture circuit.

Former Los Angeles County deputy district attorney Marcia Clark could not convict O. J. Simpson of murder, but to many she became a Champion anyway. Clark "did not fail," Kate Rounds writes in *Ms.* magazine, which named Clark a 1996 Woman of the Year. "When she came to taking hits she was by herself. And she took them with dignity and courage . . . She was angry but never irresolute, and it was this toughness that you wanted to bottle for your own future use. At a time when it's popular to seek the inner child, Clark always seems to be seeking the inner grown-up, the one we'd like to be if we, too, could be stalwart, tenacious, and strong."[3]

Lorraine Adams, in a *Washington Post* article titled "The Fight of Her Life: Marcia Clark—Working Mother and O. J. Simpson Lead Prosecutor—Takes Her Place Among Other Maligned, Adored, and Misunderstood Modern Women," approvingly quoted Clark's former boss, Deputy Los Angeles District Attorney John Lynch, as saying, "Marcia, if she beat you in Jeopardy, she'd want to beat you at tiddlywinks. She is competitive, openly competitive. In fact, Marcia's one of the most competitive people I've ever met."[4]

Shannon Faulkner was also saluted as a Champion, even after she quit The Citadel. While some young women condemned her for not being physically fit, older women rushed to her support. Kathleen Brown, for instance, who knows something about defeat from having lost her bid for California governor, said Shannon had scored a victory. "It's not unlike a woman running for governor," she said. "It's

not unlike a woman who breaks through a glass ceiling and gets somewhere no one has gotten before. Even if you run and lose, you've
paved the way." Brown added that women feel an extra burden "that
if we fail, we're failing for all women. No man ever feels that if they
fail, they're failing for all men."[5]

Susan B. Anthony said, "Failure is impossible," and she was right,
but this is true too: Failure is inevitable. She who competes loses.
She who competes eventually notices that failure is part of what happens on the way to success. Linda Stoick, a San Francisco lawyer and
former college and pro basketball player, says, "Many women in law
or business become devastated when they lose. Their whole self-
esteem is wrapped up in being competent. It's important to learn that
winning and losing are all part of the system."

University of Virginia sport psychologist and associate dean
Linda Bunker says, "Everyone I know in business and industry and
sport has sought opportunities to lose. I think of it as seeking an
opportunity to grow and to learn, but I don't know how you do that
without failure. That's the bottom line: You have to be willing to
lose.

"If I lose, I have a sense of disappointment, but I would never
get better without that competition. So at first I might be sad, but
then I focus on what I can learn. Is it something that I had control
over? If not, I try not to worry about it. If so, maybe next time I can
make a different choice."

Melanee Wagener Atkinson, a six-foot five-inch center, wanted
desperately to win a national championship with her University of
Virginia basketball team. In her sophomore, junior, and senior years,
her team made it to the Final Four (the tournament for the country's
top four teams). But each time they failed to win the championship.
After they lost again in her senior year, Melanee's spirits spiraled
downward, and she "felt depressed and angry," she says, for more
than a year.

Is something wrong with this picture? Shouldn't someone have
helped her see herself as successful, despite not having reached her

ultimate goal? She was, after all, one of the country's best college basketball players.

Robert Rotella, the sport psychologist who worked with Melanee's team, says of her response to the final defeat, "It wasn't a clinical depression. It was a disappointment. That's going to happen when you dedicate yourself to a goal and sacrifice a lot to get there. Parents often say they hate to see their kid get disappointed. I ask why. Don't you want them to feel? To experience life? To go for what they want? I tell them, 'If you don't want your kid to get disappointed, have the kid set really low goals.'"

A year later Melanee began serving as assistant basketball coach at American University, in Washington, D.C. "I've refocused my goals," she says. "Now I'd like to win a championship as a coach."

Losing hurts. Even if you're only competing against yourself, you can suffer the heartbreak of defeat. Sometimes solitude makes it worse since there's no one there to offer comfort.

But competition is like romance: If you care a lot, it's going to hurt sometimes. Most of us don't resolve: "I'll never fall in love again." (Or we sing that song for a while, then soon change the tune.) We risk loving again because the process of loving and being loved is worth the risk of loss.

Like ex-lovers, losses need to be mourned. Terry Porter competed in the 1976 Olympics in cross-country skiing and finished fortieth out of forty-four contestants. In the subsequent years she did a lot of grieving, she says, letting go of her dreams of Olympic glory and eventually letting go of competitive skiing altogether. Now she works as an adventure therapist at a psychiatric hospital in Vermont and helps retired athletes recognize and transfer their assets, such as confidence, perseverance, focus, and self-knowledge, to other aspects of life. She's especially committed to helping "empowered female athletes" become "empowered females in every aspect of life." An important part of the process, she says, is "grief work," though "it's amazing how taboo that seems to be."

Losses can be transformed into something educational, useful, inspirational, even spiritual. You forgive yourself for not winning all the time. You begin to feel grateful for the opportunity to compete. You move on.

Oprah Winfrey, in a commencement address at Wellesley College in 1997, warned the graduates that they will fail but told them, "I have learned that failure is really God's way of saying, 'Excuse me, you're moving in the wrong direction.' "[6]

Says retired Gannett executive Madelyn Jennings: "Probably the characteristic that has made me the most successful is resiliency. I once went through a divorce and typhoid fever concurrently and was able to maintain standards on my job. Resiliency is very much a part of competitiveness. When you lose, you have to pick yourself up and try again. Have you ever met a successful person who gave up when they lost? I don't think I have. It's a cliché, but even the good baseball players only bat three hundred. It helps to remember that."

Allow losing to make you stronger. Accept defeat as part of the game. Know that you can become wiser and stronger by observing what your opponents are doing right. Trust that other opportunities for success will present themselves. Search for some sort of meaning in the loss, even if it's only to make you appreciate your victories even more.

Search too for the advantages to losing. Like winning, losing can offer new opportunities: personal growth, professional development, useful perspectives you couldn't see before the competition began. Also, losers get to relax, recede, regroup. Sometimes losing is a relief.

There are ways to feel like a Champion regardless of the outcome. This is not just a strategy for protecting fragile egos from the truth. It's a method for staying positive and being gentle with yourself that will make you more likely to succeed (and be happy) in the future. Offer yourself praise for what you have accomplished. Interpret the effort itself as success. Interpret a personal best as success. Even if you drop out of a competition, congratulate yourself for accurately reassessing the situation and learning that you're not yet ready to compete in that arena.

It's tricky, though: striving for victory, feeling like a Champion, expecting to win, then—whoa!—losing. It's too late then to pretend, even to yourself, that you didn't want to win. You can look for the advantages to losing and you can reinterpret losing as a victory of some sort, but it's still going to hurt.

My friend Kimberly Carter and I joke about big losses by responding with "Oh, well!" It's not that we actually feel nonchalant about professional defeats or divorces or other major disappointments. The understated "oh, well!" just makes us laugh and lightens our moods. Laughter is a great healer. You tried your best, but someone else got the job, the bid, the invitation, the lover. You can't win 'em all. Oh, well!

Chapter 29

Notice When You're Competing
and When Others
Are Competing with You

M uch unhappiness, it seems to me, stems from a vague sense
that we're losing some contest we didn't even realize we'd entered. If we become aware of when we're competing, with whom, and
why, we can move beyond that sense of failure and make wise decisions about what to do.

Say you're angry with someone who's looking gorgeous or thriving
at work. Maybe you're feeling one down, resenting his or her beauty
or success and feeling defeated somehow. You don't have to continue
feeling uneasy around perceived competitors. You don't have to keep
disliking them or avoiding them. Ask yourself: Do you want to achieve
what they're achieving? Do you want to acquire what they possess?
Do you want to look how they look? Do you value their way of being?
In other words, do you want to compete? Or are you feeling one
down reflexively, on the basis of some old cultural conditioning? Use
your feelings as a values clarification exercise, to figure out what you
want. If, upon reflection, you determine that you do want to compete,
then go for it: Take action that will lead you to succeed, on the basis

of your definition of success. If, on the other hand, you're feeling one down only because someone reminds you of your mother or because you've slipped into the Cheerleader role and are feeling pressure to be perkier or prettier (or younger-looking or thinner) than someone else, let it go. Choose not to compete. That's not easy: to stop feeling inferior, to stop competing in futile ways that make you feel bad about yourself. But it's amazing how inappropriate competitions can dissipate once you understand the source of your feelings.

You might also be feeling one up. Sometimes competitive comparisons reassure us that we're winning, that we're not such failures after all. Yet this can also feel bad. Why be happy to learn that someone else earns less money or suffered a professional or personal loss? My advice on this one: Forgive yourself. It's natural to compare and okay to feel proud. It doesn't mean you actually want your friends and colleagues to fail. As with the one down feelings, the one up feelings can simply point you toward your values. If it's important to you to "win" in some unspoken contest over, say, popularity, then popularity is important to you—maybe more important than you're willing to admit. Maybe you've felt hurt or left out or unpopular in the past and need to know you're appreciated. That's not so awful, that's just human. Maybe you'll trace your desire to some deeper, older "need" to win in a contest involving siblings or parents or even the male-dominated culture in general. After you become aware of the source, you might be able to let it go.

What if you're certain that someone else is competing with *you*? There's a good chance that you're projecting your own competitive feelings onto that person. You're probably competing with him or her—not consciously and not successfully.

Or maybe the person is competing with you. If so, consider it a compliment. You must be doing something appealing. Try not to feel threatened or resentful. Others have every right to compete, as do you. Think of it this way: People are looking up to you. Try to offer them someone worth emulating.

Chapter 30

Pay Attention to the Process

M ountain climber and novelist Gwen Moffat has said, "Being at the top of the mountain or at the top of anything is not particularly interesting, but the process of getting there is."[1]

The process of competing can be fascinating. Analyzing why you won or lost can be engaging. Planning how and when and whether to compete again can be compelling. It's hard to remember any of that in a society that rewards results, not process.

Winners focus on excellence, on doing what it takes to excel. Olympian and physician Stuart H. Walker points out in *Winning: The Psychology of Competition*, "Winning is not the main concern of most competitors. Few actually win; few would compete if winning were their primary motivation. (Indeed, one could make a far stronger case for losing as a primary motivation.)"[2] What winners focus on is not victory itself but the daily details that they hope will lead to victory.

The American Coaching Effectiveness Program (ACEP), a national certification and training program for coaches, uses this motto: "Athletes first, winning second." Instructors train coaches to de-emphasize winning in favor of skill development, teamwork, injury prevention, and enjoyment. "Paradoxically, our coaches win more than other coaches," says Katie Donovan, former director of training for ACEP. "If you focus less on winning, you focus more on the things you need to do to win."

The danger of focusing only on winning is stated nowhere better than in the Chinese Taoist Chuang-tsu's enduring poem from about 300 B.C.:

THE NEED TO WIN

When an archer is shooting for nothing
He has all his skill.
If he shoots for a brass buckle
He is already nervous.
If he shoots for a prize of gold
He goes blind
Or sees two targets—
He is out of his mind!

His skill has not changed. But the prize
Divides him. He cares.
He thinks more of winning
Than of shooting—
And the need to win
Drains him of power.

So think of shooting arrows, or hammering nails, or selling insurance, or whatever it is that you do. Practice conscious competition, paying attention to the process. Think more about excellence than about victory. Think more about the present than the future. Think of winning and losing as just part of the life journey, not ends in themselves. "The joy of winning," Chris Evert once said, "lasts about an hour." The joy of playing tennis, however—or involving yourself fully in your passion—can last as long as you're willing to pay attention to the process.

Chapter 31

Engage in Victory Talk

"It is precisely because women have, for so long, been constrained from expressing their competitive strivings cleanly and clearly that they can become distorted into the kind of petty rivalries, jealousies, and envy that sometimes infect their relationships with each other," writes Lillian B. Rubin in *Just Friends: The Role of Friendship in Our Lives*. "As a psychotherapist, I believe one of my tasks is to help women to contact their competitive strivings more directly and to express them more openly."[1]

Women often relate to each other through "troubles talk," Georgetown University linguist Deborah Tannen has observed. Writer Naomi Wolf (in *Fire with Fire*) says women need to tell each other their successes as well as their failures. "If what Tannen calls 'troubles talk' is an accepted way for women to bond, that's not so bad; but if 'victory talk' is taboo, women have no comfortable framework for presenting their resources or skills to one another in a way that leads to consolidating political or economic power."[2]

Athletes are more likely than nonathletes to discuss competition, according to my survey, but only 32 percent of athletes and only 12 percent of nonathletes report that they "always or frequently discuss competitiveness with friends, family, or co-workers." The majority in both groups say they rarely or never discuss it. Several women wrote such comments as "I never talk about this!" and "We need to talk about these issues!"

In her women's therapy groups, "my patients rarely talk about it," reports Sarah Burton Nelson, the psychiatrist who happens to be my mother. "I bring it up. Everyone jumps up and says, 'I'm not competitive!' They look at me as if I'm accusing them of something that isn't true. The only acceptable behavior is not to be competitive, so they won't look at it in themselves."

With whom should you talk about victory? With whom should you discuss competitive feelings and behaviors? If you raise the subject of competition (including who is winning, who would like to be winning, who feels one down), you have to be ready to hear things you don't want to hear: that you're egotistical, that you're too competitive, that you want the wrong things. You have to be willing to admit feelings that I call toady frogs: ugly, embarrassing, slimy little things like envy, greed, or a desire for fame or fortune or simple attention.

You might begin by talking to friends and family members about competitions that do not involve them. Ask these people to support you in your goals and ambitions. Choose people who seem to understand competition, who use the word "compete" in a positive or neutral way, who can comfortably converse about competition in a job setting or academic setting or athletic setting.

Talking with opponents is trickier. You don't necessarily want to show them your toady frogs. The smart tennis player doesn't announce, "Gee, I wonder if I can keep up with you." Nor will she say, "I've got a weak backhand." She wants to hide her weaknesses as much as possible. She will, however, tell her practice partner, so they can work on that weak backhand together.

Sarah Burton Nelson advises against telling opponents that you feel competitive with them. If your perception is that you're winning, announcing that to the "loser" would be rude. If you feel as if you're losing and "you tell a friend you want what she has, you put her in an awkward, uncomfortable position," says Nelson. "She's not necessarily trying to compete with you at all, and she shouldn't have to apologize for having what she has, or doing what she does. It's not her fault. So it's unkind to tell her."

Your friend might also respond in hurtful ways. She might deliberately or inadvertently use your vulnerability against you, reminding you of your insecurity when you don't want to be reminded or treating you as if you still feel one down long after you've let it go.

There are times for such confessions, but these times must be carefully chosen. You must trust that the other person will neither hurt you nor feel burdened by your disclosure. You must sense that the other person is comfortable enough with her own competitive feelings that hearing yours will neither surprise nor threaten her.

I perused children's books at the Library of Congress to see if any offered girls useful advice on competition, and came across one in which Daisy Duck and Minnie Mouse openly discuss their feelings about competing with each other. In *I Want to Win* by Ruth Lerner Perle,[3] one spot opens up on a softball team, and Minnie Mouse decides to try out. Afraid that her friend Daisy Duck is better, Minnie asks Daisy not to try out. Daisy asserts her right to try out too. Three of their friends help both girls train but agonize over split loyalties. During the tryout Minnie keeps up with Daisy in throwing, catching, and batting contests. The three friends cheer for both of them. The contest comes down to one final foot race. Minnie wins. "I feel funny," Minnie tells Daisy. "I'm glad I won, but I'm sorry you lost."

"I feel funny too," Daisy responds. "I'm sorry I lost, but I'm glad you won."

Daisy shakes Minnie's hand. "Congratulations, Minnie," she says. "I tried my best, but you won fair and square. You're the lucky winner!"

Minnie responds: "You're right, Daisy. I am lucky, but it's because I have a friend like you."

Isn't that a sweet story? I think it is. And isn't it very much a *girls'* story in the best sense of the word: a successful integration of ambition and compassion? What makes their friendship succeed is that they create space for all their feelings. When Minnie asks Daisy not to try out, Daisy rejects the proposal without ridiculing Minnie for wanting what she wants. The three friends openly discuss their conflicting feelings about which girl to support, then find a way to support both of them. Everyone's allowed to feel ambivalent, but none of this complexity prevents them from pursuing their goals. The title's good too: *I Want to Win*. Nothing wrong with that.

Champions need to engage in victory talk. We need to discover ways to discuss competition that are optimistic and affirming. We need to offer support without censure and congratulations without criticism. We need to figure out when and how and to whom to reveal our competitive desires, finding new ways to say, "I feel funny," while also insisting, "I want to win."

Chapter 32

Decide When to Compete and When Not To

No one competes all the time. Or, rather, no one should compete all the time. Hence the Champion, who competes well, also chooses sometimes not to compete. She makes conscious decisions about when to compete and when not to based on an honest assessment of her own abilities and desires. She might, for example, choose not to compete in order to preserve a relationship. "Everything shouldn't be a confrontation," says retired Gannett executive Madelyn Jennings. "That's not in the best interests of your company. I know a person who does a lot of negotiations. He is so competitive he always has to win, even though he has turned off some vendors. That has probably cost his company money. He doesn't realize that sometimes the other fellow has to win. You might want to work with those vendors again."

Sometimes not competing is appropriate if the playing field is unequal. Sarah Presley, a Washington, D.C., computer programmer who has been blind since she was young, says, "My father pushed me to achieve because he didn't want me to be a shy, retiring blind person. It's why I've accomplished what I have, but I wish I didn't need the competitiveness in order to excel. It puts too much pressure on me. Like at work, all other things being equal, sighted people are going to be faster than I am. That's just the way it is. Even though I know intellectually that just being my own best is enough, I'm still upset if I'm not the best." Sarah also discounts her computer-programming skills because "lots of blind people are computer programmers." She sees her recent two-year stint with the Peace Corps in Morocco as "more of an accomplishment because not too many blind people do that."

You might choose not to compete when your competitors behave in ways that are distasteful to you. "Some tennis players are cutthroat, renowned for making bad line calls," notes University of Virginia associate dean Linda Bunker. "If I have to play them in a tournament situation, it makes me work harder to win, but generally I'll avoid playing them. Sometimes I avoid a professional situation because of how it's structured. I used to go to conferences where they'd try to nail the speaker. Eventually I quit going."

There are times to compete and times not to compete. Times to win and times to lose. Times to be a team player and times to go it alone. Decisions about when to compete and when not to must be made repeatedly, because situations change.

Competitive situations are the most problematic when we think that we must compete or that we can't. But even in a situation that is structured noncompetitively, you can find a way to create a competitive challenge, whether with others or yourself. Even after you start competing, you can almost always quit.

Even in a situation that is structured competitively, "you don't have to play that game," says University of Pittsburgh professor Mary Duquin. Duquin refuses to compete against her colleagues. "I'm setting my own standards, doing my own work, producing what I produce, period. I'm letting the boss set up the structure, do the reward thing."

Linda Villarosa, executive editor of *Essence* magazine, played basketball and ran track in high school, then played three years of competitive soccer at the University of Colorado. She still plays soccer three times a week. She describes herself as a competitive person.

"One of the skills I bring to my work here at *Essence* is being competitive. We're competitive with the black magazines and the women's service magazines: *Glamour, New Woman, Redbook, McCall's.* Also, I'm big on entering contests. I work in an all-women's office, and sometimes I tell the other women they should be more competitive than they are."

But Villarosa chooses not to compete out of solidarity with her black sisters. Her book, *Body and Soul: The Black Women's Guide to Physical Health and Emotional Well-Being,* was published by Harper Perennial in 1994, the same year that Evelyn C. White's book, *The Black Women's Health Book: Speaking for Ourselves,* was re-released from Seal Press.

"People kept setting it up as a competition," Villarosa recalls. "They'd ask me, 'Are you two feuding?'

"No. Why should we feud? We're allies. We support each other. I'm not jealous. I need her. Evelyn C. White is a health activist. She was one of the first women to talk about health issues from a personal, political, and journalistic perspective, in the spirit of *Our Bodies, Ourselves.* Definitely the first black woman to do it. Her book was first published in 1990, and it's good, so I asked her to write a section of my book. We respected each other's work. In fact we became good friends. Then her book was re-released just as mine was coming out, but I never felt competitive. She didn't either. They were different books. When I mention my book, I almost always say that hers was one of several inspirations for it."

If she were to feel competitive with another author, Villarosa says, "it would be with a white author. There are so few of us black women working as journalists, especially within the narrow field of health, there's really no room for being competitive. It's harmful. It's not good for this movement. We need to support each other."

Some women choose not to compete in certain arenas because they have been damaged by negative competitive experiences. Gale Burgess, a pseudonym for a free-lance writer, says, "I've been skiing since I was two. I'm an expert skier. I ski the steepest terrain available.

You have to make the turns correctly, or you'll slam into trees and rocks." But she no longer competes. "I don't like to compete. I always lost. I started racing at age eleven, but I was really bad for many years. I hated my body; I hated myself. I was painfully self-conscious and wanted everyone's approval. I heard negative voices in my head— 'You suck, you suck'—every time I'd go out on skis. But I really wanted to master this thing.

"In college I raced at the NCAA Division I level for two years, then quit. I never won. Our coach was terrible. She gave attention only to the winners. If I'd had the coach's encouragement, maybe the experience would have been enjoyable despite the fact that I was a consistent loser."

There were twelve members on her college team, but only five competed in races. Gale was number six. She and the other substitutes didn't compete unless someone was sick or injured. "When I did get to compete I finished dead last. For me competition became equated with negative self-worth."

After she quit racing, she accepted a job as a ski instructor. One day she was skiing in the woods with an older instructor, a poet. When they stopped, he looked around and said, "Wow, isn't this just beautiful out here!" Suddenly Gale "got it that there was this joy factor running through it all. From that moment on, my level of accomplishment skyrocketed. Now I embrace the 'feminine' principle of harmony with the mountain. My feet caress the earth. It's such a rush!"

Rosalie Hedlund, physical education professor at Ottawa University in Ottawa, Kansas, developed a course called Nontraditional Team Sports in which students must decide what games to play, what the rules are, how rules will be enforced, how to choose teams, and whether to keep score.[1] She requires them to keep a journal in which they "meaningfully reflect" on what happens in each class. It's a model I recommend in nonsport settings as well. By making conscious decisions about when and how to compete, and by writing or otherwise noting your own responses to various competitive and noncompetitive situations, you'll learn a lot about competition—and yourself.

When should you compete, and when shouldn't you? Some people compete only if they can win. Others compete only if they can "make a good showing" or not make fools of themselves. Others don't mind looking foolish and enjoy competing in virtually any arena. When deciding whether to compete, here are some questions to consider:

1. What's in it for you? Compete if you value the process, the potential rewards for success, or both. Regardless of whether you win or lose, might the process offer you valuable experience, important contacts, or a pleasurable challenge? Is it worth the risk to find out? If you do win, will you gain something you want: prestige, profit, self-esteem, or opportunities?

2. What's in it for others? If you compete, might your participation assist your teammates or advance your favorite causes or encourage the people who look to you for leadership? Is there some way in which, through your participation, others will win? Or is it important *not* to compete as a show of solidarity for people or causes you want to support?

3. What's your motivation? Are you competing to achieve a goal? To pursue excellence? For fun? Because you'd like to be number one? To demonstrate dominance or supremacy over someone you'd like to belittle?

4. Is the competition worthwhile? Is this an activity to which you care to devote your time and energy? Is it in keeping with your values?

5. How will you feel if you lose? Will you be devastated or merely disappointed? Can you cope with defeat?

6. What would constitute success? Is it achievable? Is there a way to frame the competition so you can feel successful, win or lose?

7. Who are your opponents? The most enjoyable competitions are between near equals so that the one who's slightly superior is challenged and the one who's slightly inferior has a chance to win. But you might also choose to compete with people who are far more experienced than you are. In these cases your chances for success will be fewer, but you can learn a lot by competing with the best.

8. What are the costs of winning? If you're competing against an intimate partner, is it a game? Is it all in fun? Or is there a potential for the loser to feel deeply wounded? In an article entitled "Ten Rules for Success in Marriage," Eleanor Roosevelt wrote, "Let neither husband nor wife strive to be the dominating person in the household. A victory for either means failure for the partnership." If you want the relationship to "win," you'll want to compete only in ways that amuse the two of you or strengthen the dyad. You might also be wise not to compete with your children— except when it's clearly all in fun.

9. What are the rules? Are you willing to abide by them? Can they be changed or broken without violating your code of ethics?

10. Are you having fun yet? Is there any way to adjust your attitude so you can have a good time, regardless of the outcome?

If none of these guidelines help you resolve the "to compete or not to compete" question, try doing something different. If you usually compete, back off. If you usually avoid competition, go for it. What's to lose? At the very least, you'll learn a new way of looking at the world.

Chapter 33

Define Victory and Loss
for Yourself

"Sometimes when you think you win, you haven't really won," says Rosie Perez in the film *White Men Can't Jump*. Perez is talking to her boyfriend, a basketball player and compulsive gambler played by Woody Harrelson. "And sometimes when you think you've lost, you haven't really lost. And sometimes when you tie, you've actually either won or lost."

Harrelson responds, "I hate it when you talk like that."

Winning and losing can seem mutually exclusive, but Champions understand this complexity. Sometimes when you think you've won, you haven't really won because you've lost the love or support of a man or woman who is threatened by your success. Sometimes when you think you've lost, you haven't really lost because you've won the self-esteem or admiration of others that can come from simply entering a competitive arena. Sometimes when you tie, it's actually a victory because everyone feels victorious or actually a loss because everyone feels defeated.

Victory and loss have a yin/yang relationship that many women seem to understand intuitively. If you win, someone else will lose. If you win one thing, you will lose an opportunity to do something else. If you win and everyone else loses, you might lose too because others won't want to play with you anymore. If you win by diminishing them, you might lose their friendship or respect.

Rosemary Partridge, a minister from Northern California, says "Sometimes winning means losing in the big picture. In an argument with a loved one, one could 'win' a point but lose closeness or intimacy. And vice versa. Sometimes what appears as losing is actually a win—perhaps in terms of growth experiences or even a blessing in disguise."

In early sport psychology studies, researchers equated winning with success and losing with failure. If someone won, they assumed that person felt successful. They assumed losers felt disappointed. Eventually researchers learned to ask competitors about their own perceptions of success and failure since as it turns out, some winners feel bad about their performance and some losers feel relieved, satisfied, or downright gleeful. The silver medalist who "almost won" might feel far more disappointed than the bronze medalist who almost missed winning any medal at all.

Gloria Solomon, an assistant professor of physical education at Texas Christian University, says, "As people enter into a contest, they should have realistic goals for that event, and those goals shouldn't even deal with winning. I play tennis, for example, and I want to walk off feeling great every time I compete. I usually know who my competition is, and what kind of game they have, so I set reasonable but challenging goals. If I meet those goals, I'll feel good about my performance, regardless of who wins. I try to teach my students about that, and they look at me like I'm this idealistic, out-of-touch professor. Athletes especially have a hard time embracing this concept. The coach is on their backs, saying, 'You have to win, you have to win.' I say, 'If you're not having fun, let's try something else.'"

As a professor, Solomon says, "I don't compete with my colleagues about manuscripts getting published. But I'm very competitive within myself to be productive. How most people interpret competition is how masculine society has defined it. I try to teach people to redefine it for themselves."

Wanda Oates, a teacher and coach in Washington, D.C.'s Ballou High School since 1965, won fourteen league titles in soccer, softball, and basketball as well as notoriety for being one of the first women in the country to coach boys' basketball. She recently ran for the District's Board of Education and finished fifth of fourteen at-large candidates. The top two were elected. "I don't ever lose," she says. "I've never lost a fight, ever. You have a victory in everything you do. It's how you look at it. In the election eighteen thousand people voted for me. That's a victory. I do have disappointments, but I very seldom get upset. It takes too much energy to be upset. I try to turn all negative things into positive things. The more positive you are, the happier you are."

Sportswriter Jill Lieber finished 1,282 out of 1,288 competitors in her first Ironman World Triathlon Championship in 1996. "I learned that it's okay not to be No. 1 at everything," she later wrote in *USA Today*. "In fact, at the Ironman, it means a lot more to finish at the back of the pack."[1]

Some of the ways we define victory and loss are influenced by our cultural and racial roots. John C. Walter, a professor of African-American studies at the University of Washington, has studied black women athletes and concludes that in general they define victory differently from white women athletes. "For white women, victory means equality with white men," says Walter. "Black women don't foresee equality with white men anytime soon. And they don't have equality with white women. So they have different criteria to measure success. They hope that their achievements on the playing field will set an example for their children. Not that white women don't care about their children, but black women seem to invest a lot of hope for the future in their children. And they think in terms of the community, more than individual achievement. They hope that by triumphing over the odds, their laudable victories will reflect well on the black community. This is very different from the individualistic, how-much-money-can-I-get-from-my-gold-medal sort of approach of many white women."

Define for yourself what it means to succeed, what it means to fail. Find the meaning in the competition, whether that meaning is personal or communal. If you look for the victory in each defeat and acknowledge the loss in each victory, you'll notice that your definition of success becomes more fluid and more friendly. You don't have to define victory by the final score, by the financial tally, by whether you got what you wanted. You can—and should, I believe—define victory according to your own aspirations, your own beliefs, and your own need to feel positive about any competitive experience. Once it's clear that victory and loss are two sides of the same coin, neither one seems so impressive, or permanent, or overwhelming. Chris Evert has said, "If you can react the same way to winning and losing, that's a big accomplishment."

Chapter 34

Decide What Rules to Play By

We're such good girls. We're so obedient, so ready to follow the rules, to do it right. But trying to do it right can be part of the problem. It can keep us stuck in a system that was not designed to embrace female victory. Who made up the rules? Why are we so eager to follow them?

Champions decide for themselves what rules to play by. It's something kids used to learn in neighborhood games when, without interference by adult coaches and referees, they established rules to meet the needs and desires of the players. If seven kids happened to show up, they played three-on-four basketball. They permitted Gabby, who had cerebral palsy and used a wheelchair, to play first base. They invented scads of new games. They tried to make things fair: If one team was much better, the good team would offer the other team some players or a head start. Children can be cruel, it is often observed, but children also devise rules to include people and to create balanced competitions.

Girls who were excluded from these neighborhood games, as many of us were, learned what it's like to be left out and perhaps became more compassionate and inclusive of others as a result. Those who did play learned that we too can change the rules.

Maya Townsend, a Washington, D.C., organizational development consultant who calls herself "very competitive," has learned to get creative with rules, depending on her objectives. "In my family we play these killer games of Risk. All that matters is winning. Usually my brother ends up crying, leaving the game. I sulk. My mother won't play. This year my brother and I teamed up and 'killed' my father and my cousin. You're not allowed to team up in Risk, or at least no one does it. I'm not sure it's explicitly forbidden in the rules, but it's not done. Each person is against each other person, and you're supposed to 'kill' everyone and take over the world. But we called a truce with each other and beat my father and cousin. Then, when it was just the two of us left, we decided the game was over."

In Scrabble, Townsend also changes the rules to suit her needs. "I want to keep score, but I also want to see how many interesting words I can come up with, even if they don't make a lot of points. Or how many openings I can create for others. I'm interested in the intersection of competition and conflict resolution. How to achieve win-win solutions."

You can modify rules—in board games, at work, at home, in the political arena. You won't necessarily win that way, but you won't win by playing by the traditional rules either. Remember, the original rules stipulated that women can't vote, can't speak in public, can't own property, can't seek divorce, can't wear "men's" clothes, can't attend medical school. Where would we be if we hadn't broken those rules?

So your children play on a baseball team where the rule is "Three strikes and you're out," but they come home crying because they didn't hit the ball? Change the rules. Allow everyone to bat until everyone gets a hit. Have parents pitch to the kids so the ball is more likely to go over the plate. Or set up two games: one field where the kids play by traditional rules, counting strikes and keeping score, and another field where the kids play by alternative rules, with no strike-outs and no scorekeeping. Have all the kids play on both fields, and lead them in a discussion afterward of what they think about rules and competition.

There's no reason why you can't do these things. Other parents have. Analyze when competition is working and when it's not, with feedback from the kids. Adjust the rules to accomplish your goals— in this case so the kids develop an enjoyment for sport and an appreciation of their own abilities while they practice competing in a safe, supportive setting.

You don't have to compete to win. You can play your own game or walk away from the game entirely. You don't have to compete the way men expect you to compete. You can compete to make things close and interesting; you can compete to help other people win. You can create competitions that are unique, suited to fit your needs. Men made up most of the existing rules, and they change them as they please. No reason women can't change the rules too. In fact we must.

Chapter 35

Decide Who Your Teammates Are
and Cheer for Them—Especially
When You're on the Bench

Administrator Connie Todd has two sisters. When they were growing up, they all were good-looking, but one sister, Judy, was exceptionally pretty and won beauty contests. She was also valedictorian. Their mother gave Judy a lot of attention, Connie recalls, but in response Judy would point to Connie's accomplishments with pride. Then Connie would praise the third sister, Charlene. From this supportive environment Todd learned that "sometimes it's important to let someone else shine. At work sometimes I feel a need to lay back a little bit, to be in the background. If I am constantly put up as the winner, then that can affect the team spirit. So much of competition has to do with helping everybody to win."

It's this generosity of spirit that athletes find within themselves; at least, the best ones do. Camille Duvall, the five-time world water skiing champion, names as her best friend the skier who was the five-time runner-up to Camille. That woman, Canadian Susie Graham, finally defeated Camille in their sixth world championship. "Of course I really wanted to win another year," recalls Duvall. "But I lost in the semifinals, and she got a bye. Then she won. So we never got a chance to compete head to head. And she got that bye, and I didn't. Still, even under those circumstances, I was happy for her."

Michelle Akers was long considered the best soccer player in the world. Now most people give that title to her teammate Mia Hamm. "I think that's great," says Akers. "For ten years, between 1985 and 1995, I shouldered the growth of women's soccer. To share that now is extremely gratifying. When Mia's on fire, it's true, she's the best. It's not my goal to be the number one player in the world; it's my goal to be the best player I can be. At the same time don't count me out!"

Whose side are you on? Who are your teammates? Who supports you? Once you can answer these questions, competitive decisions become easier. It's not that you won't compete with your teammates—you probably will—but you'll support them in their efforts to succeed.

A teammate is someone you want to support, or should want to support, if you really think about it. He or she is someone whose work or politics or goals or even spiritual perspective are congruent with your own. Your teammates might be friends or family members or colleagues you respect or admire. They might be people who have similar values and ambitions. Let them know you appreciate their work or simply their way of being in the world. Join the religious, professional, or social organizations that promote those goals. Support these teammates with contributions of money, time, or votes.

Feminism is about nothing so much as teamwork: women working with other women, and with men, to benefit women. Supporting female organizations and politicians (or male politicians with a feminist agenda) is a way to say, "I want all women to win."

A superwoman mentality still leads many women to believe that it's a sign of weakness, or unattractive neediness, to accept assistance from others. But athletes learn to yell, "Help!" and to trust that when they do, their teammates will pitch in.

Athletes also learn to sit on the bench and cheer for one another, even when they themselves are out of the game. This is a difficult but essential part of being a Champion: actively supporting others, even when you're not having a good day or a good year yourself.

The 1996 Olympics will go down in American history as the year of the women's team. It was the teamwork of the softball and soccer and basketball players that excited the fans. The media tried to make a hero out of Kerri Strug for vaulting on her sprained ankle, but that's not what I heard people talking about for months afterward. "Did you see the soccer team?" they asked each other excitedly. "Did you see the gold medal softball game? Did you see the fabulous basketball players?" Even synchronized swimming, long a maligned sport largely because only women do it, gained new respect when it switched to a team format. The American synchro swimmers performed incredibly impressive routines en route to the gold.

The lesson of the 1996 Olympics is this: Form alliances with women. Amazing accomplishments are possible when diverse groups of women work together and trust each other. We need to learn to depend on each other, and be each other's mentors, as men have done for each other for years.

Some of us are so used to seeing women as rivals it's hard to see ourselves as teammates. Or, conversely, we expect too much of other women, getting angry if all women don't support us, even though not all men support us. Without team sport experience, many women don't know how to work together. They're uncomfortable with female leadership, afraid of domination, unfamiliar with intrateam rivalries.

Creating teams outside the sports setting can be difficult. We want to be supportive, but at times we feel envious and inferior. We're afraid of competition among women and between women and men. We want our allies to succeed but sometimes we fear we can't all win. We forget that if others win, we can learn from their success. If others blaze new trails for women, it becomes easier for us to succeed later.

Being a team player isn't easy. Sometimes you'll feel envious and insecure. You'll even hope others fail so you feel better about your-self—except their failure won't really make you feel better. What will make you feel better is stretching, extending yourself, reaching out to support the people who are ultimately your teammates. Sometimes that support simply means silently wishing them success.

Connie Todd says, "I wish women would say to each other, 'Okay, you may have won this time, but next time I'll do better.' Or, 'I'll be happy for you because I'm glad it was you, not someone else.' You have to make the effort to be happy for someone when that person has something you wish you had. Everybody can't be in first place all the time."

She adds, "All my life, older people have nurtured and encouraged and seen the better part of me. Older people have nothing to lose by lifting you up. Sometimes it's harder to get that from your peers."

College instructor Janet Gray recently edited an anthology of nineteenth-century American women poets (*She Wields a Pen*) for the University of Iowa Press. When her manuscript was at the publisher, she learned that a similar, much bigger anthology was in progress "by someone more distinguished than I," she says. The two editors became friends. "I started sharing things with her. She started asking me about things. A couple of poets I'd selected, she decided to include also."

The other editor "raised the issue of competition," recalls Gray, saying, " 'I don't want to poach on you,' or something like that. I had to sit with myself about this, had to think it through." Gray reminded herself that the two books were different. "What it amounted to was separating my own ego from what we were making. If she can use a poet I chose, it will make that poet available to more people. By addressing different audiences, we will expand the field that we're in. We are canonizing writers. It's not about me."

If she had had tenure or money riding on the project, Gray says, she might have felt more anxious. But she's "attracted to the team concept," though she is not an athlete, and has decided that this woman is on her team. "I like her a lot. It's really special to me that I've gotten to know her."

What if you know who your teammates are and still have trouble supporting them? What if you worry that they won't support you in return? When does that magnanimous spirit kick in? How confident do you have to be before you can fully support your teammates?

Actions can sprint ahead of feelings. Sometimes, if you support someone you admire, you begin to believe that there is plenty of support to go around. You begin to feel good about yourself. You begin to feel like someone who knows when to compete, when not to, and how to be a team player. And you begin to be that sort of person.

Keep in mind that winners need support too. A few years ago I was playing Monopoly with several female friends and found myself winning, amassing more red plastic hotels than anyone else. One player went bankrupt. We let her borrow money from the bank. She went bankrupt again. I gave her a fistful of little green houses. She went bankrupt again. Someone else loaned her money. Everyone was feeling sorry for this woman, scrambling to keep her in the game and, it seemed to me, eyeing my stacks of cash critically, as if in the process of winning I were doing something wrong. In a sense something *was* wrong: with the structure of the game. All of us wanted to continue to play together until the end. We didn't want anyone to suffer the double indignities of losing and being forced to drop out. We were changing the rules so everyone could keep playing—a fine idea. But when I told my friend Katie Donovan about this incident, she asked, "Who supported the winner?"

I heard a similar story from a woman whose daughter was elected student body president of the elementary school. "The girl who lost cried, and all of that girl's girlfriends cried. My daughter ended up crying too," she said.

"Who supported your daughter?" I asked.

"It didn't seem to occur to the other kids that she needed support," the woman answered.

Women and girls so readily come to the aid of losers. But how often do we encourage winners? How often do we celebrate the victories of our friends? Aren't such celebrations often undermined with pseudohumorous remarks like "You're so good [or successful or thin] that I hate you"? It's important to sympathize with losers and to help them as we can, but in fact life is a lot like political elections and Monopoly: Not everyone can win every time.

In some ways female winners need even more support than losers do because winners are exposed and scrutinized. Their actions are more public, so their risks are more public. They need to know that they're not alone, that they have teammates who appreciate their achievements.

A Champion does it all: supports the winners and the losers, asks for help for herself, and cheers for those she considers her teammates, even when she herself is sitting on the bench. She's a team player, not sacrificing her own goals for the sake of group harmony, but asserting her affiliation with others, her loyalty to them, and her willingness to work together.

When we think of each other as teammates, women benefit from a phenomenon we rarely even name: female bonding. When we think of men as teammates, we move beyond female or male bonding and simply support other people to be Champions, just as we hope they'll support us.

Sportscaster Robin Roberts says, "I get recognized on the street, in airports. Women come up to me and say thank you. At first I was puzzled. They're not necessarily in sports or journalism, maybe in business. Now I understand it. They're saying that I'm making it easier for them."

Chapter 36

Compete with Yourself

When I asked the women I surveyed to tell me whom they "generally compete with" (they could choose more than one answer), by far the most common response was "myself; my own standards and goals" (75 percent of all respondents). The other most frequently cited answers were friends (53 percent), people at work or school (48 percent), and family members (31 percent). Only 18 percent said they competed with "my spouse or significant other," 12 percent with images of women in the media, and 4 percent said they never competed.

Later in the survey I asked, "What advice would you offer women who have difficulty with competition?" I grouped the 757 written responses into seventeen categories. The category with the most responses was "Do your personal best." (Responses included such advice as "Go out and do your best"; "Not to worry! Be the best you can!"; "Just try as hard as you can"; "Be all you can be"; "Focus on your own goals"; and "Just compete with yourself.")[1]

What does it mean to compete with oneself? If you compete with yourself, who wins?

At the end of her long speed skating career Bonnie Blair said, "Ultimately you realize that you're always competing against yourself."

This was her case because for many years no woman came close to her. In practice she competed against men. In the Olympics and world championships "I was always trying to accomplish a personal best," she says, "always racing the clock." Asked about her best race, she mentions, of all things, the fifteen-hundred-meter race in the 1994 Olympics in which she finished fourth, just missing the bronze medal. "It was my first personal best since the 1988 Olympics. I had won gold in the five hundred and one thousand [in 1994], but that was the best I could be in the fifteen hundred. I couldn't be disappointed because I had skated faster than ever."

Unlike Bonnie Blair, most of us don't have to explain to reporters that what looked like a loss was really—because we were competing against our own standards—a win. In fact that's one advantage of competing with yourself: Usually it's private. If you lose, you do not face public humiliation. No one has to know.

Another good thing about competing with yourself: You can change the rules. If you set standards, then fail to meet them, you can decide they were unrealistic and lower them. You can even change the rules in hindsight and reinterpret a loss as a victory, given what you now know about your limitations or other conditions.

Just as it's important to decide when to compete with others and when not to, so it's important to decide when to compete with yourself and when not to. Martina Navratilova has noted that it's highly unlikely that now that she has retired from tennis, she'll find any *other* occupation in which she is the world's best. If she competes against her own former accomplishments, satisfied with nothing less than being world champion, she'll feel inadequate. This would be foolish. Fortunately she knows some things about competition and seems content to try new things, to be a better than average skier and snowboarder and basketball player and spokeswoman for civil rights.

Sport psychologist Robert Rotella counsels, "You have to compete against yourself, against your own expectations. If you live life letting other people define your success, then the world will have a noose around your neck and will drag you around by that noose. The more successful you get, the more other people try to do that. You can't let them."

Sometimes competing with oneself is to competition what aerobics is to sports: a training ground, a way to test the waters without taking a huge risk. A woman who competes with herself begins to think of herself as competitive. Like the aerobicist who in the studio develops strength and endurance and confidence that she can ultimately employ on the softball field, the woman who competes with herself can eventually venture out of that protected environment and compete with others. Having learned that it's not cruel or destructive to compete with herself, she begins to notice that it's not cruel or destructive to compete with others.

But ultimately, even when you're using others for inspiration, take into consideration your own potential, your own limitations, your own desires. Compete with how you expected to do, or how you did last year, or how you'd like to do. And trust your own pace.

One day I was agonizing over the fact that I couldn't seem to come up with a good idea for this, my third book. I had finished writing my second book six months before and expected that by then I'd have an advance for the third. But I hadn't even written a proposal. I didn't even have an idea. I kept badgering my agent with bad ideas, which she gently but firmly rejected. I enjoy writing books and was eager to write another. But I couldn't seem to get going.

The truth is, writing books exhausts me. I pour all my ideas and experiences and research and interviews into each one, so naturally I feel drained afterward. But I found myself thinking enviously of my friend Meredith Maran, who, after finishing her first book, wrote and submitted a second proposal that was accepted within six weeks! My head began to fill with munchkin voices. They taunted me: "What's the matter with you? How come you can't just turn around and write another book the way Meredith can?"

Oh, happy blessed opportunity!

I thought about it while riding my bike. On a bike trail people pass you. You can sprint for a while, keeping ahead of some of them, but faster riders will eventually zip past, humbling you by courteously calling out, "Coming by on your left. . . ."

So it is with writing and many other endeavors. You can go only at your own pace. You can't go, for instance, at Meredith's pace (unless you're Meredith). You can't go at Bonnie Blair's pace (unless you're Bonnie Blair). You can emulate them, you can learn from them, you can compete with them—or you can choose not to. Ultimately you'll be happier if you challenge yourself to compete with others in appropriate arenas but also trust that your best is enough, that your own pace is the perfect pace for you.

Chapter 37

See Opponents as Opportunities

If you are a competitive woman, you will have opponents. Some of them will be women, some men. Opponents are people who, for their own reasons, try to stop you from going where you want to go.

From the Conqueror's perspective, opponents are obstacles to be demolished. But from the Champion's perspective, opponents offer opportunities. They present you with a chance to learn who you are, to notice what you want. They give you a chance to rise to the occasion. This is what athletes learn: that opponents can make us swifter, wiser, more effective. We welcome them. It's harder to do that in the rest of life.

But if welcomed as opportunities, opponents can even offer you a chance to enjoy their company and the process of striving with them. If you can find a way to see your opponents as opportunities, you'll feel less imposed upon and more grateful. You might find that you can begin to understand your opponents, rather than simply resent them. You might perceive your opponents' frailties and fears. When you see how human opponents are, they lose some of their power over you.

Gandhi perceived his political rivals as teachers, referring to them as "worthy opponents" who forced him to do his best, thereby offering a blessing.

Carlos Castaneda popularized the term "worthy opponents" in his series of books about Don Juan, the Yaquí sorcerer with whom he apprenticed in Mexico. While training Castaneda to be "a warrior, beyond victory or defeat," Don Juan teaches Castaneda to act deliberately and strategically, to be aware, to live lightly on the earth, and to use his own death as a reminder to be courageous because "you don't have much time." Don Juan obtains for Castaneda a worthy opponent, a woman with supernatural powers named La Catalina who haunts him, tricks him, and frightens him. "I didn't find you a worthy opponent because I want to play with you, or tease you, or annoy you," explains Don Juan. "A worthy opponent might spur you on; under the influence of an opponent like La Catalina, you may have to make use of everything I have taught you." Don Juan also explains that someday Castaneda will be thankful to his opponent because his opponent will have forced him to grow.[1]

What a useful concept! Any worthy opponent might ultimately be thanked because in the process of confronting a formidable challenge, one moves closer to reaching one's full potential.

Is there a difference between a worthy opponent and an unworthy opponent? Might an unworthy opponent be an enemy, someone with no sense of fair play, someone with great hostility, someone who not only seeks excellence for herself or himself but sincerely wants his or her rival to lose?

I don't think it matters. Any opponent can goad you on to greater achievements. We can't expect opponents to play fair; many of them won't. Should you still play fair? Of course. Ask not about the opponent but about the opportunity. Might this person (or group of people) provide a chance for you to move closer to obtaining your goals? Might this person inspire you to achieve more than you thought possible? Some opponents are worthy of attention, and some are not. When you ask yourself, "Is this a worthy opponent?" you might be surprised by the answer. Often the person you're perceiving as an opponent will turn out to be an ally or teammate who has somehow triggered in you feelings of inferiority. An unworthy opponent would be someone about whom you ultimately decide that it's not worth competing. Sorting out who is a worthy opponent and who is not can help you focus your attention on when and where you want to compete. In this way even unworthy opponents offer opportunities.

Chapter 38

See Men as Your Peers

One of the greatest stumbling blocks to female advancement is our reticence to challenge men. As long as we avoid competing with men, we limit our achievements. We also limit our fun.

Challenging men can be satisfying because it surprises them. It can be satisfying because it disproves a popular myth of female inferiority. Defeating men can be satisfying the same way defeating women is satisfying: It's an accomplishment, a victory.

Venus Williams, the teenage tennis pro, says, "Most guys, when they play me, know they're going to lose. They feel bad. I don't."

A twenty-nine-year-old Los Angeles secretary and runner notes, "If you're told your whole life you're physically inferior, emotionally inferior, intellectually inferior, and can't do math and science, it's very satisfying to be able to beat a man in the last six miles of a marathon. I like to count how many men I pass."

Despite the pervasive social myth that men are superior, women tend to see men as fragile. As delicate. As unable to withstand the reality that in any given endeavor, there's about a fifty-fifty chance that a woman will be better than a man. So we protect them, hiding our strengths, catering to their egos.

It's okay to defeat men. It's okay to enjoy defeating men. Don't men enjoy defeating one another? Don't men enjoy defeating women? Don't men enjoy winning contests that they're expected to lose? Relishing a victory over a man doesn't mean you hate men, that you're insensitive to men, or that you're gloating. It just means you're proud of yourself. Nothing wrong with that.

Even women who move in male-dominated domains forget sometimes to compete with men. Sportscaster Robin Roberts says she finds herself more readily competing with women. "A lot of young women call, wanting advice. My friends are, like, 'Why are you helping these people take your job?' I have to admit, in recent years, even though I'm very generous, sometimes I help a woman and she gets hired somewhere and I think, *Yikes! She's on my trail*! Then I get mad at myself. Why am I worrying only about the women? I'm being sexist. What about Bob Costas? I want his job. So I have to catch myself. In one breath I want to compete with Bob Costas, and in another breath I'm worrying about little Susie from SMU taking my job."

Yet women often hesitate to defeat men, afraid to offend their egos or suffer their wrath. Other times women refuse to compete with men because male styles of competition turn women off, or because women are afraid to lose. But competing with men doesn't have to mean competing like Conquerors, and losing is not the end of the world.

The players on the women's pro baseball team called the Colorado Silver Bullets make a living competing with men. They lose, usually, but they love the process; they love competing with men on an equal basis. Outfielder Angie Marzetta played linebacker for her high school football team. "I was a woman in a man's world, and a lot of times that's where women find themselves, so it was good practice," she says. "One of the biggest problems for women is they're not determined to win. They're socialized to be passive. Competing against men is the most important thing because you compete against men in the business world. Women need to compete in order to be equal."

Starting pitcher Lee Anne Ketcham says, "My parents taught me to go for the throat. When you've got a guy down, keep him down.

But not in a nasty way." She laughs. "We lose a lot, and I hate losing, but it's a part of life. It's more fun to play against men because in baseball they're bigger and stronger and more of a challenge."

Losing to men is okay. Defeating men is okay. Wounded male egos are okay. They're not your fault. Women and men need to learn to compete with each other, and it's going to happen only if women become willing to see men as their peers: nothing more, nothing less.

In reality men are often *not* women's peers. Men have many cultural advantages. They are less likely to have to contend with sexual assault, sexual harassment, and sex discrimination. They may have had more encouragement in math, science, technology, and sports; they may have better contacts with the people who make hiring or promotion decisions. They may be taller or stronger. Keep all that in mind. But don't enter a situation expecting to be victimized or feeling one down. Act as if you belong. Expect to be treated as an equal, and commit yourself to competing on an equal basis for what you want. See men as your peers. If you're hesitant, remember this: Whether they admit it or not, men are competing with you.

Chapter 39

Practice Right Competition

"Look at every path closely and deliberately," Don Juan advised in his teachings to author Carlos Castaneda. "Try it as many times as you think necessary. Then ask yourself and yourself alone one question: Does this path have a heart? If it does, the path is good. If it doesn't, it is of no use."

A Champion must ask herself: "Does this path have a heart? Is this an ethical path? Is it a kind, compassionate path, for my opponents *and* me? Does it honor our relationship? What's the most loving thing to do for all concerned? What's the right thing to do?"

"If you're a gracious winner, you think of ways to win so that no one feels vanquished," says Feminist Majority Foundation president Eleanor Smeal. "You can make sure the group or person who is defeated actually benefits. I don't think of competition as a zero-sum game: I win, you lose. It's all a process. Instead of thinking about getting my share of the pie, I think, *Can we make the pie big enough so everybody gets a piece?*"

Winning is not the only thing. How we win, or how we try to win, matters. Don't fool yourself into thinking that the end justifies the means or that women need to be ruthless and cutthroat or that it's okay to cheat because everybody does. It's not okay to cheat. It's not okay for women to be Conquerors. It's not okay for men to be Conquerors either, but usually you can't control other people. If you have any doubts about whether your own behavior is ethical, suppose your work habits or study habits or athletic training habits were published on the front page of a newspaper. Would you lose your job? Would you be humiliated?

One of the first people to teach me about right competition was Sandy Haddock, my tennis coach at Arcadia High in Phoenix, Arizona. Because the school had no basketball team, Sandy invited me to try out for her women's AAU team, the Phoenix Dusters. When we won the state championship, I drank some beer that my teammates offered me during our celebratory meal. But with those few sips, I violated my tennis team's code of conduct. The next day, Sandy kicked me off the tennis team. I was shocked but impressed. It was an early and memorable lesson in right competition because I had in effect cheated myself, my teammates, and my coach. I called Sandy recently to thank her again for many things, including that dismissal.

The Champion competes with a commitment to fair play. She competes skillfully, honestly, with integrity. She competes unto others as she would have them compete unto her. She finds a balance between her desire to win and her desire to help others win. Rather than narrowly focus on her own goals, she pays attention to the process and the end result, to her opponents and to herself. She chooses right competition: the path with a heart.

Chapter 40

Lighten Up

At the peak of Babe Didrikson's career in the mid-fifties, she "made it very hard on a lot of these women golfers because she'd walk right up and say, 'What are you girls practicing for? You can't win this tournament,'" reports Betty Dodd, Babe's close companion. "She did it all the time, and there were a lot of them that didn't like it one damn bit."[1]

My brother and I taunt each other when playing minigolf. "Want me to play left-handed, to make it more even?" he'll ask. Peter will even cough or sneeze when I'm putting the ball. His behavior improves my powers of concentration. It also amuses us, reminds us that minigolf is just a game, makes us feel closer, *and*, I believe, eases the tension inherent in the fact that we both crave victory, even in trivial pursuits.

Babe Didrikson also might have been joking—she did have a sense of humor—when teasing her rivals about their impending defeats. If so, the other golfers didn't get it.

Competitors need to learn to handle such teasing. Kathy Delaney-Smith tries to teach this skill to her Harvard basketball players during practice. "I'll talk about their form, their facial expressions, anything to get them thinking about the wrong thing," she explains. "They need to practice blocking out just that kind of distraction, whether it's bad officiating or comments from the fans." Delaney-Smith does not permit her players to trash-talk their opponents. She outlaws such comments as "in your face!" because they're unsportsmanlike, she says. But she believes that her own trash talk can help her players ignore distractions during games.

Trash talk can be a playful conversation, a caring connection, and a way to lighten up a tense situation. When Peter sneezes as I putt the golf ball or when Kathy Delaney-Smith tells a player there's a fly on her nose, neither one is really hoping to induce failure. Each is just upping the challenge, playing verbal defense, offering creative interference that adds intensity and connection and humor. Each is saying, "Here I am, watching you, playing with you. Can you handle some additional pressure?" It becomes part of the game.

Trash talk offers one of many ways to play with competition, to laugh about it. I also recommend gently teasing others—and yourself—about who's winning and who wants to win. Find a way to laugh out loud about your desire to have the cleanest desk in the office or to beat someone else to the copier, and others will laugh with you. Following your lead, they might even begin to admit the simple daily ways that they're trying to win. Competitiveness doesn't have to be a shameful boogeyman hiding under the bed. It can be a game, a way to laugh and connect with other people about the human desire to excel.

Chapter 41

Say, "Yes, I Can!"

When Connie Todd first arrived at her job as program director of the Foster Grandparent Program of Washington, D.C., morale was low. "The staff was not ready to do hard work," recalls Todd, whose federally funded nonprofit program matches senior volunteers with children with special needs. "The ninety foster grandparents were agitated, anxious about what was going to happen." At the first meeting Todd communicated her goal to the staff and the grandparents: "We're going to be the best program in the country." Then she got everyone chanting: "Yes, we can! Yes, we will! Yes, we can! Yes, we will!"

It was helpful, says Todd. "It energized us. Now our staff will go around saying that we're the best program in the country. There are about two hundred programs, and no one else awarded us that. We just claimed it. We bought into it, and now everyone has."

Some people in other programs resent Todd's chutzpah. "They think, *Who is she to say she's the best?*" reports Todd. "They think our egos are big. They think we're pretentious, boasting on ourselves. In fact one lady—and this is a friend—said, 'Oh, you're so full of yourself!' "

Todd says, laughing: "I told her, 'And you gotta love me anyway!' "

Todd's unabashed "Yes, we can!" attitude inspired me on a golf course recently. I was waiting at the red tees of 214-yard par four with a water hazard. Most recreational golfers would hit the ball 100 yards or so, laying it up in front of the 100-yard pond, then lob over the pond on the next shot. I was planning to hit the ball the entire 200 or so yards, over the fairway and over the water and onto the edge of the green. On a good day I can hit it that far. It seemed like a good day. I was standing at the tee waiting for the foursome ahead of me to finish putting. I didn't want to hit them with my drive.

From somewhere behind me, I heard men yelling. Men have often tried to instruct me on a golf course, but I'd never before been yelled at (except when someone shouts, "Fore!"), so it took me a while to understand what the commotion was about and that it was directed at me. Finally I looked around and saw two men standing at the white tees, about fifty yards behind me. "You can't hit the ball that far!" they were yelling. "Go ahead and drive! You can't hit the ball that far!"

Without thinking, I cupped my hand to the side of my mouth and shouted back, "Yes, I can!"

That felt great—for about five seconds, because then I had to do it. I wasn't sure I could. I am not a good golfer. I'm not even comfortable using my driver.

But how dare they tell me, "You can't hit the ball that far!" Would they ever have said that to a man?

During a lifetime of athleticism I've hit many balls with sticks. I'm coordinated, strong, and flexible. I've often performed under pressure. I know how not to choke. I was reminding myself of all this as I waited for the foursome on the green to finish putting.

Finally I addressed the ball and pulled my three-wood slowly overhead. When it whipped around, I heard the club-face hit the ball with that satisfying "ping" sound that Ping clubs are named for. Then I watched with delight as the tiny white moon arched over the fairway, over the water, and onto the green grass on the other side. I didn't even mind that it was about thirty yards off to the left.

As I sauntered toward my ball, trying to refrain from skipping, I didn't glance back at the jerks behind me. I had nothing more to say to them—except, perhaps, "Thank you." The men—and Connie Todd—had given me a gift: the words "Yes, I can." I'd never said them before, and now I say them all the time. I recommend it, whether your opponents are strangers on golf courses or colleagues at work or family members who lack confidence in your abilities or annoying negative voices inside your own head. Say, "Yes, I can," or, "Yes, we can," especially when you're not sure if you can or not. Then give it a shot.

Chapter 42

Think of Yourself as a Champion

When I give public presentations, I ask the women, "How many of you think of yourselves as athletes?" Some raise their hands. Then I ask, "Of those who did not raise your hands, how many of you swim, walk, lift weights, do aerobics, play softball, do yoga . . . but don't think of yourselves as athletes?" Many more raise their hands. "I recommend that all of you think of yourselves as athletes," I say. An athlete is someone who engages in athletic activity. She doesn't have to do it well. She doesn't have to win. She doesn't even have to compete. When you begin to think of yourself as an athlete, you act more like an athlete, making physical fitness a priority. You begin to walk as an athlete walks, with pride. It changes you.

Now I have a new question: Do you think of yourself as a Champion? What would it take for you to feel like a Champion? If you thought of yourself as a Champion, how might you behave differently?

A Champion is someone who is willing to compete in public arenas. She takes that risk. She seizes that opportunity: to challenge herself, to challenge her opponent, to get to know herself and her rivals, male and female. She doesn't have to win. She wants to win and gives herself permission to win and seeks victory unapologetically but pays attention to the process of competing, the process of dedicating herself to the pursuit of excellence. Remembering that competition is a relationship, the Champion competes with compassion, for herself and her rivals.

She doesn't have to compete all the time. She makes conscious decisions about when to compete and when not to, how to compete and how not to. She's aware of the cultural and political factors that discourage women from competing and refuses to be limited by them. Or she competes to change them.

If you think of yourself as a Champion, you'll act more like a Champion, competing with courage and commitment. If you have never felt like a Champion—if you have never excelled at sports or music or science contests in which you felt victorious—that's even more reason to claim the word now. Try it on for size. See how it feels to think of yourself as a Champion. See how it changes the way you walk. See how it changes the choices you make. See how it changes your life.

Part Six

Passing
the
Torch

Chapter 43

Embracing Victory: An Epilogue

When I was five and Mom was eager for someone to compete with, she taught me that competition can be about love, fun, seeking excellence together. If I had kids, I'd probably do the same for them, challenging them to races and telling them stories about how Grandmom Sarah and I used to compete, how she'd slap the end of the pool and say, "Ha! Beat you!" But I don't have kids and Grandmom Sarah has become a real athlete, not just someone messing around in a backyard pool. It's time to return the favor, seems to me. So instead of going to a daughter or son's Little League games, I go to Mom's swimming meets. Instead of teaching kids about victory and defeat, I teach Mom. Or try to.

Mom's athletic career bloomed late. Way late. She joined a swim team at age sixty-nine but waited until she turned seventy before entering her first meet so she'd be at the bottom of her age-group (seventy to seventy-four). Mom likes to win.

"I've always had an intense desire to be the best," says Sarah Burton Nelson. Now that she's finally competing against women her own age she's winning a lot. Gold medals in the fifty-meter and hundred-meter breaststroke in the 1996 Arizona Senior Olympics, which qualified her for the 1997 National Senior Olympics, where she placed fifth and sixth. Four gold medals in the Grand Canyon State

Games in 1995, and another four in 1996 and again in 1997. Five victories, one third place in the Arizona State Championship in 1996.

She's getting noticed too. The *Arizona Republic* ran a feature story about the local psychiatrist turned athlete on the front page of its sports section.

I had been encouraging my mother to enter meets for decades. "You'd love it," I said. "It's called masters swimming, and you race against women your age. There are lots of meets. You'd improve. You'd love it!"

"I'm too slow!" she'd protest. "I wouldn't win!"

"Mom! You don't have to win! And besides, you probably would."

It's not that my mother lacks courage. She attended Cornell Medical School in the 1940s, with fewer than a dozen women in her class ("hen medics" the male students called the women derisively). When I was growing up, she was the family doctor for the townspeople of Blue Bell, Pennsylvania. She and my father—who became a physician after they married, because she made it seem like a good idea—opened a practice together. Many patients initially refused to believe she was a doctor or demanded to see the "man doctor" instead. Eventually "Dr. Sally" gained the respect of the community. But by age forty-seven Mom had grown bored with general medicine—too many sore throats, she said—and she returned to school for three years to become a psychiatrist.

She's got athletic courage too. One time when she was about forty-two, she challenged another physician to a race in our neighbor's pool. She had quit smoking and wanted to prove he should quit too. Who could swim the farthest underwater before needing air?

Dr. Miller, an athletic young man, went first, swimming for a long time, then finally jerking his head out of the water, gasping. The small gathering of friends and family clapped politely, but we were betting on Mom. After taking one huge breath, she submerged, then breast-stroked back and forth. At each end she calmly turned around underwater, pushed off, and continued swimming. My lungs felt desperate just watching.

"How many laps did you swim underwater?" I asked her recently. "Three?"

"Four," she recalled immediately. "He swam three and a half, so I had to swim four."

At about age fifty-two, while vacationing in Colorado, Mom dived off a three-meter diving board. Without practicing from a lower board, and without *jumping* off the board first—as I always do—Mom executed a swan dive but hit the water askew, partially dislocating her left shoulder. In great pain Mom sat on the bottom of the pool's deep well and rammed her right fist into her left armpit to push the ball of her humerus back into its socket. She then rocketed to the surface, her arm securely in place.

Yet Mom was reluctant to enter a real swimming meet. She was afraid, I now realize, the way I get afraid of writing sometimes: When you want to succeed at something very much, it can be scary to try it. You might fail.

What ultimately inspired her to join a team, I believe, was her visit with me. I invited Mom to participate in one of my D.C. Masters practices. After receiving assurances that she wouldn't be the slowest person in our pool, she agreed. It was no small commitment. We had to arise at 5:15 A.M. in order to stretch, drive to the pool, and be in the water by 6:30.

When I sent Mom over to Lane 1, where the slowest swimmers swim, she was welcomed by Lorraine Murphy and Helen Hummer, two friendly, athletic women in their late seventies. Both are about Mom's speed, and both have competed in meets. Mom was so nervous that she swam too close to the buoyant lane line, banging her arm on the hard plastic and tearing her fragile skin. But she refused to bandage it, instead pausing at each end to apply pressure in a vain attempt to stop the blood. Despite the odd sight of red liquid oozing down my mother's forearm, Helen and Lorraine were encouraging. "You're fast!" they kept telling her. "You ought to try a meet!" Mom began to believe that she was not in fact slow for her age and that she might, if she entered a meet, win.

Upon returning home, she joined the Phoenix Swim Club, where she learned how to dive off a starting block ("I was shaking so hard I had to hold someone's hand, but I did it!"). She began keeping a log of her fastest times, scrupulously comparing them with the times printed in *Swim* magazine. "Here's a sixty-five-year-old who swims fifty meters in thirty-six seconds!" she told me during one of our weekly (sometimes daily) training talks.

"Are you sure?" I asked.

"It says right here—and it's a world record! And my fastest is only fifty-five seconds!"

"Mom, you don't have to beat a world record holder," I assured her. "Besides, she's only sixty-five years old. She's not in your age-group."

"Yes, and she never will be," she noted, relieved. "But look at this! Here's a woman, Matilda Gray, who's seventy-two, and she swims the fifty in fifty seconds. That's five seconds faster than my very fastest!"

"Your times will come down, Mom," I predicted. "Besides, you don't have to beat her either. Maybe you'll come in second."

"Oh," she said. It was a novel and unpleasant idea.

Two weeks after turning seventy, my mother entered her first meet. She was a wreck ("Do you think if I take just a quarter of one Valium before the meet?" "No, Mom." "I do it at the dentist's office." "No, Mom"), but she won all three events she entered.

Mom brought Bernie, her fifty-nine-year-old fiancé, to her second meet, the Arizona State Championships, warning him that she would be too nervous to be good company until after the meet ended. Bernie came in handy because he reminded Mom, just before she stepped on to the starting block for her first race, to remove her shoes.

Mom dominated her age-group again, and these victories thrilled her. They thrilled me too, secretly, but sometimes I withheld praise, not wanting early success to make her too smug. "You're a big fish in a small pond," I told her. "I'd like to see how you do against the best women in the country."

Accepting the challenge, she agreed to meet me in Mount Hood, Oregon, for the U.S. Masters Swimming Long Course Championships. There she was lapped by speedy septuagenarians, who graciously offered her pointers afterward. Mom did finish in the top ten in all six events she entered. Not bad for a novice.

Still, like any novice, Mom can lack confidence. She frets about Clara Lamore Walker, a sixty-nine-year-old Younger Woman. "She's moving up into my age-group!" Mom tells me, distraught. "I might never win again!" Clara's a 1948 Olympian who swims the fifty-meter freestyle in 35.86; Mom's best is now 48.16. "She's way out of my league," Mom moans. "Your mother is just a rinky-dink swimmer."

"You don't have to win all the time," I remind her.

"Good thing Clara doesn't enter my best events," she says, ignoring me.

Mom's best events are the fifty- and two-hundred-yard breaststroke. In those she set two Arizona state records, one of which she later broke. (Her records are now 55.31 for fifty breast; 4:41.37 for two hundred breast.) She has learned the "wave" breaststroke that Olympians do; she can push her head high above water, like a volcano, hands out front in prayer. She's also working on her butterfly since her time for the hundred-yard individual medley is within 0.6 seconds of the state record.

Like any parent and child, we've had to sort out who is competing for whom. "I hope I don't disappoint you," she told me before one meet.

"You can't!" I assured her. "I'll just be happy to be there, watching you fulfill a lifelong dream."

"Yeah, yours!" she said.

Truth is, her competitive swimming *is* my dream. Mom's from the three-dribble basketball generation, when girls were forced to "grow up and be ladies" long before they perfected their hook shots. I've always wanted Mom to enjoy what sports have given me: fun, friends, physical ecstasy, a sense of accomplishment and success.

Now that she's finally competing, the thrill is clearly hers as well.

Long gone are her "old lady" suits and the half-mile (eight hundred meters) she used to paddle for fitness. She logs up to twenty-two hundred meters per workout at timed intervals. She swims in a slick black Speedo, packs her bag with goggles, fins, pull buoy, and chamois towel. She's even weight training now; if you meet her at a party, she'll insist you squeeze her biceps. "Sarah, you're a warrior!" her personal trainer said recently.

"I'm tickled pink!" she told me that day. Perhaps the world's first pink warrior.

I'm her informal coach; her real coach is Troy Dalbey, former coach of 1996 Olympian Gary Hall. Dalbey won two gold medals himself in the 1988 Olympics. "Come on, Nelson, get off the wall!" He'll cajole Mom, grinning. Mom grins back, loving the encouragement, the teasing. Dalbey told me that if Mom "had had the opportunity to swim as a young lady, she could have been great—on the Olympic level." That made me sad in a way. How tragic that so many women like Mom never got to fulfill their potential.

Mom doesn't waste time crying over what might have been. She's too busy studying *Swim* magazine, practicing her flip turns, training for her next meet. Like any happy kid—and any successful Champion—she's savoring what is. And imagining what might be.

Acknowledgments

If it weren't for my friends, family, and colleagues, I wouldn't be able to write books. Thanks to all of you for the many ways you sustain me with your enthusiasm, your laughter, and your support.

If it weren't for my readers, I'd be sitting here talking to myself! Thanks to all of you, especially those who have written to tell me your responses to my work.

This book would not have been possible without the generosity of the more than two hundred women and men who allowed me to interview them as they thoughtfully shared their experiences, insights, and feelings.

Also indispensable were the many people who helped me conduct quantitative research for the book. Thanks to those who tested early drafts of my surveys: Kimberly Carter, Chris Cerf, Nancy Kass, Rosemary Partridge, Kim Price-Nuñoz, Ann Rasmussen, Palma Strand, Dave Sylvester, Mary Farmer and the Lammas softball team, and the 1995 conference participants at the Women's Institute on Sports and Education.

Many thanks to the people who graciously volunteered to distribute and collect my 2,150 surveys: David Armstrong, Heather Barber, M. Deborah Bialeschki, Amy Chinitz, Doris Corbett, Donetta Cothran, Robin Cunningham, Valerie Cushman, Sue A. Daggett, Tracy Davis, Lynne Emery, Bill Finney, Judith A. Flohr, Susan L. Forbes, Deborah Hambly, Trish Harvey, Barbara High, Marge Holman, Karen Hovan, Bill Johnson, Shawn Ladda, Suzanne Lainson, Linda S. Levy, Susan J. Loftus, Shauna McGhie, Jan Meyer, Judy Morey, Barb Motes, Jo Oliver, Tracy Santanello, Maryanne H. Schiffman, Sheila E. Schroeder, Patricia A. Shewokis, Cheryl Silva, Winifred Simon, Gloria B. Solomon, Teri Staloch, Bessie Stockard, Sanya Tyler, Ann-Marie Wehrer, Chris Weller, and Dianna Wilkerson.

Thanks also to Gigi Ransom, who helped me gain access to minority students in Washington, D.C.

Thanks to computer programmer Janet Goldstein, who designed a program and entered the data for me; Fern Dickman, who introduced me to Janet; and Karen Hill, who helped me understand computerized data entry.

A very special thanks to sport sociologist Cynthia Hasbrook, an associate professor of physical activity with the Department of Human Kinetics at the University of Wisconsin, Milwaukee. Professor Hasbrook, who teaches undergraduate- and graduate-level statistics courses, analyzed, organized, and guided me through reams and reams of survey data. This massive job involved not only analyzing the data in various ways but explaining to me (repeatedly, patiently) what it meant.

Thanks to Nancy Kass for reviewing my survey design and offering suggested revisions. Thanks to Carole Oglesby, who reviewed my survey design and offered helpful comments on my survey results.

Thanks to many friends, colleagues, and family members, including Nancy Barnett, Carol and Ray Biggs, Cathy Breitenbucher, Amy Chinitz, Carol Galbraith, Trish Harvey, Susan Reifer, Gail Whitaker, and especially Terry Dale, for supplying me with a steady stream of competition-related articles.

Thanks to Nancy Barnett, Carol Galbraith, Meredith Maran, Nancy Nerenberg, Carole Oglesby, and Ellen Wessel for reading and commenting on one or more chapters.

Thanks to Linda Brock-Nelson, Felicia Eth, Cynthia Hasbrook, Mary Jo Kane, Arthur Nelson, and Sarah Nelson for giving me valuable feedback on the entire manuscript.

Thanks to my longtime agent Felicia Eth, for coming up with the title for this book, freely sharing her time and wisdom, and always challenging me to do my best, and to my editor, Claire Wachtel, for her early and enduring enthusiasm for this project.

Thanks to my friends on the D.C. Masters and DCAC swimming teams, for keeping me healthy and happy.

Thanks to Martha Nelson for saying, many years ago, "Write about your mother," and for shepherding my first story to *Ms.* magazine.

For spiritual guidance, thanks to Cheri Huber.

Finally, for many helpful discussions about this book, many playful competitive games, and a lifetime of love and support, I'm deeply grateful to my family: Sarah, Art, Carol, Peter, Bernie, Linda, Bill, Teagan, Alex, Annaliese, Chris, and especially Katherine.

Appendix:
Survey Methodology and
Demographics

In 1995, with feedback from the Temple University physical education professor Carole Oglesby, the Johns Hopkins University public health professor Nancy Kass, and about forty friends, neighbors, and acquaintances, including a Washington, D.C., softball team, I designed, tested, and revised four drafts of what ultimately became a five-page, sixty-question anonymous survey entitled "Mariah Burton Nelson's Confidential Competition Survey for Women."[1]

To distribute the questionnaires, I created a team of forty-two professors, teachers, and coaches in nineteen states plus the District of Columbia and three Canadian cities in two provinces.[2] Thirty-five of these volunteers subscribe to an Internet list called WISHPERD (Women in Sport, Health, Physical Education, Recreation, and Dance), where I posted a notice asking for help. (More than sixty people offered; I chose those who responded first and those most likely to have access to the population I wanted to sample.) These distributors fell into two groups: those who knew of my previous work and those who were simply interested in this proposed project on women and competition.

Each person agreed to distribute between 25 and 185 written surveys, which I mailed to them. Because I wanted to compare athletic and nonathletic students in middle school, high school, and college, I asked distributors to hand the questionnaires to (1) college, high school, or middle school sports teams or (2) required college, high school, or middle school classes. (I also asked some people to distribute questionnaires to women who were not students, but later discarded these.) In order to survey a sufficiently large minority population, I recruited another seven coaches and teachers to distribute copies to their students or athletes, and I personally distributed the questionnaires at the Richard England Metropolitan Police Boys and Girls Club of Washington, D.C., and to the women's basketball teams at Howard University, Marymount University, and the University of Maryland.

None of my volunteers reported any trouble gaining access to the students. Only one school, a public high school in Arlington, Virginia, rejected my request. (After asking me to fill out a twelve-page questionnaire about my research, the principal denied my proposal, explaining that she objected to the survey question in which I asked "Sexual orientation: a) heterosexual/straight; b) bisexual; c) homosexual/lesbian/gay; d) not sure/don't want to say").

In this way we distributed the survey to a total of 2,150 women and girls (1,900 surveys in the first distribution, then 250 in the minority oversampling). After discarding surveys that were not completed by students, those not completed by females, and those not completed, I was left with a 1,030 usable surveys (a 48 percent response rate).

It was not a random sample. My academic consultants tell me this qualifies as a convenience sample, purposive sample, or targeted sample. In other words, the results are not generalizable to all women and girls.

Janet Goldstein entered the data into a computer program she designed herself, and sport sociologist Cynthia Hasbrook computed statistically significant differences for me and helped me interpret three huge loose-leaf binders full of data.

Using a variety of tests, Hasbrook analyzed all of the questions for statistically significant differences. She explains it this way: "Independent-samples Pearson chi-square tests and post-hoc tests were conducted to determine if various subject groups (e.g., athletes v. nonathletes) significantly differed ($p < .05$) in their proportional responses to a number of categorical variables." All differences discussed in this book were deemed statistically significant.

Most of the questions were in a true-false or a multiple-choice format on a five-point Likert scale (agree strongly, agree somewhat, don't have an opinion, disagree somewhat, and disagree strongly). Later I combined "agree strongly and agree somewhat," as well as the two disagree categories, for each of these questions. I usually refer to these simply as "agree" or "disagree." When comparing women of different races or ethnic backgrounds, we controlled for age and athletic identity.

I also asked an open-ended question: What advice would you offer women who have difficulty with competition? I received more than seven hundred written responses, which I categorized and tallied.

All the respondents were female, and all were students between the ages of eleven and forty-nine. A majority (64 percent) were of traditional college age (eighteen to twenty-one). High school kids constituted 16 percent of the sample. The rest were older students (12 percent were twenty-two to twenty-nine, 3 percent were thirty to thirty-nine, and 1 percent were forty to forty-nine) or middle school students (4 percent were eleven to thirteen). College athletes constituted 30 percent of the sample (314 respondents).

Sixty-five percent of the sample is white. In the book I use the term "European-American" interchangeably with "white." (I prefer the term "European-American," unwieldy though it may be, and even though it is not entirely accurate, because it defines people by their historical and cultural roots rather than by their skin color.) Twenty percent of the population is African-American. (I use the terms "African-American" and "black" interchangeably because they seem to be the preferred terms at this point in history.) Another 4 percent of the sample is Asian-American; 3 percent is Hispanic, Latina, or Chicana (I use the terms "Hispanic" and "Latina" to refer to this group), and a total of 8 percent identified itself as Native American, Pacific Islander, biracial, multiracial, "other," or "don't know/don't want to say." I did not make any comparisons based on these final groups since they were too small or, in the case of the "biracial" category, not meaningful enough.[3]

Most (93 percent) had no children. In response to my question about sexual orientation, 91 percent identified as heterosexual; 3 percent as bisexual, 3 percent as gay; and 3 percent answered "not sure/don't want to say."

Most respondents identified as liberal or moderate, with 31 percent calling themselves "somewhat liberal," another 14 percent "very liberal/radical," and 40 percent "moderate." A total of 15 percent identified as "somewhat conservative" or "conservative."

The women and girls seemed enthusiastic about answering my questions. Hundreds of them scrawled unsolicited comments in the margins of the surveys, eager to be understood. (Their spelling was atrocious. One example: "Don't wery, be happy.") Many commented that "we need to talk about this subject." Though I tried to frame questions in a neutral way, the very act of being asked to answer questions about competition proved inspiring for some. One fifteen-year-old girl wrote, "I think this survey is very good for women to take so they don't feel so down compared to men. Men do everything. Now it's time for women."

Notes

Chapter 1: Seeking Excellence Together: An Introduction

1 "Know Your Enemy: A Sampling of Sexist Quotes," in Robin Morgan, *Sisterhood Is Powerful: An Anthology of Writings from the Women's Liberation Movement* (New York: Vintage Books, 1970), pp. 35–36.

2 Audre Lorde, *Sister Outsider: Essays and Speeches* (Freedom, CA: Crossing Press, 1984), p. 45.

3 Susan Faludi, *Backlash: The Undeclared War Against American Women* (New York: Crown, 1991), p. xxiii.

4 For more information about the survey methods, overview, and demographics, see the Appendix.

Chapter 2: What Men Are Doing in This Book

1 Natalie Angier, "Gene Defect Tied to Violence in Male Mice," *New York Times*, November 23, 1995.

Chapter 3: Conquerors

1 Gerald Posner, *Citizen Perot: His Life and Times* (New York: Random House, 1996).

2 In *Are We Winning Yet?* (New York: Random House, 1991) I describe what I called the military model of sports, in which competition is about winning and winning is about domination. Opponents are enemies, games are battles, and outcome is all that counts: "Who won?" Now expanding this concept beyond sports, I'm calling it the Conqueror's way.

3 Tracy Wallach, "Competition and Gender in Group Psychotherapy," *Group* 18:1 (Spring 1994).

4 Paul Monette, *Borrowed Time: An AIDS memoir* (San Diego: Harcourt Brace Jovanovich, 1988), p. 59.

5 Mona Harrington, *Women Lawyers: Rewriting the Rules* (New York: Plume/Penguin Books, 1995), pp. 129–32.

6 Pat Heim with Susan K. Golant, *Hardball for Women: Winning at the Game of Business* (New York: Penguin Books, 1992), p. 29.

7 Carolyn G. Heilbrun, *Reinventing Womanhood* (New York: W. W. Norton, 1979), p. 97.

Chapter 4: Cheerleaders

1 For information about upcoming performances of the fascinating, entertaining, high-energy troupe called the X-Cheerleaders, contact choreographer Jody Oberfelder (212-777-6227; JodyOber@inch.com) or founder Kim Irwin (919-382-8745; KimIrwin@mindspring.com).

2 Martha Burk, *Washington Feminist Faxnet*, May 16, 1996.

3 "Oh Baby! Big Gains for Little Outfits," *Sporting Goods Business* (March 1997), p. 21.

4 Laurel R. Davis, "Male Cheerleaders and the Naturalization of Gender," in Michael A. Messner and Donald F. Sabo, eds., *Sport, Men, and the Gender Order: Critical Feminist Perspectives* (Champaign, IL: Human Kinetics Books, 1990), p. 157.

CHAPTER 5: CHAMPIONS

1 Mariah Burton Nelson, *Are We Winning Yet? How Women Are Changing Sports and Sports Are Changing Women* (New York: Random House, 1991), p. 9.
2 Mary Jo Festle, *Playing Nice: Politics and Apologies in Women's Sports* (New York: Columbia University Press, 1996), p. 14.
3 Ibid., p. 139.

CHAPTER 6: COMPETITION IS A RELATIONSHIP; IT REQUIRES COMPASSION

1 Emmy A. Pepitone, *Children in Cooperation and Competition* (Lexington, MA: Lexington Books, 1980), p. 5.
2 Valerie Miner, "Rumors from the Cauldron," in Miner and Helen E. Longino, eds., *Competition: A Feminist Taboo?* (New York: The Feminist Press, 1987), p. 193.
3 Gail Whitaker, "Feminism and the Sporting Experience: Seeking Common Ground," Judith Andre and David N. James, eds., *Rethinking College Athletics* (Philadelphia; Temple University Press, 1991).
4 Brenda J. L. Bredemeier, Gloria S. Desertrain (a.k.a. Gloria Solomon), Leslee A. Fisher, Debby Getty, Nancy E. Slocum, Dawn E. Stephens, and Jaimie M. Warren, "Epistemological Perspectives Among Women Who Participate in Physical Activity," *Journal of Applied Sport Psychology* 3 (1991), pp. 87–107.
5 Charles Johnson, *The Middle Passage* (New York: Atheneum, 1990), p. 140.

CHAPTER 7: COMPETITION IS A PROCESS; IT REQUIRES AWARENESS

1 Paul Farhi, "Tuning Out Testosterone," *Washington Post*, July 23, 1996, p. A1.
2 Walter Tevis, *The Queen's Gambit* (New York: Random House, 1983).
3 D. L. Gill and D. A. Dzewaltowski, "Competitive Orientations Among Intercollegiate Athletes: Is Winning the Only Thing?," *Sport Psychologist* 2 (1988), pp. 212–21; D. L. Gill, "Competitiveness and

Competitive Orientation in Sport," in R. N. Singer, M. Murphey, and L. K. Tennant, eds., *Handbook on Research in Sport Psychology* (New York: Macmillan, 1993), pp. 314–27.

4 Tim Keown, "When Winning Isn't Enough," San Francisco *Chronicle*, March 22, 1995, p. D1.

5 Thanks to Warren P. Fraleigh for making a somewhat different analogy between sex and sport. In *Right Actions in Sport: Ethics for Contestants* (Champaign, IL: Human Kinetics, 1984), pp. 84–91, Fraleigh describes the difference between perceiving the "opponent as obstacle" and the "opponent as facilitator." In the opponent as obstacle approach, sexual intercourse is seen as a conquest of one person by another. The winner "scores" and moves on to another conquest; "there is little regard for the welfare of any one seduced person." In the opponent as facilitator approach, "the partners oppose each other through the actions and reactions of lovemaking" and "the success of the act is incomplete without mutual satisfaction."

CHAPTER 8: COMPETITION IS AN OPPORTUNITY; IT REQUIRES A SENSE OF HUMOR

1 Drew Hyland, "Competition and Friendship," *Journal of the Philosophy of Sport* (Fall 1978), pp. 27–37.

2 Luise Eichenbaum and Susie Orbach, *Between Women: Love, Envy, and Competition in Women's Friendships* (New York: Penguin Books, 1988), p. 121.

CHAPTER 9: COMPETITION IS A RISK; IT REQUIRES COURAGE

1 Susan E. Cayleff, *Babe: The Life and Legend of Babe Didrikson Zaharias* (Urbana: University of Illinois Press, 1995), p. 65.

2 Ibid., p. 192.

3 Ibid., pp. 47, 78–98.

4 Anna Seaton [Huntington], "Grace, Sass, and the Many Forms of Competitive Spirit," *New York Times*, February 6, 1995, p. S9.

5 Simone de Beauvoir, *The Second Sex* (New York: Vintage Books, 1952), p. 331.

6 Robert Horn, "No Mountain Too High for Her," *Sports Illustrated* (April 29, 1996), pp. 18–20.

CHAPTER 10: COMPETITION IS A FEMINIST ISSUE;
IT REQUIRES UNDERSTANDING

1 Barrie Thorne, *Gender Play: Girls and Boys in School* (New Brunswick, NJ: Rutgers University Press, 1993), p. 179.
2 Gloria Steinem, *Revolution from Within* (Boston: Little, Brown, 1992), p. 189.
3 Letty Cottin Pogrebin, *Among Friends* (New York: McGraw-Hill, 1987), p. 75.
4 bell hooks, *Ain't I a Woman?*, cited in Susan Ostrov Weisser and Jennifer Fleischner, *Feminist Nightmares: Women at Odds* (New York: New York University Press, 1994), p. 88.
5 Audre Lorde, *Sister Outsider: Essays and Speeches* (Freedom, CA: Crossing Press, 1984), p. 50.
6 Elizabeth Debold, Marie Wilson, and Idelisse Malave, *Mother-Daughter Revolution: From Betrayal to Power* (New York: Addison-Wesley, 1993), p. 184.

CHAPTER 11: FEMALE ATHLETES GET COMFORTABLE
WITH COMPETITION

1 William Rhoden, "Sports of the Times: Mission Reaffirmed in Nation's Capital," New York Times News Service, December 7, 1995.
2 Debbie Becker, "Triumphs Could Pave the Way for New Programs for Girls," *USA Today*, August 5, 1996, p. 12C.
3 Ibid.
4 Christine Brennan, "U.S. Women Look Good in Gold," *Washington Post*, August 5, 1996, p. C5.
5 Naomi Wolf, *Fire with Fire: The New Female Power and How It Will Change the 21st Century* (New York: Random House, 1993), p. 207.
6 Jean Baker Miller, *Toward a New Psychology of Women* (Boston: Beacon Press, 1976; updated 1986), p. 117.
7 Donald Sabo, Merrill Melnick, and Beth Vanfossen, *Women's Sports*

Foundation Report: Minorities in Sports: The Effect of Varsity Sports Participation on the Social, Educational, and Career Mobility of Minority Students (New York: Women's Sports Foundation, 1989).

8 D. L. Gill and D. A. Dzewaltowski, "Competitive Orientations Among Intercollegiate Athletes: Is Winning the Only Thing?," *Sport Psychologist* 2 (1988), pp. 212–221.

9 Eighty-eight percent of pros and Olympians and 81 percent of college athletes said they had enjoyed competing with a loved one.

10 The more athletic experience women have, the more likely they are to feel good about comparing their achievements with those of others. Only 29 percent of women who have never played sports described this comparison as positive. By contrast, 55 percent of former college athletes and 63 percent of former Olympic or professional athletes said comparing their achievements to those of others yielded a positive feeling.

11 Seventy-seven percent of community league athletes and 75 percent of college athletes defined themselves as "bold, willing to make their presence felt and desires known."

12 "Tall Tales," *PrimeTime Live*, ABC, July 23, 1997.

13 Jane Gottesman, "Fit for Office," *Women's Sports + Fitness* (December 1994), pp. 43, 84.

14 "Can You Find Donna?," *Sports Illustrated Women/Sport* (Spring 1997), p. 170.

15 Linda K. Bunker, "Lifelong Benefits of Youth Sport Participation for Girls and Women," presented at the Sport Psychology Conference, Charlottesville: University of Virginia, June 22, 1988.

16 Bruce Kirkcaldy and Cary Cooper, "Work Attitudes and Leisure Preferences: Sex Differences," *Personality and Individual Differences* (March 1992), pp. 329–34.

17 Amy Miller, "The Knockout Lesson," *Inc.* (June 1995), p. 21.

18 Jane Gottesman, "Local Legend," *Women's Sports + Fitness* (December 1994), p. 42.

19 Jane Gottesman, "Fit for Office," *Women's Sports + Fitness* (December 1994), p. 43.

20 Michele Kort, "Where Are They Now?," *Women's Sports + Fitness* (September 1992), p. 53.

21 Joan Biskupic, "Women Are Still Not Well-Represented Among Lawyers Facing Supreme Test," *Washington Post*, May 27, 1997, p. A3.

22 Debbie Becker, "Triumphs Could Pave the Way for New Programs for Girls," *USA Today*, August 5, 1996, p. 12C.

23 Michael Wilbon, "U.S. Women's Issue: Playing for Inclusion," *Washington Post*, July 30, 1996, p. D4.

24 Ibid.

25 Ibid.

26 Peter Brewington, "Player of the Year Honor for Stephanie White," *USA Today*, April 15, 1995, p. 13C.

CHAPTER 12: FEMALE ATHLETES LEARN TO COMPETE WITH MEN

1 Laura Friedman, "Fast Laura," *Los Angeles* magazine (February 1995), p. 79.

CHAPTER 13: EVEN ATHLETES ARE AMBIVALENT ABOUT COMPETITION

1 Ann Gerhart and Annie Groer, "The Source's Hot Shots Club: No Duffers, Please," *Washington Post*, June 11, 1997, p. D3.

2 Of the older athletes, 33 percent answered "true" to "competitive situations tend to make me uncomfortable," compared with only 16 percent of the college athletes.

3 Of the older athletes, 27 percent (and only 10 percent of the college athletes) responded "true" to "I tend to avoid competitive situations."

4 There were sixteen paddlers and twenty-five COWS.

5 Mary Jo Festle, *Playing Nice: Politics and Apologies in Women's Sports* (New York: Columbia University Press, 1996), p. 12.

6 Ibid., p. 133.

7 In my survey, 81 percent of lesbians described themselves as "bold . . . willing to make [their] presence felt and desires known," compared with 74 percent of straight women and 68 percent of bisexuals.

8 Joli Sandoz recently compiled some of these stories in a book entitled *A Whole Other Ballgame: Women's Literature on Women's Sport* (New York: Farrar, Straus & Giroux, 1997).

Chapter 14: "I'm Not Competitive, But . . ."

1 Mimi Murray and Hilary Matheson, "Competition: Perceived Barriers to Success," in Greta Cohen, ed., *Women in Sport: Issues and Controversies* (Newbury Park, CA: Sage Publications, 1993), p. 220.
2 Jean Baker Miller, *Toward a New Psychology of Women* (Boston: Beacon Press, 1976, updated 1986).

Chapter 15: Family Games, Cultural Games

1 Joseph LaBarbera, "Seductive Father-Daughter Relationships and Sex Roles in Women," *Sex Roles* (November 1984), pp. 9–10.
2 U.S. Census Bureau, 1995.
3 Women's Sports Foundation, *The Wilson Report: Moms, Dads, Daughters and Sports*, June 7, 1988.
4 Elizabeth Debold, Marie Wilson, and Idelisse Malave, *Mother-Daughter Revolution: From Betrayal to Power* (New York: Addison-Wesley, 1993), p. 183.
5 Ibid., p. 164.
6 Judith Arcana, *Our Mother's Daughters* (London: Women's Press, 1981), p. 173, cited in Debold, op. cit., p. 25.
7 Jane Greer with Edward Myers, *Adult Sibling Rivalry: Understanding the Legacy of Childhood* (New York: Crown 1992), p 12.
8 Doug Smith, "Newest Entry Gets Own Room in Hall of Fame," *USA Today*, July 14, 1995, p. C1.
9 Frank Sulloway, *Born to Rebel: Birth Order, Family Dynamics, and Creative Lives* (New York: Pantheon Books, 1996), p. 86.
10 Greer, op. cit., p. 13.
11 Patricia Harrison, ed., *America's New Women Entrepreneurs: Tips, Tactics, and Techniques of Women Achievers in Business* (Washington, DC: Acropolis Books, 1986).
12 Greer, op. cit., p. 12.
13 Ibid., p. 129.
14 Ibid., p. 118.
15 Ibid., p. 123.

16 Luise Eichenbaum and Susie Orbach, *Between Women: Love, Envy and Competition in Women's Friendships* (New York: Viking, 1988), p. 94.

17 Maria Allison and G. Luschen, "A Comparative Analysis of Navajo Indian and Anglo Basketball Sport Systems," *International Review of Sport Sociology* 14: 3–4 (1979), pp. 75–85, cited in Jay Coakley, *Sport in Society: Issues and Controversies* (St. Louis: Times Mirror/Mosby, 1990), p. 72.

18 Don Sabo, Merrill Melnick, and Beth Vanfossen, *The Women's Sports Foundation Report: Minorities in Sports: The Effect of Varsity Sports Participation on the Social, Educational, and Career Mobility of Minority Students* (Eisenhower Park, NY: Women's Sports Foundation, August 15, 1989), p. 14.

19 Black women were the least likely to want their daughters to play sports (92 percent of white women, 86 percent of Hispanic women, 84 percent of Asian-American women, and only 76 percent of black women wanted their daughters to play sports).

20 Women's Sports Foundation, op. cit.

CHAPTER 16: BEAUTY CONTESTS

1 Mary Pipher, *Reviving Ophelia: Saving the Selves of Adolescent Girls* (New York: Grosset/Putnam, 1994), p. 55.

2 Susan Brownmiller, *Femininity* (New York: Linden Press, 1984).

3 Martha Burk, *Washington Feminist Faxnet*, May 16, 1996.

4 Megan Rosenfeld, "Games Girls Play: A Toy Chest Full of Stereotypes," *Washington Post*, December 22, 1995, p. C1.

5 Naomi Wolf, *The Beauty Myth* (New York: William Morrow, 1991), p. 75.

6 In my survey 50 percent of heterosexuals, 54 percent of bisexuals, and only 26 percent of lesbians said they "always or frequently" compared themselves with other women regarding physical attractiveness; 57 percent of heterosexuals, 54 percent of bisexuals, and only 32 percent of lesbians said they compared themselves with other women in regarding to weight, fat, or body size; and 40 percent of heterosexuals, 27 percent of bisexuals, and only 21 percent of lesbians said they compared themselves with other women regarding clothing.

7 The figures on this comparison: 34 percent of heterosexuals, 23 percent of bisexuals, and only 3 percent of gay women.

8 Only 38 percent of African-American women said they "always or frequently" compare themselves with other women regarding physical attractiveness, contrasted with 52 percent of white and Hispanic women and 59 percent of Asian-American women. Only 43 percent of African-Americans said they always or frequently compared themselves with other women regarding weight, fat, or body size, compared with 59 percent of white women, 69 percent of Hispanic women, and 72 percent of Asian-Americans.

9 Nancy Hellmich, "Looking Thin and Fit Weighs on More Women," *USA Today*, September 25, 1995.

10 Nancy Friday, "The Age of Beauty," *New York Times Magazine*, May 19, 1996, p. 82, excerpted from *The Power of Beauty* (New York: HarperCollins, 1996).

11 Roxanne Roberts, "Beauty and the Ballot Box: Miss America to Let Public Have a Vote," *Washington Post*, July 16, 1996, p. D1.

Chapter 17: Catfights

1 Peter Johnson, "Lunden, Vargas Say All Is Sunny at 'GMA,'" *USA Today*, July 11, 1996, p. D1.

2 Peter Johnson, "A 20/20 Look at Two Decades of Stellar Chats," *USA Today*, April 25, 1996, p. D1.

3 Susan J. Douglas, *Where the Girls Are: Growing Up Female with the Mass Media* (New York: Times Books, Random House, 1994), p. 222.

4 Melanie Thernstrom, "The Glass Slipper," in Cynthia Baughman, ed., *Women on Ice: Feminist Essays on the Tonya Harding/Nancy Kerrigan Spectacle* (New York: Routledge, 1995), p. 151.

Chapter 18: "I Won, but I'm Sorry": The Femininity Game

1 Aurelia Schosber Plath, ed., *Sylvia Plath: Letters Home* (New York: Harper & Row, 1975), p. 297.

2 Jan Felshin, "The Triple Option for Women in Sport," *Quest* 21

(1974), p. 36; Jan Felshin, "The Social View," in E. Gerber, J. Felshin, P. Berlin, and W. Wyrick, eds., *The American Woman in Sport* (Reading, MA: Addison-Wesley, 1974).

3 Bruce Horovitz, "Burning Up the Ice," *USA Today*, January 19–21, 1996, p. 1A; E. M. Swift, "Wild Thing," *Sports Illustrated* (January 6, 1997).

4 Horovitz, op. cit.

5 Melanie Thernstrom, "The Glass Slipper," in Cynthia Baughman, ed., *Women on Ice: Feminist Essays on the Tonya Harding/Nancy Kerrigan Spectacle* (New York: Routledge, 1995), p. 161.

6 Christine Brennan, "Ito Passes 1st Comeback Test," *Washington Post*, March 19, 1996, p. D3.

7 Abigail M. Feder, "A Radiant Smile for the Lovely Lady," in Baughman, op. cit., p. 42.

8 Mary Jo Festle, *Playing Nice: Politics and Apologies in Women's Sports* (New York: Columbia University Press, 1996), p. 61.

9 Ibid., p. 60.

10 Susan K. Cahn, *Coming on Strong: Gender and Sexuality in Twentieth-Century Women's Sports* (New York: Free Press, 1994), p. 122.

11 Carolyn G. Heilbrun, *Reinventing Womanhood* (New York: W. W. Norton, 1979), p. 203.

CHAPTER 19: DO WOMEN CARE TOO MUCH?
FEMALE FRIENDSHIPS

1 Deborah Tannen, *You Just Don't Understand: Women and Men in Conversation* (New York: William Morrow, 1990), p. 274.

2 Carol Gilligan, *In a Different Voice: Psychological Theory and Women's Development* (Cambridge, MA: Harvard University Press, 1982), p. 159.

3 Jean Baker Miller, *Toward a New Psychology of Women* (Boston: Beacon Press, 1976; updated 1986), p. 83.

4 David Leon Moore, "Streets Tough It Out Through Peaks, Valleys," *USA Today*, November 27, 1996, p. 2C.

5 Mary E. Duquin, "Power and Authority: Moral Consensus and Conformity in Sport," *International Review for the Sociology of Sport* 19 (1984), pp. 295–304.

6 Stephanie Grant, "Posting-Up," in E. J. Levy, ed., *Tasting Life Twice: Literary Lesbian Fiction by New American Writers* (New York: Avon Books, 1995), p. 20.

7 Ibid., p. 21.

8 Luise Eichenbaum and Susie Orbach in *Between Women: Love, Envy, and Competition in Women's Friendships* (New York: Viking Books, 1988), p. 98.

9 Marianne Williamson, *A Woman's Worth* (New York: Random House, 1993), p. 29.

10 Liz Chandler, "North Carolina Begins Another Quest for National Title," Knight-Ridder/*Tribune* newspapers, September 1, 1995.

11 Julia Lawlor, "Gender Raises Tough Issues in Workplace," *USA Today*, July 6, 1994, p. 2B.

12 Mark Blaudschum, "The World at Their Feet," Boston *Globe*, November 14, 1995.

13 Johnette Howard, "In Chapel Hill, Kicks Are Still the Best," *Washington Post* (October 5, 1994), p. B6.

14 Chandler, op. cit.

15 Blaudschum, op. cit.

16 Ibid.

17 Lawlor, op. cit.

CHAPTER 20: BUT HOW DO WOMEN COMPARE WITH MEN?

1 Diane L. Gill and D. A. Dzewaltowski, "Competitive Orientations among Intercollegiate Athletes: Is Winning the Only Thing?" *Sport Psychologist* 2 (1988), pp. 212–21; D. L. Gill, "Competitiveness and Competitive Orientation in Sport," in R. N. Singer, M. Murphey, and L. K. Tennant, eds., *Handbook on Research in Sport Psychology* (New York: Macmillan, 1993, pp. 314–27; D. L. Gill and T. E. Deeter, "Development of the Sport Orientation Questionnaire," *Research Quarterly for Exercise and Sport* 59 (1988), pp. 191–202.

2 Gill, "Competitiveness and Competitive Orientation in Sport," loc. cit.

3 Thelma Horn, ed., *Advances in Sport Psychology* (Champaign, IL: Human Kinetics, 1992), p. 149; J. T. Spence and R. L. Helmreich, *Masculinity and Femininity* (Austin: University of Texas Press, 1978); Michael Platow, "Observing Social Value Orientations: A Social In-

terdependence Approach," *New Zealand Journal of Psychology* 22 (December 1993), pp. 101–9; Marita Inglehart and Donald R. Brown, "Competition and Gender Differences in Academic Achievement," *Contemporary Education* (Summer 1989), pp. 213–15; and Doris Bischof-Kohler, "(A Psycho-biological Viewpoint of Women and Careers)," *Zeitschrift fur Arbeits und Organisationspsychologie* 34 (1990), pp. 17–28.

4 David Stimpson, Wayne Neff, Larry Jensen, and Timothy Newby, "The Caring Morality and Gender Differences," *Psychological Reports* (October 1991), pp. 407–14.

5 Joanne Coutts, "Masculinity-Femininity of Self-Concept: Its Effect on the Achievement Behavior of Women," *Sex Roles* (January 1987), pp. 9–17; Eleanor Emmons Maccoby and Carol Nagy Jacklin, *The Psychology of Sex Differences* (Stanford, CA: Stanford University Press, 1974), p. 254.

6 Susan Pollack and Carol Gilligan, "Images of Violence in Thematic Apperception Test Stories," *Journal of Personality and Social Psychology* 42 (1982), pp. 159–67.

7 Timothy Church and Marcia Katigbak, "The Cultural Context of Academic Motives: A Comparison of Filipino and American College Students," *Journal of Cross-Cultural Psychology* (March 1992), pp. 40–58.

8 Diane E. Gill, "Gender and Sport Behavior," in Horn, op. cit., p. 151.

9 Mimi Murray and Hilary Matheson, "Competition: Perceived Barriers to Success," in Greta Cohen, *Women in Sport: Issues and Controversies* (Newbury Park, CA: Sage Publications, 1993), p. 220.

10 Ibid., p. 220.

11 Emmy A. Pepitone, *Children in Cooperation and Competition*, (Lexington, MA: Lexington Books, 1980); Alfie Kohn, *No Contest: The Case Against Competition* (Boston: Houghton Mifflin, 1986).

12 Barrie Thorne, *Gender Play: Girls and Boys in School* (New Brunswick, NJ: Rutgers University Press, 1993).

13 Ibid., pp. 94–95.

14 John Evans, "Gender Differences in Children's Games: A Look at the Team Selection Process," *Canadian Association for Health, Physical Education, and Recreation Journal* 52 (1986), pp. 4–9, cited in Thorne, op. cit., p. 131.

15 Pepitone, op. cit., pp. 317–18; Maccoby and Jacklin, op. cit.

16 Janet Lever, "Sex Differences in the Complexity of Children's Play and Game," *American Sociological Review* 43 (1978), pp. 471–83; Janet Lever, "Sex Differences in the Games Children Play," *Social Problems* 23 (1976), pp. 478–87, cited in Thorne, op. cit., p. 93.

17 Pepitone, op. cit., pp. 317–18.

18 Thorne, op. cit.

19 Deborah Tannen, *You Just Don't Understand: Women and Men in Conversation* (New York: William Morrow, 1990).

20 Brenda J. L. Bredemeier, Gloria S. Desertrain, Leslee A. Fisher, Debby Getty, Nancy E. Slocum, Dawn E. Stephens, and Jaimie M. Warren, "Epistemological Perspectives Among Women Who Participate in Physical Activity," *Journal of Applied Sport Psychology* 3 (1991), pp. 87–107.

21 Carol Tavris, *The Mismeasure of Woman: Why Women Are Not the Better Sex, the Inferior Sex, or the Opposite Sex* (New York: Simon & Schuster, 1992), p. 90.

22 Maccoby and Jacklin, op. cit.

23 Linda Hughes, "But That's Not Really Mean: Competing in a Cooperative Mode," *Sex Roles* 19 (1988), pp. 669–87; Thorne, op. cit.

24 Amy Sheldon, "Conflict Talk: Sociolinguistic Challenges to Self-Assertion and How Young Girls Meet Them," *Merrill-Palmer Quarterly* 38 (1992), pp. 95–117, cited in Thorne, op. cit., p. 106.

25 Thorne, op. cit., pp. 95, 102.

26 Pepitone, op. cit., pp. 317–18.

27 Thorne, op. cit.

28 Linda Carli, "Gender, Language, and Influence," *Journal of Personality and Social Psychology* 59 (1990), pp. 941–51, cited in Tavris, op. cit., p. 299.

29 Tavris, op. cit., p. 43.

CHAPTER 21: "MANY MEN FEEL THREATENED BY
FEMALE VICTORY"

1 Lawrence Naumoff, *Taller Women* (New York: Harcourt Brace Jovanovich, 1992), pp. 24–26.

2 Frank Swoboda, "'Glass Ceiling' Firmly in Place, Panel Finds," *Washington Post*, March 16, 1995, p. A1.

3 Peter T. Kilborn, "Women and Minorities Still Face 'Glass Ceiling,' Study Says," *New York Times*, March 16, 1995, p. A1.

4 Orlando Patterson, "The Crisis of Gender Relations Among African-Americans," in Anita Faye Hill and Emma Coleman, eds., *Race, Gender, and Power in America* (New York: Oxford University Press, 1995).

5 Ellen Neuborne, "Complaints High from Women in Blue-Collar Jobs," *USA Today*, May 3–5, 1996, p. 1A.

6 Ibid.

7 Dana Priest, "Abuse in Army 'Not That Unusual,' " *Washington Post*, November 21, 1996, p. A21.

8 Ibid.

9 Mariah Burton Nelson, *The Stronger Women Get, the More Men Love Football* (New York: Avon, 1995).

10 See the "My Coach Says He Loves Me" chapter in *The Stronger Women Get, the More Men Love Football*.

11 Beverly Smith, "Female Athletes in School Study at Disadvantage," *Toronto Globe and Mail*, July 24, 1996. This study was supported by the Canadian Interuniversity Athletics Union.

12 When this woman complained, "I don't know what to tell them," I responded: Tell them that they're limiting their thinking to how they can win in traditional terms—by overcoming an opponent or by maintaining their masculine privilege and place in the gender hierarchy. Tell them there are other ways to win. Tell them that if they wrestle against a woman and perceive and appreciate her strength and competence, they could win a newfound respect for female athleticism, persistence, courage—or for women in general. Tell them that if they defeat a woman, and if she is inspired and challenged to improve, they could win a friend, just as they might win a male friend who appreciates the challenge and the contest. Tell them that if they lose to a woman, they could win for themselves a psychological advantage over men who feel a need to reign supreme all the time, an advantage noted by the hearing officer who ruled back in 1973 that Little League must be sexually integrated: "The sooner little boys begin to realize that little girls are equal and that there will be many opportunities for a boy to be bested by a girl, the closer they will be to mental health."

13 Janet Lever, "Sex Differences in the Complexity of Children's Play

and Games," *American Sociological Review* 43 (1978), pp. 471–83; Janet Lever, "Sex Differences in the Games Children Play," *Social Problems* 23 (1976), pp. 478–87, cited in Barrie Thorne, *Gender Play: Girls and Boys in School* (New Brunswick, NJ: Rutgers University Press, 1993), p. 93.

14 Carol Tavris, *The Mismeasure of Woman: Why Women Are Not the Better Sex, the Inferior Sex, or the Opposite Sex* (New York: Simon & Schuster, 1992), p. 291.

15 Thorne, op. cit., p. 168.

16 Alfie Kohn, *No Contest: The Case Against Competition* (Boston: Houghton Mifflin, 1986), p. 168.

17 Matina S. Horner, "Towards an Understanding of Achievement-Related Conflicts in Women," *Journal of Social Issues* 28: 2 (1972), pp. 157–75.

18 M. Zuckerman and S. N. Allison, "An Objective Measure of Fear of Success: Construction and Validity," *Journal of Personality Assessment* 40 (1976), pp. 422–30.

19 M. A. McElroy and J. D. Willis, "Women and the Achievement Conflict in Sport: A Preliminary Study," *Journal of Sport Psychology* 1 (1979), pp. 241–47.

20 D. Tresemer, "The Cumulative Record of Research on 'Fear of Success': Popular but Unproven," *Sex Roles* 2 (1976), pp. 217–36.

21 Kohn, op. cit., p. 71.

22 Georgia Sassen, "Sex Role Orientation, Sex Differences, and Concept of Success," master's thesis, University of Massachusetts, 1981, cited in Kohn, op. cit., p. 172.

23 "Women in Corporate Leadership: Progress and Prospects," 1996, Catalyst, 250 Park Avenue South, New York, NY 10003-1459.

24 Carol McPhee and Ann FitzGerald, eds., *Feminist Quotations: Voices of Rebels, Reformers, and Visionaries* (New York: Thomas Y. Crowell, 1979), p. 10.

25 Jill Adler and Kristen Ulmer, "Should You Pamper the Fragile Male Ski Ego?," "Crush it like a Bug" (Ulmer), and "Treat it like the Eggshell It Is" (Adler), *Powder* magazine (March 1997).

26 Jean Shinoda Bolen, *Goddesses in Everywoman: A New Psychology of Women* (New York: Harper & Row, 1985), p. 48.

27 Jean Baker Miller, *Toward a New Psychology of Women* (Boston: Beacon Press, 1976, updated 1986), p. 120.

28 Mary Jo Festle, *Playing Nice: Politics and Apologies in Women's Sports* (New York: Columbia University Press, 1996), p. 68.
29 Five percent said they never compete.

CHAPTER 22: DESPERATE TACTICS TO WATCH OUT FOR

1 James P. Gustafson, M. D., and Lowell W. Cooper, Ph.D., *The Modern Contest: A Systematic Guide to the Pattern That Connects* (New York: W. W. Norton, 1990), p. xiii.
2 Tama Starr, *The "Natural Inferiority" of Woman: Outrageous Pronouncement by Misguided Males* (New York: Poseidon Press, 1991).
3 Ibid.
4 Ibid.
5 Ibid.
6 Leonard Shapiro, "For Women Analysts, Networks Mostly Off Course," *Washington Post*, September 23, 1995.
7 Tom Green, "Unabashed Barkin," *USA Today*, December 11, 1995, p. 2D.
8 "Women on the Verge of a Power Breakthrough," *Washington Post Magazine*, May 10, 1992, p. 31.

CHAPTER 23: TOO COMPETITIVE

1 Nancy Colasurdo, "Fragile Knees?" *Trenton Times*, 1996.
2 Dusty Miller, *Women Who Hurt Themselves: A Book of Hope and Understanding* (New York: Basic Books, 1994).
3 Richard H. Cox, *Sport Psychology: Concepts and Applications* (Dubuque, IA: Wm C. Brown Communications, 1994), p. 370.
4 Arnold D. LeUnes and Jack R. Nation, *Sport Psychology: An Introduction* (Chicago: Nelson-Hall, 1989), p. 428.
5 D. Layman and A. Morris, "Addiction and Injury in Runners: Is There a Mind-Body Connection?," paper presented at the annual convention for the Psychology of Sport and Physical Activity, Scottsdale, AZ, 1986, cited in LeUnes and Nation, op. cit., p. 429.
6 Caroline Knapp, *Drinking: A Love Story* (New York: Dial Press, 1996).

Chapter 24: Give Yourself Permission to Compete

1 Audre Lorde, *Sister Outsider: Essays and Speeches* (Freedom, CA: Crossing Press, 1984) p. 57.

Chapter 27: Forgive Yourself Immediately for All Mistakes

1 Bruno Bettelheim, *A Good Enough Parent: A Book on Child-Rearing* (New York: Knopf, 1987). Bettelheim was modifying the "good enough mother" concept of the British psychologist D. W. Winnicott.

Chapter 28: Be Willing to Lose

1 Karen Karbo, "Polite, Feminine, Can Bench Press Dennis Conner," in John Feinstein, ed., *The Best American Sports Writing* (Boston: Houghton Mifflin, 1996); first appeared in *Outside* magazine, 1995.

2 Angus Phillips, "Mighty Mary Is Now Looking Mighty Fast," *Washington Post*, March 21, 1995.

3 Kate Rounds, "Marcia Clark: For Her Ongoing Efforts in the Service of Justice," *Ms.* (January–February 1996), p. 64.

4 Lorraine Adams, "The Fight of Her Life: Marcia Clark—Working Mother and O. J. Simpson Lead Prosecutor—Takes Her Place Among Other Maligned, Adored, and Misunderstood Modern Women," *Washington Post*, August 20, 1995, p. F1.

5 Sara Rimer, "Nation Analyzes and Agonizes over Citadel Dropout, but 29 Men Who Quit Escape All Scrutiny," *New York Times*, August 21, 1995.

6 "Commencement Kudos," *Time* (June 16, 1997), p. 84.

Chapter 30: Pay Attention to the Process

1 Nina Winter, *Interview with the Muse: Remarkable Women Speak on Creativity and Power* (Berkeley, CA: Moon Books, 1978), p. 122.

2 Stuart H. Walker, *Winning: The Psychology of Competition* (New York: W. W. Norton, 1980), p. 4.

CHAPTER 31: ENGAGE IN VICTORY TALK

1 Lillian Rubin, *Just Friends: The Role of Friendship in Our Lives* (New York: Harper & Row, 1985), pp. 83–89.
2 Naomi Wolf, *Fire with Fire: The New Female Power and How to Use It* (New York: Fawcett Columbine, 1993), p. 285.
3 Ruth Lerner Perle, *I Want to Win* (Middletown, CT: Walt Disney Co., 1991).

CHAPTER 32: DECIDE WHEN TO COMPETE AND WHEN NOT TO

1 Rosalie Hedlund, "Nontraditional Team Sports—Taking Advantage of the Teachable Moment," *Journal of Physical Education, Recreation, and Dance*, April 1990.

CHAPTER 33: DEFINE VICTORY AND LOSS FOR YOURSELF

1 Jill Lieber, "Finishing Race Personal Quest," *USA Today*, October 30, 1996, p. 3C.

CHAPTER 36: COMPETE WITH YOURSELF

1 Other advice categories, in order of popularity, included: "Believe in yourself"; "Define winning and losing for yourself"; "Go, girl"; "You don't have to compete"; "Lighten up"; "Persevere"; "Get tough"; "Don't worry what others say"; "Life is a competition, so get used to it"; "Don't be afraid"; "Be yourself"; "Think of the advantages"; "Go ahead and compete"; "Try playing sports"; "Network with others"; and "Examine why you're uncomfortable."

CHAPTER 37: SEE OPPONENTS AS OPPORTUNITIES

1 Carlos Castaneda, *Journey to Ixtlan: The Lessons of Don Juan* (New York: Simon & Schuster, 1972), pp. 225–26.

CHAPTER 40: LIGHTEN UP

1 Susan E. Cayleff, *Babe: The Life and Legend of Babe Didrikson Zaharias* (Urbana: University of Illinois Press, 1995), p. 194.

APPENDIX

1 By labeling the survey that way, I was trying (1) to establish credibility for those who might know of me or my books, (2) to promise confidentiality, to ensure the most honest responses possible, and (3) to take responsibility, so they'd know that it was my project, not their teacher's. It occurred to me later that the use of my name might have influenced whom these girls and women thought they were talking to. They might have been more willing to admit competitive attitudes to me than to a male researcher. Or they might have been trying to please me by claiming to be more or less competitive than they thought I wanted them to be.

2 Surveys were distributed in Windsor, Ontario; Waterloo, Ontario; Edmonton, Alberta; California, Colorado, Connecticut, Indiana, Massachusetts, Minnesota, Maryland, Missouri, Nebraska, New Hampshire, New Jersey, New York, North Carolina, Ohio, Pennsylvania, Texas, Virginia, Washington, Wisconsin, and the District of Columbia.

3 Definitions of race are in flux right now, and in hindsight I can see that there might have been better ways to acquire racial data. For instance, some people are rewriting questionnaires to offer a "check all that apply" option, which tends to validate survey respondents who want to acknowledge a diverse heritage without being lumped into a biracial or multiracial category. But that system too has its limitations.

Index